"Imagination, capability, and opportunity take on a new dimension in the digital age. *Leading Digital* provides a framework for creating sustainable business differentiators across the value chain. A must-read for all those who aspire to become Digital Masters."

> —**Manish Choksi**, President of Home Improvement,
> Supply Chain and IT, Asian Paints

"Westerman, Bonnet, and McAfee have done a masterful job of describing the essential characteristics of Digital Masters and presenting a thoughtful and pragmatic leader's playbook for digital transformation. This book is an exceptional contribution to strategy and management practice."

> —**John Glaser**, CEO, Health Services, Siemens

"The authors have lived on the cutting edge of how global organizations use digital technology to change and improve the way they do business. With this book, they bring us along on the transformation journey. If you want to prepare yourself to lead your organization through this profound change, *Leading Digital* is a must-read."

> —**Jean-Christophe LaLanne**, Executive Vice President and
> Chief Information Officer, Air France–KLM Group

"Using powerful examples, this impactful, evidence-based book demonstrates that mastery of digital technologies drives significantly high levels of profit and productivity across almost all industries—and shows you how to become a Digital Master yourself."

> —**F. Warren McFarlan**, professor, Harvard Business School

"We are living in a time where technology is impacting everything we do and touch like never before, where being connected is becoming a basic human right, and where the unshared certainties of all businesses are turning into shared uncertainties. *Leading Digital* offers a powerful and refreshing approach to what needs to be done during each stage of this journey."

> —**Osman Sultan**, CEO, Du, United Arab Emirates

LE▲DING
DIGITAL

LE▲DING
DIGITAL

TURNING TECHNOLOGY
INTO BUSINESS TRANSFORMATION

GEORGE WESTERMAN | DIDIER BONNET | ANDREW McAFEE

HARVARD BUSINESS REVIEW PRESS

Boston, Massachusetts

21 20 19 18 17 16 15 14 13

The web addresses referenced in this book were live and correct at the time of the book's publication but may be subject to change.

Library of Congress Cataloging-in-Publication Data

Westerman, George, 1963-
  Leading digital : turning technology into business transformation / George Westerman, Didier Bonnet, Andrew McAfee.
      pages cm
   ISBN 978-1-62527-247-8 (hardback)
  1. Information technology—Management. 2. Strategic planning. 3. Organizational change. I. Bonnet, Didier. II. McAfee, Andrew. III. Title.
  HD30.2.W4645 2014
  658.4'038--dc23

                                                                    2014013859

The paper used in this publication meets the requirements of the American National Standard for Permanence of Paper for Publications and Documents in Libraries and Archives Z39.48-1992.

CONTENTS

PART I:
BUILDING DIGITAL CAPABILITIES

PART II:
BUILDING LEADERSHIP CAPABILITIES

PART III:
BACK AT THE OFFICE:
A Leader's Playbook for Digital Transformation

*Let us be grateful to the people who
make us happy; they are the charming gardeners
who make our souls blossom.*

—Marcel Proust

From George

*To Clare, Henry, and Marilyn, who transformed my
life in ways I never could have envisioned.*

From Didier

*To my wife Kathryn, for her immeasurable love and
support, and to my two own digital masters,
Alexandra and William, for keeping me on the
right side of the digital divide.*

From Andy

*To my coauthors, who have taught me much about
scholarship, writing, professionalism, and good cheer.*

ARE YOU READY?

Technology is the biggest story in business today, plain and simple.

There are other big stories, of course. The Great Recession of 2007–2009 and subsequent sovereign debt crises were hugely important events; they affected the fortunes of countless people and companies, and their impact is far from over. Globalization and offshoring are also key forces shaping strategy and structure both now and for some time to come. Demographics are shifting in ways that will cause deep and lasting changes in markets.

These are big deals, but technology is bigger. It's bigger because recent progress in all things digital is removing constraints and creating exciting new possibilities that affect everyone's lives and enterprises. Do you want to finally hear the voice of your customers and escape the narrow lenses of surveys and focus groups? Social media let you. Do you want all of your people to be available and productive no matter where they are? Mobile computing makes that possible. Want significantly better forecasts, judgments, and decisions in key areas? That's the promise of big data. Want to roll out entirely new organizational structures, business processes, and customer offerings, and to quickly modify them over time as circumstances change? We all know these things are possible because we've seen companies doing all of them.

The tech wave has been building for a long time, but has accelerated in recent years. The past decade has witnessed a remarkable run of progress in digital technologies. The phrase *Web 2.0* entered popular use in 2004 to signify a deep change under way on the World Wide Web: a great democratization of content creation. The rise of Facebook, Twitter, *Wikipedia*, and many other utilities full of user-generated content shows that there really is a new version of the Web. Moreover, a new generation of computing devices seems likely to challenge, if not completely overturn, the decades-long dominance of the personal computer as the device of choice for knowledge workers. Apple's twin breakthroughs—the iPhone in 2007 and the iPad in 2010—ushered in the era of the smartphone and the tablet and made real the long-standing promises of mobile computing. These technology advances are staggering, but the real impact is how they are changing the way we live and work. Companies, and people, can do things that would have been impossible a decade ago.

The data center has been disrupted as much as the desktop has in recent years, thanks to the rapid rise of cloud computing, which is calling into question the standard assumption that you have to own technologies like servers, operating systems, and applications if you want to use them. Enterprise applications, social networks, mobile devices, sensors, and just about every other element of modern digital infrastructure generate scads of data—so much that we really do need to use the modifier *big* now to distinguish the current era. These and many other innovations are being combined to bring us the sharing economy, supercomputers that win game shows, cars that drive themselves, and a host of other novelties that fundamentally challenge our thinking about business structure, labor costs, and the relationship between people and machines.

The last time there was this much technological innovation hitting the business world was the first time. It was the Industrial Revolution, when new machines bent the curve of commerce, capitalism, and, indeed, human history. Today, innovation in digital technologies is bringing our world into what one of us (Andy) and his coauthor Erik Brynjolfsson called "the second machine age" in their 2014 book of the same name.

Are you ready for the second machine age? With all due respect, you're probably not.

We say this because for the past three years, we've been conducting research on how firms around the world and in many industries work with digital technologies. We've collected data and interviewed people at hundreds of companies. We've talked with executives and examined the companies' performance. We've studied both how the companies approach all things digital and the results of their efforts.

Our most fundamental conclusion is that *Digital Masters*— companies that use digital technologies to drive significantly higher levels of profit, productivity, and performance—do exist, but they're rare. For reasons that we'll explain here, most firms fall short of digital mastery. That's the bad news, and it's why we believe you're probably not ready to survive and thrive in the second machine age.

Here's the good news: the reasons that companies fall short of digital mastery aren't mysterious or too numerous to list. In fact, the reasons are pretty easy to categorize. Companies that struggle with becoming truly digital fail to develop digital capabilities to work differently and the leadership capabilities required to set a vision and execute on it. The firms that excel at both digital and leadership capabilities are Digital Masters.

If you read the business press about technology, you might well surmise that most Digital Masters are American; that most American masters reside in Northern California, the Pacific Northwest, or New England; and that most of these companies are in the hardware and software businesses. And certainly, giants like Apple, Facebook, and Amazon.com, and start-ups from San Francisco to Boston are excellent users of technology. But these aren't the Digital Masters we're talking about.

In fact, we didn't even include them in our research. We wanted to understand how technology was being adopted and used *in the 90-plus percent of the economy that doesn't do technology for a living*. So we didn't look at Silicon Valley's stars. And we didn't look at start-ups and other small companies either, because their tech-related opportunities and challenges are quite different from those faced by large enterprises.

We focused on big companies, in industries from finance to manufacturing to pharmaceuticals. These companies power much of the economy, but are rarely mentioned in the technology news. Not all of them are Digital Masters, but still, many are doing amazing things with technology. We also spent a lot of our time looking outside the United States, for the simple reason that most of the world is there. The diffusion of business technology is a global phenomenon, and we wanted to understand what was happening around the world. So we conducted research at large enterprises from around the globe to understand their approaches to harnessing the many recent waves of innovation in information and communication technology and to see which approaches worked best. We discovered all kinds of companies, both those struggling and those succeeding in the great challenge of becoming digital. As we explained above, the companies that are succeeding—and they range across industries and sectors—we're calling Digital Masters. And Digital Masters outperform their peers. Our work indicates that the masters are 26 percent more profitable than their average industry competitors. They generate 9 percent more revenue with their existing physical capacity and drive more efficiency in their existing products and processes.

As we'll show, achieving digital mastery is not an impossible task or arcane art. It doesn't require that you hire away Google's top talent or spend 20 percent of revenue on technology every year. It does require some level of human capital and investment, of course, but the main requirements are time, tenacity, and leadership. With these, knowledgeable companies can assemble the elements of technological progress into a mosaic not just once, but continuously over time. Digital Masters, in short, keep making digital technologies work for them even though the technologies themselves keep changing.

Our research has convinced us—and with this book, we hope to convince you—that digital mastery is an achievable goal for any enterprise. We'll give many examples of what digital mastery looks like, why it's important, and how it can be developed. We hope that you'll find the examples compelling, and that you'll use our work to help you embark on your own journey toward becoming a Digital Master.

This is an important journey because when it comes to the impact of digital technologies on the business world, we ain't seen nothin' yet. The innovations and disruptions of the past ten years have been nothing short of astonishing, but they're just the warm-up acts for what's to come.

Robots will become more dexterous, mobile, and aware of their surroundings. They will start showing up not only on factory floors, but also in warehouses, stockrooms, and retail environments. Their close cousins, autonomous vehicles, will start driving and flying at first in remote areas, and then probably in populated ones.

The data these drones generate will be combined with the streams from countless sensors as we instrument (in other words, slap a sensor on) just about everything. As the entrepreneur Gil Elbaz puts it, "The world is one big data problem."[1] The coming years will show that if Elbaz's comment is an overstatement, it's not much of one. Digital Masters will take this torrent of data; combine it with the latest innovations in artificial intelligence, machine learning, and visualization; and use the resulting insights to make smarter decisions, see the future more clearly, drive out inefficiencies, and better understand their customers. Everyone else will fall behind.

No one can predict all the digital innovations that the coming years will bring. Perhaps the best general prediction is an expansion of what inventor, entrepreneur, and venture capitalist Marc Andreessen wrote in a 2011 *Wall Street Journal* column: "Why Software Is Eating the World."[2] We wholeheartedly agree and just want to expand on his point: the elements of the digital world—software, hardware, networks, and data—are pervading the business world, and they're doing so quickly, broadly, and deeply. Regardless of industry or geography, businesses will become much more digitized in the future. It's inevitable— so the time to start pursuing digital mastery is now.

If you want to become a Digital Master, read on. Chapter 1 defines digital mastery: what it is, what it means, and how it varies from company to company and from industry to industry. Our research has identified the key characteristics that make companies Digital Masters. What these masters have done, though not easy, can be adopted by any company willing to follow a similar path. Digital Masters excel at two essential capabilities. They build digital capabilities by rethinking and improving their business processes, their customer engagements, and their business models. They also build strong leadership capabilities to envision and drive transformation. Each dimension of capability is important on its own. Together, they make you a Digital Master.

The next two parts of the book examine the two critical capabilities that constitute the DNA of digital mastery in turn. Part I focuses on digital capability. It is the *what* of digital mastery—the investments and initiatives that executives have undertaken to transform the way their companies operate. Chapter 2 examines the most visible aspect of digital capabilities—*how you engage with customers*. This capability goes beyond websites and mobile apps to truly change the customer experience. Chapter 3 explores a far less visible, but equally important element of digital capability, namely, *operational processes*. Digital technology allows companies to break some of the traditional paradoxes of operational excellence, helping you to build capabilities that improve efficiency and agility, power new customer engagements, and enable new business models—all while remaining largely hidden from your competitors. Finally, chapter 4 discusses *new business models*, from reconfiguring delivery models to creating new products and services to reinventing whole industries. Through these models, you can gain an advantage over your competitors and outwit new entrants.

Part II focuses on the other critical dimension, leadership capabilities. These are the *how* of digital mastery—the ways in which executives are driving change. Large companies are prone to both inertia and entropy; it can be tough to get started, and even tougher to keep things moving in the same direction. The only effective way we've seen to drive transformation is top-down, through strong senior executive direction coupled with methods that engage workers in making the change happen. Chapter 5 shows how to create a *transformative digital vision*. Vision sets the aspirations for your company, but many companies lack this essential part of driving transformation. Chapter 6 then describes a distinctive approach to *engagement*, which is the process of energizing employees to make the vision a reality. Chapter 7 examines *digital governance*. Vision and engagement are just part of the story of leadership capabilities. An energized workforce, believing strongly in a shared vision, may still proceed in many directions. Governance provides the guardrails and steering wheel to keep the transformation on the right track. Finally, chapter 8 examines the *technology leadership capabilities* you will need to power your transformation forward: the strong relationship that Digital Masters build between their IT and business leaders, and the way these companies use that relationship to drive change in their internal platforms and digital skills.

Part III constitutes what we call the *leader's playbook for digital transformation*. This toolset, synthesized from the insights in previous sections, provides concrete management guidance to help get you started in creating your own digital advantage. Chapter 9 is the starting point: *framing* the digital challenge. It shows how to build awareness, understand your starting point, craft a vision, and align your senior executive team around it. Chapter 10 shows how to *focus your investments*. It provides advice on how to translate your vision into action, build the required governance, and fund your transformation. Chapter 11 is about *mobilizing the organization* to make the transformation happen—signaling your ambitions, earning the right to engage, setting new behaviors, and starting to evolve the company's culture. Finally, chapter 12 discusses how to *sustain the change*. It includes building foundation skills, aligning incentives and reward structures, and continuously monitoring progress. Although each topic in Part III could be a book on its own, each chapter contains a self-diagnostic exercise, as well as some useful examples and techniques to help you get started.

Our overarching conclusion from this work is simple: we ain't seen nothin' yet. Within the next ten years, industries, economies, and probably entire societies will be transformed by a barrage of technologies that until recently have existed only in science fiction, but are now entering and reshaping the business world. Becoming a Digital Master is challenging, but there has never been a better time. The longer you wait, the more difficult it will become.

CHAPTER 1

WHAT IS DIGITAL MASTERY?

If people knew how hard I worked to get my mastery, It wouldn't seem so wonderful at all.

—MICHELANGELO

Sporting goods company Nike has built its business on innovation. According to CEO Mark Parker, "We're an innovation company . . . Innovation and design is at the epicenter of all we do."[1] That innovation focus goes beyond Nike's products to include the way it engages with customers and even the way it manages internal operations. And digital technology is making new kinds of innovation possible.[2]

Online customers can order personalized shoes in hundreds of color combinations. Digital tools have made product design and manufacturing faster and more efficient than ever before. Additional digital capabilities have helped Nike to improve visibility and performance in its operations, increasing efficiency, reducing waste, and enhancing corporate social responsibility in the company' global supply chain.

Social media enable Nike to be an integral part of the conversation around major sports, sporting events, and sporting apparel. And Nike's digital products, such as the FuelBand, allow athletes to track their workouts, share their performance online, and even receive advice from digital "coaches." Meanwhile, both social media and digital products provide Nike with rich data on customers, their activities, and their preferences.

These innovations arise in different parts of the company as managers constantly seek new ways to improve. According to CEO Parker, "I always like to say that we focus on our potential and the distance between where we are and our potential, not the distance between us and our competition. That's where a leader should be. And as you focus on that space, you're gonna create some incredible things."[3]

Yet in 2010, Nike executives decided to invest in something different. They created a new business unit, called Nike Digital Sport, to build new digital products and reimagine how Nike could engage with customers across its categories. Marketers, designers, and engineers work together to develop and launch products under the Nike+ banner. The unit also helps other parts of Nike develop their digital efforts. Its "innovation kitchen" produces new designs and techniques ranging from marketing to manufacturing. Its accelerator program is building the firm's digital ecosystem. Analysts mine mountains of data, gathered from Nike's digital products and marketing efforts, to get ever closer to customers around the world.

According to Nike's global digital brand and innovation director, Jesse Stolak, "The goal hasn't changed since the beginning of Nike—we want to connect with athletes to inspire and enable them to be better."[4] No longer just a seller of products, Nike is becoming part of its customers' lives.

Nike's story is not unique. Asian Paints is India's largest paint company and Asia's third-largest paint company, with revenue of $1.8 billion.[5] It has been able to globalize and maintain fast growth, more than 15 percent annually for a decade, while increasing efficiency, transforming customer experience, and reducing its environmental impact.[6]

Having built a digital advantage serving India's billion-person economy, Asian Paints has expanded to seventeen countries around the world. None of this would have been possible without successive waves of digital transformation over the past decade.

According to CIO and head of strategy Manish Choksi, a challenge of the company has been "to drive efficiency and growth in a business spread over 120 locations, which deals directly with twenty thousand to thirty thousand retailers."[7] After first unifying the company through strong IT systems for manufacturing, order processing, and supply chain, the company was on a good foundation for growth. This set the stage for a series of transformations. Centralizing the routine customer order-taking process into a single corporate call center increased efficiency and customer service. The firm's salespeople then transformed from clipboard-carrying order takers to always-connected relationship managers. New automated plants produced higher product quality and environmental safety than labor-intensive plants did. Expanding into services—selling painted walls instead of cans of paint—provided benefits beyond new revenues. Providing the service ensured that high-end products were applied properly, thereby improving customer satisfaction, and helped the firm get closer to end consumers that it didn't typically meet.[8] As Asian Paints' website affirms, digital transformation will continue into the future: "The road ahead is to integrate all our stakeholders including suppliers, employees and customers and create an extended enterprise."[9]

Nike and Asian Paints are in very different industries. The companies have very different products, customers, and histories. But they have something in common: the way they use digital technologies to drive their businesses forward. As two examples of Digital Masters, Nike and Asian Paints are using digital technologies to transform the way they do business. Digital Masters use technology better than their competitors do and gain huge benefits. The benefits occur not only in visible customer interactions, but also in less visible internal operations. The advantages are apparent in the financials; Digital Masters are substantially more profitable than their peers.[10]

But what do Digital Masters do differently? How can you become a Digital Master? Nike and Asian Paints did not start as Digital Masters. They built their digital advantage over time. And they did it through different paths. But both came to realize what our research has shown: Digital Masters do more than just invest in digital capabilities. They create the leadership capabilities to get the most from their digital activities. We'll show you how.

THE DNA OF DIGITAL MASTERS

We started our research with a simple but broad question: how are large companies around the world using fast-evolving new digital technologies in their businesses? When we started our research, we didn't have specific dimensions or practices in mind. We just knew that big companies were doing far more than we were hearing in the media. And we were intrigued by the juxtaposition of speeds between the digital technology industries and the slower, more deliberative cultures of large firms in many other industries.

We've learned over the years that when we are faced with a big question that doesn't have clear answers, the best thing to do is see how executives are actually answering the question for themselves. So, we talked with executives in large companies—150 executives in fifty companies around the world—to understand how these leaders were thinking about new digital challenges, and what they were doing with new technologies.

We found that most of the companies were already investing in technologies such as social media, mobility, analytics, and embedded devices. But some—the firms we call Digital Masters—were making far better progress than others. Comparing these companies and the rest of the pack helped us identify differences in how the masters conceptualized and managed their digital activities. We found that it's not just what they invest in, but it's how they lead change that makes these companies Digital Masters.[11] After testing our theory in a global survey of nearly four hundred companies, we became even more convinced.

Digital Masters excel in two critical dimensions: the *what* of technology (which we call *digital capabilities*) and the *how* of leading change (which we call *leadership capabilities*). These are two very distinct dimensions of digital mastery, and each plays its own role. What you invest in matters, to a point. How you use those investments to transform your company is a key to success. Neither dimension is enough on its own. Each is associated with different types of financial performance, and each provides only partial advantage.[12] Taken together, they combine to give Digital Masters a clear advantage over their competitors.

Digital Capabilities

Digital Masters know where and how to invest in the digital opportunity. The size of the investment is not as important as the reason—and the impact. Digital Masters see technology as a way to change the way they do business—their customer engagements, internal operations, and even business models. To these companies, new technologies such as social media, mobility, and analytics are not goals to attain or signals to send their customers and investors. These technologies are tools to get closer to customers, empower their employees, and transform their internal business processes.

But more than technology is needed. While the changes possible through smart digital investment are impressive, they are not enough. Companies that invest in the right areas have higher revenue for each unit of their existing physical capacity (such as people and facilities) than their competitors, but they are no more profitable. Gaining the true digital advantage also requires leadership.

Leadership Capabilities

For Digital Masters, committed leadership is more than just a buzzword. It is the lever that turns technology into transformation. Despite the advice of many gurus to "let a thousand flowers bloom" in your company, we saw no examples of successful transformation happening bottom-up. Instead, executives in every Digital Master steered the transformation through strong top-down leadership: setting direction, building momentum, and ensuring that the company follows through.

Top-down leadership does not mean that you need to plan out the transformation in complete detail from the start. Nor does it mean that you can just energize the company and wait for great things to happen. In the Digital Masters we studied, leaders created a clear and broad vision of the future, started some critical initiatives, and then engaged their employees to build out the vision over time. The leaders stayed involved throughout the transformation to make the case for change, to drive the change forward, and to redirect activities and behaviors that went against the vision. And they continually looked for ways to extend the vision and move the company to the next level of digital advantage. As Asian Paints, Nike, and others have learned, every step on the road to transformation opens up new possibilities to exploit and extend the company's digital advantage.

Top-down leadership does mean strong governance and coordination. It is very difficult to ensure that all parts of a complex company move in the right direction at the right pace. People in different units often do their own thing or wait before committing to a new way of action. The true advantage comes from linking different digital activities, and that can only happen if people are on the same page. Nike built Nike Digital Sport in 2010 to provide coordination, innovation, and some shared resources for the company's many digital efforts.[13] Coffee powerhouse Starbucks created the position of chief digital officer in 2012 for the same reason.[14] Asian Paints extended the role of the chief information officer (CIO) to cover strategy as well as IT. Other firms find that digital steering committees are enough. The roles are less important than the results. All Digital Masters find ways to build a clear vision of a radically different future, engage their employees in the goal, foster strong bonds between technical and businesspeople, and steer the course through strong governance.

FOUR LEVELS OF DIGITAL MASTERY

If Digital Masters like Nike and Asian Paints represent excellence on both digital and leadership dimensions, what about other firms? Each dimension is different, and each is important for different reasons. Putting the two dimensions together yields four levels of digital mastery (figure 1-1). Digital Masters excel at both dimensions, but most companies do not. Some companies are strong on digital capabilities but weak on leadership capabilities. Some are the reverse. Still others are weak on both dimensions; they have not yet begun the digital journey.

Beginners are just at the start of the digital journey. Many of them adopt a wait-and-see strategy, trying to gain certainty before they act. Some believe the digital opportunity is right for other industries, but not for theirs. Others lack the leadership to make something happen. As a result, Beginners have only basic digital capabilities. And they

FIGURE 1.1

Four levels of digital mastery

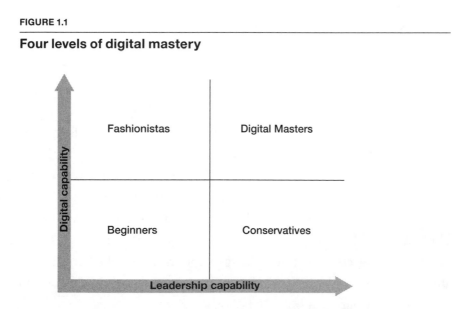

Source: Adapted from George Westerman, Maël Tannou, Didier Bonnet, Patrick Ferraris, and Andrew McAfee, "The Digital Advantage: How Digital Leaders Outperform Their Peers in Every Industry," Capgemini Consulting and MIT Center for Digital Business, November 2012.

lag behind their competitors on multiple measures of financial performance.

Many Beginners use regulation or privacy as an excuse for inaction. Meanwhile, their competitors are not waiting to act. Many insurance companies have been slow to adopt social media because of regulatory challenges in allowing their agents to use blogs and social media messages. But Northwestern Mutual found a safe way to put its agents on LinkedIn so the financial representatives can build and maintain relationships.[15] Similarly, many medical and pharmaceutical companies are wary of regulatory and privacy concerns in using social media. But a medical device company used social media to inform medical providers about a game-changing new device far faster than traditional media could have done.[16]

Fashionistas are not waiting to act. They buy every new digital bauble. They flaunt their technological trendiness but don't change what's behind the veneer. However, because they lack strong digital leadership and governance, they waste much of what they spend. Or they find that they need to reverse what they've done so that they can integrate and scale their capabilities. One company we studied built employee collaboration platforms in different parts of the business using different (and incompatible) technologies. Employees could collaborate within their silos, but couldn't share knowledge across the company. Another company had three mobile marketing initiatives, in different parts of the company, addressing overlapping markets. The mobile solutions used different vendors and different technology sets, so they could not build on each other.

Although there is nothing wrong with trying experiments to find the best solution, neither of these Fashionistas had mechanisms to coordinate their activities or build synergies across their investments. Building a wide variety of incompatible processes and systems may seem like progress, but it limits bigger opportunities. This incompatibility impedes a coordinated approach to customer engagement and a unified view of operations.

Conservatives have a capability profile that is the opposite of Fashionistas. Although Conservatives have useful digital leadership capabilities, excess prudence prevents these firms from building strong digital capabilities. Unconcerned about technology fashion, the companies focus on ensuring that every digital investment is carefully considered and strongly coordinated. Leaders in these companies don't want to make mistakes that would waste their scarce time, effort, and money. This caution can be useful, especially in highly regulated industries such as health care and financial services. But it can also create a governance trap that focuses more on controls and rules than making progress. By focusing on control and certainty, Conservatives find it hard to mobilize top management—and the rest of the organization—to see the bigger prize that digital transformation can bring. In trying to prevent failure, these companies fail to make much progress at all.

DIGITAL MASTERY MATTERS

Digital Masters have overcome the difficulties that challenge their competitors. They know how and where to invest, and their leaders are committed to guiding the company powerfully into the digital future. They are already exploiting their digital advantage to build superior competitive positions in their industries.

To quantify the digital advantage, we conducted a survey of 391 companies in thirty countries.[17] We limited the survey to large companies only—those with revenues of $500 million or higher. We used statistical methods on specific questions in the survey to construct factors representing subcomponents of the two dimensions of digital mastery, to cluster the component factors, and then to make the two dimensions as statistically independent of each other as possible. Then, we split the sample at the median on each dimension to place each company into one of the four categories, with each category containing approximately 25 percent of the firms.

Next, we analyzed the financials of the 184 publicly traded firms in our sample. We mean-adjusted the performance of each firm by subtracting the average performance of all firms in its industry that were larger than $500 million in annual revenue. Then we compared the average mean-adjusted performance of companies in each quadrant.

We found a striking performance difference for Digital Masters (figure 1.2). The two critical elements of digital mastery—digital capabilities and leadership capabilities—are associated with different types of performance; companies that excel in a particular dimension outstrip industry competitors in some performance measures while lagging in others. Meanwhile, Digital Masters—companies that excel in both dimensions—have the highest performance, far outstripping other firms on multiple financial measures. Digital Masters are 26 percent more profitable than their industry peers and generate 9 percent higher revenue from their physical assets.[18]

FIGURE 1.2

Digital Masters outperform their peers

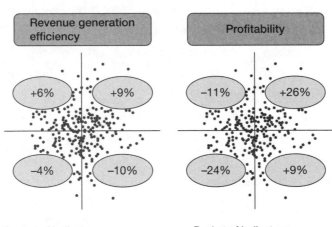

Basket of indicators:
• Revenue/employee
• Fixed-assets turnover

Basket of indicators:
• EBIT margin
• Net profit margin

Note: Average performance difference for firms in each quadrant versus the average performance of all large firms in the same industry for the 184 publicly traded companies in our sample. EBIT: earnings before interest and taxes.

Source: Adapted from George Westerman, Maël Tannou, Didier Bonnet, Patrick Ferraris, and Andrew McAfee, "The Digital Advantage: How Digital Leaders Outperform Their Peers in Every Industry," Capgemini Consulting and MIT Center for Digital Business, November 2012.

Digital Capability and Revenue Generation

Companies with stronger digital capabilities are better at driving revenue with their physical assets. On a basket of measures including revenue per employee and fixed-asset turnover, Fashionistas and Digital Masters outperform average industry performance by 6 and 9 percent, respectively. Meanwhile, Beginners and Conservatives, both of which lag in their digital capabilities, trail their industry competitors by 4 and 10 percent, respectively.

These differences between high and low digital capability make sense; digital activities can improve and extend the reach of physical ones. With e-commerce, companies big and small now have access to a global marketplace for their goods and services. Digital business can help companies to manage more volume with a unit of existing physical capacity. And digital capabilities can also help companies grow revenue by reaching out to new customers or engaging with existing customers in new ways. Nike's ability to generate buzz through social media, or Asian Paint's use of call centers and mobile devices to leverage its salespeople, helps these companies grow revenue without investing in more employees or facilities.

The revenue-generation difference is substantial. For example, Fashionistas—strong on digital investment but not on leadership—gain 16 percent more revenue per unit of human and physical assets than Conservatives do, and 10 percent more than Beginners. Conservatives, being weak on digital investment, have lower revenue leverage, but they excel in other ways.

Leadership Capability and Profitability

Moving in the other dimension, companies that excel in leadership capability are significantly more profitable than their peers. On average, Conservatives and Digital Masters are, respectively, 9 and 26 percent more profitable than their average industry competitors on a basket of measures including EBIT (earnings before interest and taxes) margin and net profit margin. Meanwhile, Beginners and Fashionistas, with their weaker leadership capabilities, trail their average competitors by 11 and 24 percent, respectively, on these profitability measures.

For companies that excel at leadership capability, strong vision and disciplined governance help drive digital investments in a common direction. These firms weed out activities that run counter to the future vision of the transformed firm. They scale successful investments enterprise-wide. And they engage their employees in identifying valuable new opportunities.

Asian Paints built on efficiencies it gained through strong governance and IT–business relationships to launch new digital capabilities that moved the company into the Digital Master category. Nike's digital unit develops digital products and capabilities, helps other units, and manages digital activities that cut across organizational silos. Each firm found that strong digital leadership created efficiency and scalability in its digital efforts.

THE PERFORMANCE ADVANTAGE
OF DIGITAL MASTERS

Firms that excel in either dimension outperform their competitors in specific and different ways. Digital Masters—firms that excel in both dimensions—far outperform the others. On average, Digital Masters are 26 percent more profitable than their industry competitors. They generate 9 percent more revenue with their employees and physical assets. For the large, traditional companies we studied—with revenues of $500 million or larger—the difference can be many millions of dollars on the bottom line.

Digital Masters combine digital capabilities and leadership capabilities to achieve performance that is greater than either dimension can deliver on its own. Strong digital capabilities make new digital initiatives easier and less risky, while providing revenue leverage that can generate new cash. Meanwhile, strong leadership creates synergies that free up money for investment, while also engaging employees to identify new opportunities. Together, the two capabilities spiral in a virtuous cycle of ever-increasing digital advantage.

Our analysis shows correlation, not causality. Excelling in digital capability and leadership capability may lead to higher financial performance for the firm. On the other hand, we may be seeing that companies that outperform their peers financially tend to excel in the two dimensions of digital mastery. The direction of causality is important from an academic research standpoint. But from a management standpoint, either direction of causality leads to the same advice.

So, let's say it this way: the best-managed companies in the world—those that significantly outperform their peers in both revenue generation and profitability—tend to manage their digital activities in a common way. They build both digital capabilities and leadership capabilities that are better than other companies. If the best-managed companies in the world do digital this way, then it's a good idea to manage your digital activities this way too.

DO YOU HAVE TIME TO WAIT ?

Digital transformation is moving much more rapidly in some industries than in others. If you are in the travel or publishing industries, you have been dealing with digital competitors and digital sales for years. But what if you are in an industry like pharmaceuticals or utilities, where strong digital threats have yet to materialize? Can you afford to wait?

Figure 1.3 shows digital mastery, by industry, for our survey. Each dot represents the average mastery of companies in each industry for which we have twenty or more data points. Some industries are already squarely in the Digital Masters quadrant, while others still lag. Many firms in the high-tech industry are already Digital Masters, while digital mastery in pharmaceuticals is far lower. Other industries, such as telecom or consumer packaged goods, are on the cusp of digital mastery, but need more digital or leadership capabilities, or both, to get there.

FIGURE 1.3

Digital mastery by industry

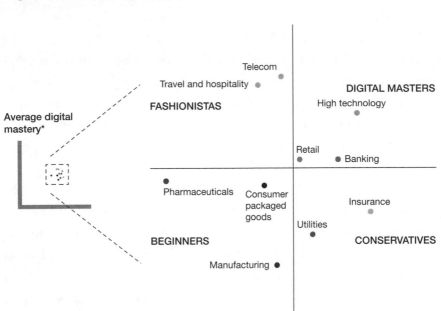

*Average digital mastery of industries for which we received at least twenty survey responses.

Source: George Westerman, Maël Tannou, Didier Bonnet, Patrick Ferraris, and Andrew McAfee, "The Digital Advantage: How Digital Leaders Outperform Their Peers in Every Industry," Capgemini Consulting and MIT Center for Digital Business, November 2012.

If your company is trailing your industry's average digital mastery, then you need to get moving fast. But what if you are not behind in your industry? If you are an executive in a Beginner industry, such as consumer packaged goods, pharmaceuticals, or manufacturing, you might be tempted to believe you can wait. After all, why invest the cost and effort to become a Digital Master if your whole industry is lagging? This kind of thinking is sensible. And it's wrong.

You might think that if your industry is not in the Digital Master quadrant, then you have an opportunity to grab digital advantage before anybody else does. Such thinking is a bit more accurate, but still wrong.

You might even think that you can watch your competitors and be a fast follower. This attitude, too, is not quite right. It's too late to beat all of your peers to the punch, and you can't be a fast follower in digital mastery unless you are already there.

If you are not a Digital Master, figure 1.4 has bad news. It shows, for each industry, the percentage of firms in each quadrant. In most industries, more than one-fourth of all large firms are already Digital Masters. Even more important is this: every industry already hosts at least one Digital Master. In other words, in every industry—from pharma to manufacturing to high-tech—some company is already reaping the benefits of the digital advantage. Every other company is behind.

This situation should be a call to action. Think about it. Even if it only takes you three or four years to become a Digital Master, some firms in your industry are already enjoying a digital advantage. Even worse, while you start to build the capabilities you need, the masters can exploit the capabilities they already have. These companies can accelerate ahead of you even as you try to catch up.

FIGURE 1.4

Digital mastery by industry

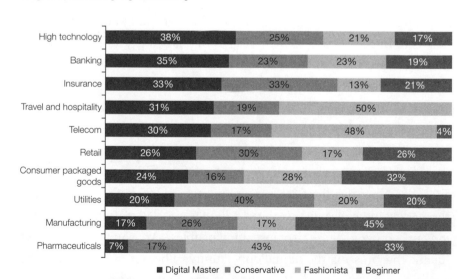

Note: Distribution of digital mastery for all industries with more than twenty respondents in our survey. Note that there are Digital Masters in every industry studied.

Source: George Westerman, Maël Tannou, Didier Bonnet, Patrick Ferraris, and Andrew McAfee, "The Digital Advantage: How Digital Leaders Outperform Their Peers in Every Industry," Capgemini Consulting and MIT Center for Digital Business, November 2012.

HOW TO GET STARTED NOW

Digital mastery matters. It matters in every industry. We've found that the DNA of Digital Masters is clear, and any company can adopt it. But it takes time to become a Digital Master, and time is a fast-diminishing commodity for many firms.

How will you become a Digital Master? Companies take different paths to get there. Nike was a Fashionista before it became a Digital Master. Initially, it developed digital capabilities in silos. Then, through its Nike Digital Sport unit, it added new leadership capabilities to link the silos and launch new digital capabilities.

Asian Paints went the other way; it was a Conservative before it became a Digital Master. Executives in Asian Paints created the vision to become a more unified company and then built governance and IT capabilities to help it get there. Then they repeatedly built on the company's capabilities to transform its customer engagement, internal operations, and business models. Both Asian Paints and Nike are reaping huge benefits from their digital mastery.

Although it is less common, some companies have made the leap directly from Beginner to Digital Master. They did not stop in between. Burberry, which we'll discuss in chapter 2, did it. And while making a direct leap is difficult and risky, sometimes it is the only way forward. This is especially true if you have a crisis situation—a "burning platform" such as in media, entertainment, or information services; in this case making the leap may be the best way out.

Figure 1.5 shows the four quadrants of digital mastery in more detail, including challenges that each quadrant can face. Take a minute to think about it. What quadrant is your company in? Decide for yourself, and then ask some colleagues. Are your digital efforts creating real change in your company, or are they just shiny baubles? Are you being too careful and thus missing the digital opportunity? The self-assessment in the appendix can help you identify your position in the matrix.

If your firm is a Fashionista, you should start to build leadership capabilities and gain synergies across your digital efforts. Find a unifying vision, and invest in governance to coordinate across

FIGURE 1.5

What is your level of digital mastery?

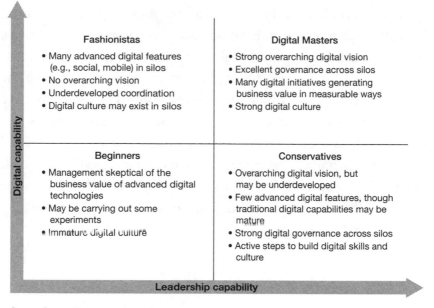

Source: George Westerman, Claire Calméjane, Didier Bonnet, Patrick Ferraris, and Andrew McAfee, "Digital Transformation: A Roadmap for Billion-Dollar Organizations," Capgemini Consulting and MIT Center for Digital Business, November 2011.

your company. You may want to hire a chief digital officer like Starbucks did or create a digital unit like Nike did. Moving from Fashionista to Digital Master may require some investment as you refocus disconnected digital initiatives and technologies into a unified and coherent digital program. This kind of refocusing and rework, however painful in the short term, will pay off later in terms of lower costs, lower risk, and greater agility.

If your firm is a Conservative, you can take advantage of your digital leadership strengths to build new digital capabilities in a smart way. Every company has areas that executives know they can improve, whether in customer engagement or internal operations. Try some experiments to address these issues. Then scale the successful trials to enterprise level. Like the executives at Asian Paints, you can continually think about how to expand your digital vision. What else can you do with your new digital capabilities? Engage your employees, through meetings or innovation contests, to identify new digital opportunities. Then implement.

If your firm is a Beginner, you can try some experiments to test the digital waters, either with customers or in your internal operations. Then build a vision of your digital future and start to create the capabilities to make it happen. Often the best course is to start with the capability that is most natural for your company. Then you can move in the more challenging direction once you are ready. Insurers and banks could leverage their conservative cultures to build committed leadership capabilities first, and then expand their digital investments. Fast-moving, customer-focused industries such as fashion or media could start by innovating new digital capabilities and then building strong leadership capabilities.

WHAT'S NEXT

You've seen the benefits of being a Digital Master. You've started to think about your level of digital mastery. Now it's time to plot your digital transformation strategy. In the rest of the book, we'll show you how.

Part I shows, in depth, what it means to build your digital capabilities. Our research has identified three broad areas in which companies are building new digital capabilities—customer experience, operational processes, and business models. We thus devote a chapter to each area, including examples from many companies around the world such as Air France, Burberry, Caesars Entertainment, and Codelco. Part II shows how to build your leadership capabilities. We've identified four elements: shared transformative vision, strong governance, deep engagement, and solid technology leadership. We devote a chapter to each element, including examples of how companies such as Caesars, Codelco, P&G, Pages Jaunes, and Starbucks are making it happen. Then, part III helps you build your roadmap. We provide concrete management guidance—plus self-assessments you can complete with your colleagues—to help you create your own digital advantage.

PART I

BUILDING DIGITAL CAPABILITIES

The DNA of Digital Masters is clear. One element of the DNA shows that digital transformation cannot happen without astute digital investments—the *what* of digital transformation. But too many companies confuse digital advantage with the digital technologies themselves. Digital Masters focus on making their businesses different through technology, not on the technologies themselves.

Part I shows, in depth, how executives have transformed the way their companies operate. You can differentiate your company through three broad categories of digital capability: customer experience, operational processes, and business models. Let's look at each in turn.

CHAPTER 2

CREATING A COMPELLING CUSTOMER EXPERIENCE

One of the deep secrets of life is that all that is
really worth doing is what we do for others.

—LEWIS CARROLL

Transforming the customer experience is at the heart of digital transformation. Digital technologies are changing the game of customer interactions, with new rules and possibilities that were unimaginable only a few years back.

Do you want to finally hear the voice of your customers and escape the narrow lenses of surveys and focus groups? Social media let you. Do you want your clients to continue their engagement with your brand on the move? Mobile computing lets you. Do you want to know where your customers physically are? Geolocalization lets you. Do you want to make better predictions to deliver a truly personalized experience? Customer analytics lets you.

For Digital Masters, these new technologies are not goals to attain or signals to send to investors. Instead, the technologies are tools that can be combined to get closer to customers. Digital mastery goes well beyond websites and mobile apps to truly transform the customer experience and how you steer customers effortlessly through it.

Delivered properly, an engaging customer experience creates value for both customers and firms. It drives retention and stimulates customer loyalty. But delivering a differentiated customer experience in large organizations is a complex task. Why? First, customer expectations have increased substantially; of the 150 executives we interviewed early in our study, 70 percent highlighted the ever-rising tide of customer expectations as a key driver for change.[1] Second, integrating new digital channels into existing operations can be organizationally challenging. Third, these digital interactions force an evolution in culture—new clock speed, new decision-making methods, new rules—that can run counter to the way large traditional companies have managed customer relationships. So, like our Beginners or Conservatives, you can choose to do only a few experiments here and there. Or, like our Fashionistas, you can invest in every new shiny object that's available. But you would be missing the big prize.

Despite the challenges, huge benefits are available to those companies that create compelling customer experiences.

LEADING THE DIGITAL REBIRTH
OF AN OLD ICONIC BRAND

In 2006, when Angela Ahrendts took the helm at Burberry, the company's top-line growth was significantly behind its peers.[2] While the overall sector was growing at around 12 to 13 percent a year, Burberry's growth was only 1 to 2 percent. The company was not keeping pace with the rapid development in the luxury goods market, neither in terms of innovation nor in terms of products and services. Burberry was up against tough competition from much larger French and Italian peers, each of which had multiple brands and many times the company's own revenue and profit. Something had to be done to reverse this trend.

Burberry's management team began by asking itself a fundamental question: "What is our vision?" From there, the team members began the development of a five-year strategy-making process looking at Burberry's unique assets and strategic direction. Ahrendts explained: "What do we have that our peers don't? First, we're British. Second, we were born from a coat. Finally, our peers were all targeting 'ladies who lunch' and focusing mainly on the baby boomers. There was no way we could meet them head on with their much larger advertising budgets. We decided to go after the millennial customers."[3]

This last strategic choice proved critical to Burberry's digital journey. The company decided to target its marketing spending on millennial consumers—those in their twenties. They chose to focus on emerging economies, where the average high-net-worth customer is typically fifteen years younger than in traditional markets. To engage and communicate effectively with this population, Burberry had to use millennials' mother tongue: digital. That's when the digital vision became reality and the digital transformation started for Burberry.

Ahrendts identified that, to be successful, there had to be a pure, global brand vision. Christopher Bailey, the digital-savvy chief creative officer, became the "brand czar," meaning anything that the customer sees goes through his office. Working together, Ahrendts and Bailey communicated this vision internally. Ahrendts explained: "We said we would no longer do what was best for a person or what was best for a region. We would do what was best for the brand. We talked about the 'digital tsunami' coming, and used this to drive home why and where we needed to focus, and how united and pure our global brand expression had to be."[4]

With the top team aligned around this new vision, Ahrendts and Bailey decided to focus on digital marketing to target their customers. They hired a young, dynamic marketing team whose members mirrored the millennial customer. The company allocated a substantial portion of its annual marketing budget to digital media, shifting away from traditional media.

The company has excelled in digital marketing, launching several successful and innovative initiatives: revamping Burberry.com in eleven languages;[5] launching a fragrance with innovative Facebook sampling;

developing Tweetwalk, live-stream fashion shows, with Twitter; collaborating with Google to create Burberry Kisses, allowing users to capture and send their "kiss" to anyone in the world;[6] and partnering with Chinese social media platform WeChat in the autumn/winter 2014 runway show to launch a series of mobile content experiences. Empowered by a closely connected, creative thinking culture, the company used digital technologies to share the excitement of key brand moments with its worldwide customers.

At the same time, Burberry's retail investment was keeping pace—opening twenty to thirty new stores a year. How could the company use digital innovation to engage its customers seamlessly in its physical real estate as well as online? This is where Burberry's retail-theater concept came into play. Ahrendts explained: "We began to partner with technology companies to make the 'retail theater' concept real, enabling us to broadcast our multifaceted content to our stores globally. We used technology to bring our brand to life in our stores: from the music to the rich video content on giant internal and external screens to the iPads carried by all sales associates that gave access to the full global collection regardless of what was available in-store. We invited our customers to watch our runway shows live in stores and enabled them to shop the collection on iPads immediately afterwards for delivery in six to eight weeks. In this way, we have developed our stores to showcase our digital innovations."[7]

Prior to this wave of digital innovations, Burberry had spent several years implementing a backbone enterprise platform to consolidate its systems and make its global operations transparent. It was critical for the company to have a single view of the customer in order to improve the experience across all channels, media, and platforms. "Had we not put that in place," Ahrendts said, "we would not have been able to do so much of the front-end digital innovation we have been doing."[8] The company also made big investments in customer service not only by training salespeople in stores, but also on its website, where customers can click to call or click to chat with customer service representatives 365 days a year, 24/7, and in fourteen languages.[9]

Burberry's next challenge was analytics. The company layered on new communication and analytics tools. It promoted a chief customer officer to optimize insights from all physical and digital interactions. It launched a "Customer 360" program—a data-driven shopping experience that invites customers to digitally share their buying histories, shopping tendencies, and fashion preferences—to allow Burberry to profile and personalize the experience. Retail assistants can access customers' digital profiles through tablets, knowing, for example, what a Brazilian customer last bought on a stopover to Paris and what she said about Burberry on Twitter.[10]

According to Ahrendts, "Our vision was that any person, any constituency, needing to interact with Burberry would come to Burberry.com and enjoy exactly the same experience as in-store customers. We wanted them to come into our world—Burberry World—and be able to visit all the different parts of the business as they would do in our HQ."[11]

Today, more people see the Burberry brand via digital than they do through any other medium. In luxury, 60 percent of people shop online and pick up in a store. As Ahrendts pointed out, "If the store doesn't look or feel the same as it does online, are you truly behaving like a great brand?" In 2013–2014 Burberry was named by think tank L2 as the fashion brand with the number one "digital IQ" for the second year running, included in *Fast Company*'s list of the top ten most innovative retail companies globally for the second consecutive year, and named one of Interbrand's best global brands for the fifth consecutive year.[12]

WHAT DO DIGITAL MASTERS
DO DIFFERENTLY?

Burberry is an outstanding example of a company that blurs the lines between its digital and physical customer experiences. It is not an isolated case. Our research shows that Digital Masters transform their customer experiences through the sum of four related interventions. Together, these interventions fundamentally change the customer value equation. First, Digital Masters spend time understanding customer behavior and *designing the customer experience from the outside in*. A Digital Master figures out what customers do and why, where, and how they do it. The company then works out where and how the experience can be digitally enhanced across channels.

Second, Digital Masters use digital technologies to increase *reach and engagement* through smart investments in new digital channels. They provide user-friendly mobile apps, develop rewarding social media experiences, and rebalance their marketing spending to reinforce the engagement.

Third, they put *customer data at the heart* of the whole customer experience. They become more scientific, using metrics and analytics to inform the change—everything from understanding current usage of their products and services to segmenting the customer base and proactively offering personalized deals and designing predictive marketing campaigns.

Finally, Digital Masters work to *seamlessly mesh the physical and digital experiences*, not by replacing the old with the new, but by using digital technologies to enhance the customer experience by leveraging valuable existing assets.

DESIGNING THE CUSTOMER EXPERIENCE FROM THE OUTSIDE IN

Designing a good experience is, of course, based on a clear vision of what you are trying to achieve. As Gary Loveman, CEO of global gaming company Caesars Entertainment, pointed out, "The experience has to be what our customers want it to be."[13]

Digitally engaged customers expect that products, services, and information will be timely and tailored to their specific needs. They want all of these at the precise moment they are looking, and on whatever platform they are using at the time. The more touch points you have, the greater the complexity of the interactions across channels and the greater the need to understand them in detail. So how can you define the kind of engaging experience your customers really want?

You need to thoroughly understand both customer behaviors and the organizational requirements to deliver the new customer experience.

Take the time to systematically learn how people interact with your products, services, channels, brand, infrastructure, and employees—deep insights into customer decisions and usage journeys. How do customers behave before, during, and after an interaction with your company? Where are the pain points? How can you alleviate them? What part of the experience can be digitally enhanced? Which customers are more prone to engage digitally, and how?

Joe Gross, head of group market management at insurance group Allianz, pointed out: "We started by identifying touch points that digital impacted, and of course, these touch points spanned the entire spectrum of the value chain—right from the customer-awareness stage to distribution to actual sales, product offers to pricing, et cetera. Once we identified these touch points, we devised assessment criteria against each of them."[14]

Adam Brotman, chief digital officer at Starbucks, adopted a similar approach. "We tend to look at what are the needs of our customers, what's the strategy of our business, what are all the different digital touch points that are already in place versus ones we need to put in place, and then we'll roadmap out how we want to prioritize our time and effort against this backdrop."[15]

Behaviors across large customer bases are rarely homogeneous. Data and analytics should inform the segmentation of your customer base, defining targeted experiences according to specific behavior patterns. Burberry, for example, understood early that high-net-worth millennial consumers in emerging markets would require a different, digital-rich, experience than would traditional fashion consumers.

Similarly, Kirsten Lynch, chief marketing officer of Vail Resorts, realized that to improve the customers' experience, she had to get a more granular understanding of skiers' behavior: "For years we've had a CRM [customer relationship management] system that gives us basic demographic and behavioral data . . . Skiing is such a passion-based business that we need to go beyond basic data to understand why our guests come to the mountain."[16] She decided to use personae to segment her customer base.[17] "We have the 'Alpine A-Listers,' who are hard-core about skiing and also passionate about the luxury experience," she said. "Then there are 'Village Sophisticates,' who tend to care more about dining, shopping and spas than skiing. The 'Shred Heads' care only about making the most of their ski day—it's not about luxury for them. For each segment, we know how many days they ski a year, where they ski and what they spend their money on. We can personalize what we talk to them about . . . We are piloting some new technology that pre-populates the agent's screen with everything we know about our guests."[18]

You also need to focus on delivery from the start. How big is your organizational challenge? What process, people, and technology changes are required to make the new customer experience work? What power needs to be in the hands of customers so they can use whichever technology they prefer to reach your company? For instance, self-service facilities can be used to track a package delivery, configure a complex industrial product online, or know precisely when a pizza will be delivered.

Unfortunately, too few companies do what it takes to succeed. Forrester Research reports that although 86 percent of customer-experience executives believe that customer experience is a top strategic priority, less than half of the companies have a companywide program to address it, and only 30 percent have a dedicated budget to fund the change required.[19]

Digital Masters do it right; they invest in designing a compelling customer experience from the outside in. They are also prepared to do what it takes to adapt the organization to deliver on the promise.

CREATING REACH AND CUSTOMER ENGAGEMENT

Digital transformation cannot happen without digital investment. Digital Masters make smart digital investments to creatively enhance customer experiences. The size of the investment is not important, but the impact is. To these companies, new technologies such as social media, mobility, and analytics are only tools to get closer to their customers.

Since opening its first location in Seattle in 1971, Starbucks has grown into one of the world's most globally recognized brands. Starbucks has built a multi-billion-dollar enterprise on more than just coffee; it has succeeded in creating a unique "Starbucks experience" in its stores and online. But Starbucks has not always been a Digital Master.

Following a rapid expansion, Starbucks faced declining same-store sales in 2008, and its share price had been cut nearly in half over the prior two years. The picture wasn't much better on the technology front. Unintuitive point-of-sale systems still ran on antiquated technology, and store managers had no access to e-mail. To turn the tide, senior leaders, under the helm of CEO Howard Schultz, took a number of strategic actions, key among them using digital technologies to engage customers in new ways. Adam Brotman, the company's chief digital officer, explained: "Digital for Starbucks was not just about a website or a point-of-sales system, but about an ability to connect with customers and transform their experience and drive the company."[20] The company decided to lead the way with mobile and social channels.

The first Starbucks foray into mobile was the company's myStarbucks app, released in 2009, which allowed customers to locate the nearest store, learn more about the company's coffees, and even build their own drinks. In January 2011, Starbucks took its loyalty program digital with the introduction of its Starbucks Card mobile app. This app allowed Starbucks customers to pay for in-store purchases with their mobile phones. App users could present an on-screen version of their prepaid loyalty card and could top up their funds online, on their smartphones, or in stores. This approach integrated easily with existing point-of-sale technology, which was already set up for reading bar codes. Since its launch, the program has been extremely successful, with 20 percent of all loyalty card transactions conducted via mobile in 2012.[21]

Keeping pace with advances in mobile technology, Starbucks has continued to expand its mobile payment capabilities. In 2012, it announced that customers would be able to make payments at the register via Square—an app-based mobile payment system—following a $25 million investment in the service.[22] Starbucks has also enabled integration of its application with Apple's native Passbook feature, which consolidates ticket, coupon, and loyalty card information on an iPhone or iPod Touch for convenient access.

Mobile payments at Starbucks have been a success for customer convenience, but they are proving to have financial benefits as well. Processing fees for transactions through its mobile app and Square have been substantially reduced. With over three million mobile payment transactions per week in 2012, the mobile-payments introduction has significantly reduced transaction fees.[23] The reduction benefits both coffee drinkers and Starbucks.

Starbucks has also built a leading presence in social media. By 2012, the company's 54 million Facebook fans, 3.4 million Twitter followers, and 900,000 followers on Instagram earned Starbucks a number one ranking among socially engaged companies.

Digital Masters like Starbucks do not just invest smartly in technology and channels. They maximize these investments by optimizing their marketing media mix. Burberry took the plunge by redirecting a substantial portion of its annual marketing budget to digital media. Procter & Gamble, the consumer products giant, is investing almost a third of its media spending on digital, social, and mobile.[24] Not a small decision from one of the world's biggest advertisers! Not all companies have to be that bold. Research firm Gartner estimated that on average, large US companies spend about 25 percent of their marketing budgets on digital.[25] Whatever the amount, a rebalancing is needed if a firm is to get full benefits from the increased channel reach.

The social media presence of Starbucks has earned the company more than just fans. The company also uses social media to fuel customer-driven innovation. Through its My Starbucks Idea site, Starbucks has collected more than 150,000 customer-submitted ideas to improve its products, customer experience, and corporate initiatives.[26] Once an idea has been submitted, the site's customer community can vote the idea up or down, helping Starbucks identify and implement the best ideas. The company closes the loop with its *Ideas in Action* blog, where employees respond to ideas personally, and it lets customers know when they can expect to see their ideas realized in stores. For example, one community member suggested making it easier for customers to manage multiple orders—especially useful for people going on midday Starbucks runs for their coworkers. In less than a month, Starbucks introduced its Runner Reward program. The program provides runners with a convenient form to manage orders and offers them a fifth drink (their own drink) free of charge.[27]

Brotman summed it up: "Everything we are doing in digital is about enhancing and strengthening those connections [with our customers] in only the way that digital can and only the way that Starbucks can."[28]

PUTTING CUSTOMER DATA AT THE HEART OF THE EXPERIENCE

The digitization of just about everything we do or use these days has created a deluge of information. Executives now have access to precious data that can substantially increase their insights into the customer experience. Data should be the lifeblood for designing compelling customer experiences. By adding science to the art, data helps companies move from guesswork to inspired predictions and continuous hypotheses testing.

Digital Masters rely heavily on data-driven insights. But making your customer experience more scientific requires difficult organizational learning. CEO Gary Loveman of Caesars explained: "When I showed up at Caesars, we were collecting a tremendous amount of transactional data about our customers who were anxious for us to do something useful with it. And we couldn't figure out how to do that. The organization had a loyalty program that collected a bunch of information so that we could give customers certain things in return for their business, like free meals and hotel rooms and the like. But we couldn't figure out how first to architect the data in a constructive fashion and then apply analytics against it that would allow us to get a guy named X to make an incremental visit under certain conditions and someone named Y to make a different visit under different circumstances."[29]

Today, the picture at Caesars is different. The company collects vast amounts of transactional, demographic, and game-play data through its loyalty program to create a detailed profile for each Caesars guest. Employees then use this information throughout the company to make better customer decisions.

For example, Caesars marketers can create and target special offers with precision. Meanwhile, the hospitality staff can use the same information to personalize nearly every aspect of a guest's stay, from how he or she is greeted on arrival, to how the room is made up. Should a guest have an unlucky evening at the casino, managers on the floor can even perform a cost-benefit analysis and offer complimentary services to improve the experience.

While it is common across the industry to lavish this kind of personalized attention on big spenders (or whales, in industry parlance), most casino-goers receive a relatively undifferentiated experience. The Caesars data-driven approach, on the other hand, allows the company to scale its personalized touch to a far larger group of customers. Gary Loveman said, "You can't just fail to service the tens of millions of people that constitute the middle of the market."[30]

Mobility and location-based data also play a key role in driving customer intelligence at Caesars. A customer's mobile experience begins before he or she even walks through the door. Before arriving at one of the forty Caesars properties, guests who have opted into the company's Texpress service can check in via SMS (short messaging service, or texting). This service enables them to bypass registration lines and pick up their keys at the bell desk. Texpress also combines mobile location data and SMS to deliver timely and relevant special offers. "If you're at Paris, we could send you two free admissions to the

Eiffel Tower ride or if you're at Caesars Palace after 6 p.m., we could send you an offer for the Bette Midler show," explained a member of the Caesars marketing team. "We might have some additional show tickets left over, so knowing where the customer is, is a great way to get those tickets pushed."[31]

The digital world has multiplied the sources and volume of data available to corporations. There is a need to harness the wealth of structured and unstructured data from usage and social media. What's more, the data can be enriched when it is meshed with location-based data from mobile devices. The key is your ability to integrate this data to make better decisions, increase the quality of the personalized experience, and create true competitive advantage.

US financial institution Capital One is known for its sustained growth in the credit card market. At the heart of its performance is an advanced data analytics capability. Capital One employs both internal and external data to effectively segment the market for credit cards.

The company's Card Lab gives direct insight into every user's individual preferences. The lab's users have the freedom to modify the visual appearance of their card, and to select from a combination of rewards, interest rates, and fees.[32] With its acquisition of data aggregator Bundle Corp, Capital One can track usage data from more than twenty million Visa and MasterCard branded cards.[33] In addition, the company has been able to combine banking services with coupons.[34] Capital One helps consumers get the best mobile-payment offers based on their geographical location and purchase history. And, of course, all this data mining helps Capital One understand consumers better.

With this mass of data, Capital One gets very granular insights into individual consumer preferences. But the story goes further. With its Digital Innovation Lab, Capital One continually finds innovative ways to use these consumer insights to improve the customer experience.[35] The company analyzes up to sixty thousand different product configurations every year and follows through on the most promising.[36]

The digital contact centers can use the insights to predict requirements better, thus providing better customer support.

Capital One's strategy has improved its financial performance. Its net profit grew at a compound annual growth rate of 19.3 percent between 2000 and 2010. And Capital One has continued to thrive after the financial crisis of 2009, achieving 10.7 percent growth from 2010 to 2013.[37]

As the preceding examples show, the culture of Digital Masters is rooted in a common pursuit. Whether drawing on insights from demographic, mobile, or social media data, or good old-fashioned attention to detail, Digital Masters use information and advanced analytics to deliver a superior customer experience.

SEAMLESSLY MESHING PHYSICAL AND DIGITAL EXPERIENCES IN NEW WAYS

Companies with multiple channels to customers—physical, phone, mail, social, mobile, and so on—are experiencing pressure to provide an integrated experience. Delivering these omni-channel experiences requires envisioning and implementing change across both front-end and operational processes. Innovation does not come from opposing the old and the new. But as Burberry has shown, innovation comes from creatively meshing the digital and the physical to reinvent new and compelling customer experiences and to foster continuous innovation.

Similarly, the unique Starbucks experience is rooted in connecting with customers in engaging ways. But Starbucks does not stop with the physical store. It has digitally enriched the customer experience by bridging its local, in-store experience with attractive new online possibilities. Delivered via a free Wi-Fi connection, the Starbucks Digital Network offers in-store customers premium digital content, such as the *New York Times* or *The Economist*, to enjoy alongside their coffee. The network also offers access to local content, from free local restaurant reviews from Zagat to check-in via Foursquare.[38]

Combining physical and digital to enhance customer experiences is not limited to just commercial enterprises. Public services are getting on the act. The Cleveland Museum of Art is using technology to enhance the experience and the engagement of visitors. "EVERY museum is searching for this holy grail, this blending of technology and art," said David Franklin, the director of the museum.[39]

Forty-foot-wide touch screens display greeting-card-sized images of all three thousand objects on display in the museum. Visitors touch an image; the screen enlarges it, arranges itself near similarly themed objects, and offers information like the location of the actual piece. By touching an icon on the image, visitors can transfer it from the wall to an iPad (their own, or rented from the museum for $5 a day), creating a personal list of favorites. From this list, visitors can design a personalized tour, which they can share with others.

"There is only so much information you can put on a wall, and no one walks around with catalogs anymore," Franklin said. The app can produce a photo of the artwork's original setting—seeing a tapestry in a room filled with tapestries, rather than in a white-walled gallery, is more interesting. Another feature lets you take the elements of a large tapestry and rearrange them in either comic-book or movie-trailer format. The experience becomes fun, educational, and engaging. This reinvention has lured new technology-savvy visitors, but has also made seasoned museum-goers come more often.

FACING A TALL ORDER FOR TRADITIONAL ORGANIZATIONS

This digital age has both informed and amplified customer expectations. In the last few years, many digital-savvy companies have set a high bar. Whether you are e-hailing a taxi through a mobile app or buying personalized insurance for your pet online, it's simple, it works, it meets your personal needs, and it can even be a pleasurable experience. And the expectation gap is increasing. A study by Harris Interactive found that

89 percent of consumers in 2011 quit doing business with a company because of a bad customer experience, up from 68 percent in 2006.[40]

Customers don't separate their online experiences from their physical experiences. They see products and services as a whole; they search for objective advice and compare. They want to engage with brands that care, and they share feedback openly—good or bad. Forrester Research found that a quarter of American consumers who had unsatisfactory service interactions in 2010 shared their experiences through social networks, a 50 percent increase over 2009.[41] Unfortunately, there is no indication that these rising expectations will slow down anytime soon. Get prepared.

Creating a compelling customer experience is one of the key pillars of digital transformation. Opportunities abound, but getting it right is organizationally complex. It takes a thorough understanding of customer behavior, smart channel investments, a grasp of customer data, and creativity in blending the old and the new. As we will show in part II, it takes strong operational capabilities and great IT systems. And it takes strong vision and leadership to create organizational change. Whatever stands in the way of delivering a compelling customer experience, fix it. In the long run, doing so will contribute to delivering good performance and changing your company culture from the inside.

In the next chapter, we'll show how Digital Masters create the right kinds of operational capabilities to increase efficiency, flexibility, and customer satisfaction. Later, in part II, we will describe how to build the right leadership capabilities so that you, like Burberry, can transform your customer experience, and your company as a whole.

LEADING DIGITAL CHECKLIST: CUSTOMER EXPERIENCE

✓ Put customer experience at the heart of your digital transformation.

✓ Design your customer experience from the outside in.

✓ Increase reach and customer engagement, where it matters, through new digital channels.

✓ Make data and analytics the lifeblood of your customer experience reinvention.

✓ Seamlessly mesh your digital and physical experience in new ways

✓ Keep on innovating—it's never over. Every digital improvement in customer experience will open up new possibilities.

CHAPTER 3

EXPLOITING THE POWER OF CORE OPERATIONS

*What lies behind you, and what lies in front of you,
pales in comparison to what lies inside of you.*

—RALPH WALDO EMERSON

Codelco, the world's largest copper producer, did not choose customer experience as the focus of its digital transformation. It looked inward, transforming its operational processes to increase both its efficiency and its innovativeness.[1] The company, which is owned by the government of Chile, employs nearly eighteen thousand people and produces 10 percent of the world's copper. In 2012, it produced 1.8 million metric tons of copper, generating $15.9 billion in revenue.[2]

Mining can be a dirty, dangerous, and labor-intensive process. Coordination is difficult because up-to-date information is often only available where the work is happening, whether it is underground with miners, on trucks that move around the mines, or at the machines that process copper ore. Facing challenges around mining productivity, worker safety, and environmental protection, Codelco's executive team took a hard, strategic look at what the future could bring. The team wanted to transform mining operations, moving from a physical model to one powered by digital technology.

To turn that vision into reality, executives initiated Codelco Digital. The initiative's goal was to drive radical improvements in mining automation and to support executives in developing, communicating, and evolving a long-term digital vision. CIO Marco Orellana, the leader of Codelco Digital, worked with the executive team, employees, vendors, industry partners, and sometimes even Codelco's competitors, to innovate operational processes. He said, "Our business in the past was related to physical labor, and today our business is more related to knowledge and technology . . . We introduced new innovations, new ways of working, and new ways of relating with the people inside the mines."[3]

After improving its internal administrative systems, the company shifted focus to transforming the mining process. The first step was to implement real-time mining, that is, a comprehensive real-time view of operations with the goal of improving operational performance.[4] In four mines, experts in a centralized operations center coordinate activity remotely, using data feeds from different parts of the mines. Operators capture and share information in real time to tune their operations and to adjust production schedules as needed.

These advances set the stage for more radical change. Immense mining trucks now drive autonomously, arriving at their destinations on time and with fewer accidents than human drivers. The lessons learned from building autonomous trucks have led to autonomous mining machinery. And work processes are changing to take advantage of the possibilities that mobile technology, analytics, and embedded devices make possible. Already, according to Orellana, many workers "don't travel to the mines. They travel to the [control center in the] city . . . they apply their knowledge, not their physical strength."[5]

The transformation continues, leading to even more radical changes in Codelco's operations. Integrated information networks and fully automated processes will let the company design future mines differently. The company is moving toward an intelligent-mining model, where no miner may ever need to work in the dangerous underground environment again. Intelligent mining is an important goal, especially after 2010, when thirty-three miners from a different mining company were trapped underground for sixty-eight days.[6] Fully autonomous machines, connected through a wide information network, will operate twenty-four hours per day, while being controlled remotely from the central control center.[7]

But the benefits of digitally transforming mining operations go far beyond safety. Removing humans from underground mines will allow Codelco to design mines to different specifications. After all, if a tunnel collapses on a person, it's a terrible tragedy. But if it collapses on a driverless truck, it's not so bad. Human-free mining designs are cheaper and faster to build, with implications for the economics of the company. If Codelco can dig more cheaply and with lower risk, it can exploit huge caches of ore that are not economically feasible today. What started as better process information and driverless trucks is now changing the economics of the entire company.

At the same time that Codelco is automating processes and removing humans from dangerous locations, the company is engaging employees far differently from before. CIO Orellana said, "Our company is very conservative, so changing the culture is a key challenge."[8] Leaders are working to speed execution, become more data-driven in decision making, and increase the firm's innovativeness. According to Orellana, "We created internal innovation awards to promote new ideas and encourage our workers to innovate." When workers create an innovation in one mine, Codelco publicizes the innovation, and the workers, across the company.

While not immune to the union-versus-management challenges common in many mining companies, Codelco's managers and workers are joining together to identify and implement digital opportunities. "We needed more safety conditions for the workers," Orellana said, "and we needed to create a more attractive business for the new workers who don't like working inside the mines and inside the tunnels."[9]

Codelco executives are now reaching for new frontiers through model-driven management in mining. Instead of making decisions based on past results, they are moving to real-time predictive management. According to Orellana, "This is very challenging because the tools as we know them today, such as ERP, must be adjusted to collect, process, and deploy this new information. We are sure that this ability will become a competitive advantage, allowing us to be even more productive and more efficient than we are today."

Digital transformation is already paying huge dividends at Codelco. Operational efficiency and safety are increasing steadily. The firm is extending the life of older mines and identifying new opportunities. It is working with vendors from inside and outside the industry to create innovative ways of performing and orchestrating activities. Through vision and execution, this government-owned enterprise is transforming its internal operations, its industry, and, potentially, the nature of mining throughout the world.

Codelco's story, like that of Burberry, Asian Paints, and Caesars, shows how the first step in digitally transforming operational processes sets the stage for further transformation. We've seen this pattern in dozens of companies that use digital tools ranging from basic IT to leading-edge mobile and embedded technologies. Digitally transforming operations requires a strong technology backbone that integrates and coordinates processes and data in the right ways. Then it takes rethinking how you can manage your business better through technology and information. New opportunities follow, ranging from customer experience to operations to business models.

THE POWER OF DIGITALLY
TRANSFORMED OPERATIONS

Let's face it: transforming operations is less sexy than transforming customer experience. Your internal technologies and processes may not be as pretty and polished as what you show your customers. Your best operations people may be more gritty and gruff than your salespeople. But we all know that what's sexy on the outside isn't always good on the inside (and vice versa).

In industry after industry, companies with better operations create a competitive advantage through superior productivity, efficiency, and agility. What's more, strong operational capabilities are a prerequisite for exceptional digitally powered customer experience, as the Burberry and Caesars examples in chapter 2 showed. Yet operational capabilities are far less visible to outsiders than changes in customer experience.

The hidden nature of operations makes it a particularly valuable source of competitive advantage. Competitors can see the outcome—better productivity or agility—but cannot see how you get it. The operational advantage is difficult to copy, because it comes from processes, skills, and information that operate together as a well-tuned machine. Simply adopting a technology or process alone won't do it. For example, it took US car manufacturers many years to get good at Toyota's lean manufacturing methods, even though Toyota willingly gave factory tours to its rivals' executives.[10] More recently, traditional companies continue to struggle to adopt the digitally powered methods of online leaders like Amazon.com and Google, although the outlines of these methods are well known. As these cases show, even when competitors start to understand your hidden operations advantage, it may be years before they can make the advantage work for themselves.

Opportunities abound. Companies in every industry and country are already capturing the digital operations advantage. Executives are making better decisions because they have better data. Employees routinely collaborate with people they've never met, in places they've never visited, and stay connected with the office anywhere and anytime. Frontline workers, armed with up-to-date information, make decisions and creatively resolve operational issues in ways never possible before. Technology, from robots to diagnostics to workflow management, can outperform human workers along dimensions ranging from cost to quality to safety to environmental protection. Other technology is augmenting human labor, improving human productivity, and making work more fulfilling in jobs ranging from customer service workers to attorneys to surgeons. By virtualizing business processes—separating the work process from the location of the work itself, and providing decision makers with the information they need regardless of the source—companies are using technology to truly leverage their global knowledge and scale.

So where do you start? A great first step is to digitally optimize your internal processes. You can digitize core processes, change the way employees work, create real-time transparency, or make smarter decisions. But this should just be a start. The best firms, like many of the Digital Masters we have studied, go well beyond simple process improvements. They see technologies as a way to rethink the way they do business, breaking free of outdated assumptions that arose from the limits of older technologies.

OPERATIONAL PARADOXES
OF THE PREDIGITAL AGE

To many executives, improving operational performance represents a paradox of competing goals. Do you focus on the needs of the global company or the needs of local units? On today's efficiency or tomorrow's growth? On risk management or on innovation? It may seem that you can optimize one or the other, but not both. Six levers of operational improvement have traditionally created three key managerial paradoxes (figure 3.1). The limits of nondigital technologies and management methods forced managers to make trade-offs on each dimension, choosing "either-or" instead of "both-and."

For example, the ideas of *standardizing* and *empowering* have traditionally been seen as a paradox: artisans empowered to choose their own methods were considered less efficient than workers at production lines, yet the standardized nature of production tasks can make workers far less empowered (and fulfilled) than artisans. Standardization can lead to automation that further deskills workers, reduces wages, or eliminates jobs.[11] In a world where computers can do more and more jobs that people once did, what happens to the workers?[12]

Another pair of operational goals often seen as a paradox is *controlling* and *innovating*. Controlling processes tightly—ensuring they

FIGURE 3.1

Three operational paradoxes of the nondigital world

run exactly as designed and detecting any variation—can improve efficiency and reduce risk. Yet controlling variation can prevent people from innovating the process in useful ways.[13] Employees may be unable to adjust global processes for local customers or to conduct experiments that would improve the processes. On the other hand, loosening controls to enable innovation can open the door to inefficiency or fraud.

A third paradox comes from the need to synchronize steps in complex processes. Paper, offices, and status meetings were the coordinating technology of the twentieth century. That is why, for example, salespeople, field service workers, and police investigators had to visit their offices regularly in person and fill out numerous paper forms. It's also why so many employees can feel buried in status meetings and e-mail. Traditionally, however, unleashing employees from their offices or workstations made coordinating their activities very difficult.

As a result, *orchestrating* (which managers want) and *unleashing* (which employees want) represent another paradox of the nondigital world. In the past, tighter orchestration required tying people closer to the places and methods that did the orchestrating. It created overhead that could reduce peoples' productivity, restrict their sense of freedom, and sap their energy. Unleashing people or processes from old technology tethers can allow workers to focus on more important activities. But unleashing people can introduce problems in the handoffs between them.

Wouldn't it be nice if these paradoxes didn't represent stark either-or trade-offs? When asked whether you want standardization or empowerment (or control or innovation, or orchestration or unleashing), wouldn't it be nice if you could answer yes?

DIGITAL TRANSFORMATION BREAKS OPERATIONAL PARADOXES OF THE PAST

Facing daunting operational paradoxes, managers typically choose to reduce variation and flexibility rather than increase it. They redesign processes to be more standardized, better controlled, and more tightly orchestrated than before. This approach made sense in the days before computers and was the focus of many computerization efforts over the past fifty years.

However, the newest wave of digital technologies is different. Technologies such as smartphones, big-data analytics, social media collaboration, and embedded devices can break the paradoxes of the predigital age. Mobile and collaboration technologies that *unleash* workers from desks, paper reports, and status meetings can also *orchestrate* workers more closely. *Standardization* that removes creativity from some tasks can also *empower* workers to be more creative in other ways. Technology that imposes strict *controls* to reduce process variation and fraud can also help you to *innovate* those processes. Let's look at how companies are approaching each paradox.

Standardizing and Empowering

Ever since the days of Frederick Taylor, engineers have seen standardization as a way to improve process efficiency. Through time-and-motion studies and other methods, they broke each process into its component parts, standardized each step, eliminated unnecessary activity, and asked workers to follow a precise cookbook of actions.

This kind of activity, even in the precomputer age, enabled radical manufacturing innovations such as interchangeable parts and the moving assembly line.

Standardization also makes automation possible. Process reengineering and enterprise resource planning (ERP) efforts of the past twenty-five years have led to dramatic financial benefits.[14] Robots have made inroads in standardized assembly-line tasks, working twenty-four-hour days without complaint and making fewer mistakes than humans do. Robots can also make hazardous tasks, such as automotive painting, more efficient by removing the need for worker protection safeguards. As computer capabilities increase, machines will be able to substitute for workers in more and more tasks.[15]

But standardization can make humans more efficient without replacing them. By providing consistent information on process performance and the status of every order, ERP systems help humans do their jobs better. Similarly, standardized processes in cockpits and pharmacies can help people conduct their work more efficiently and safely without eliminating their jobs.

Let's look at how companies are managing the standardizing-versus-empowering paradox. It's sensible to start with standardization, since newer technologies are creating huge opportunities that did not exist before. For example, mobile phones, e-business, and embedded devices produce billions of data points that you can mine for insights on how to standardize and improve your processes. But while some companies continue to drive efficiency through standardization, others are breaking the paradox to both standardize and empower.

Improving Efficiency Through Standardization at UPS

The success of global package delivery company UPS is based largely on standardization and operational efficiency. The company operates in 220 countries, with nearly four hundred thousand employees. In 2012, it served 8.8 million customers and delivered some 4.1 billion items. UPS controls a complex logistical web with millions of possible permutations in service options and delivery routes. Jack Levis,

UPS director of process management, explained: "We not only aim to deliver every package on time, but we provide customers with multiple service options to meet their needs. We even allow adjusting of delivery choices while the shipment is in route. Executing this mission means constantly orchestrating orders, adjusting route schedules and following up on package deliveries with a massive fleet of ground and air vehicles."[16]

For decades, UPS has been a leader at optimizing its processes. By standardizing its processes, even to the extent of telling drivers how to step off the truck, UPS continually improves efficiency, safety, and quality.[17] New data analytics capability is enabling even further optimization. According to Levis, UPS generates "huge amounts of data feeds, from devices, vehicles, tracking materials and sensors. Our goal is to turn that complex universe of data into business intelligence."[18]

Route optimization is a key opportunity and a complex challenge, as Levis explained: "We have 106,000 package car drivers globally and we deliver more than 16 million packages daily. When you consider the fact that every driver at UPS has trillions of ways to run their delivery routes, the number of possibilities increases exponentially. The question becomes: how do you mine the sea of data from our sensors and vehicles to arrive at the most effective route for our drivers?"[19] Cracking the puzzle can have huge payoffs, as a reduction of one mile per driver per day translates into savings of up to $50 million per year.[20]

Levis and his team used advanced algorithms to shave millions of miles from delivery routes. The project crunches business rules, map data, customer information, and employee work rules, among other factors, to optimize package delivery routes within six to eight seconds. An optimized route might look very similar to the driver's normal route—a quarter mile saved here, a half mile there—but the real benefit lies in the accumulated distance saved across thousands of deliveries.

The project is a huge endeavor for UPS, employing some five hundred people. But it generates significant operational advantage. So far, analytics has helped UPS to reduce eighty-five million miles driven per year. The reduction equates to over eight million fewer gallons of fuel used.

The systems reduced engine idle time by ten million minutes, thanks in part to onboard sensors that help determine when in the delivery process to turn the truck on and off. This technology alone saved more than 650,000 gallons of fuel and reduced carbon emissions by more than 6,500 metric tons.

Levis said, "We don't look at initiatives as 'analytics projects,' we look at them as business projects. Our goal is to make business processes, methods, procedures and analytics all one and the same. For the front line user, the use of analytics results becomes just part of the job."[21]

Breaking the Standardizing-Versus-Empowering Paradox

UPS has generated millions of dollars of savings through standardizing its internal processes. Many other companies are making similar improvements and getting substantial savings. Yet, these changes, while valuable, sometimes focus on only one side of the standardization-empowerment paradox.

Other companies have managed to break the paradox. Even if standardizing can deskill or disempower workers, it does not have to do so. Companies can shift routine tasks to workers who find the routine tasks fulfilling. And if standardizing eliminates some workers, it can empower the others to do more-fulfilling work.

The changes can be small or large. A manufacturer we studied started to standardize, and then automate, many of the tasks in its human resources (HR) function. The company reduced HR staff from more than a hundred to fewer than thirty, while improving employee satisfaction. Employees found it easier to manage routine HR tasks through self-service systems. According to the vice president of HR, the remaining HR employees are happier too. They can now focus on "enlarging manager skills, rather than counting days off."[22] Looking forward, HR plans to hire new employees as the volume of these more-empowered HR tasks grows.

Asian Paints standardized the process of taking orders from the retailers it serves. Formerly, a sales force of hundreds visited thousands of retailers regularly.[23] Salespeople took orders for paint and other products, answered questions, and contacted local distribution centers to deliver each order. Orders were then fulfilled by local distribution centers, which operated largely independently from each other.

Seeing an opportunity to improve operations, company executives implemented a single ERP system to manage the whole order-to-cash process, as well as advanced supply chain management capabilities. Implementing the new system required the company to standardize the way it worked, both within and across regions. It also provided better information and efficiency. According to CIO and head of strategy Manish Choksi, "During this period, we built an extremely strong financial and operational foundation for growing the company."[24]

Executives soon found another opportunity to standardize processes. Analysis showed that the company could improve customer experience and sales performance by having workers in a centralized call center—instead of salespeople in the field—take routine orders. The change eliminated steps in the process and created economies of scale in order-taking personnel.

As an added bonus, the change also improved service quality. Formerly, customer satisfaction varied across regions and salespeople. But the centralized call center, and its enabling technology platform, changed the situation. For the first time, executives had a single view of all customer-related activity across the company. They could ensure that every retailer got the same level of service, regardless of the retailer's location. Managers could monitor the performance of each phone representative, providing training and making adjustments as needed. The improvement extended beyond order taking, as the system allowed executives to understand whether some distribution centers were outperforming others, and why.

But what about the people? Workers in the call centers perform highly routinized processes managed by automated systems. Yet, jobs in call centers are considered far better than the jobs many of the call-center workers could have obtained before. And although salespeople lost a key component of their former jobs, eliminating routine order-taking empowered them to do something more. Now, armed with mobile access to the company's systems, plus training and support from the company, salespeople have transformed from low-skilled order takers to empowered relationship managers. They can give greater service to retailers and be more fulfilled while call center workers are happy to perform routine order-taking.

We have seen this kind of simultaneous standardization and empowerment in many companies we have studied. In online pharmacies, automated production lines do much of the routine work, empowering pharmacists to do more fulfilling tasks: advising patients and managing complex orders, not putting pills in bottles. At Caesars, strong standardization and automation make processes more efficient, but also arm employees with up-to-date information about each customer. Customer representatives can decide to provide an upgrade or a free meal without having to check with supervisors. They even receive information in real time about customers who may need an intervention, and can choose how to serve them best.[25]

Controlling and Innovating

Codelco's centralized operations center allows its managers to know, in real time, the status of all activities in a mine. Because information is available in one place, managers can spot potential problems, coordinate activities, and make better planning decisions. Controlling variation makes processes more efficient and safe, while real-time control capabilities allow Codelco to adjust to changes in workload, ore composition, machinery efficiency, and other factors. Yet integrated information also helps Codelco identify areas to target for innovation.

In many industries, automation is particularly well suited to applications that require control. Autopilots make minor adjustments to thrust and direction to keep an aircraft on course. Process automation mixes chemicals in the right quantities and temperatures to optimize reactions and safeguard product quality. Accounting systems ensure that people can only enter transactions for valid accounts and amounts.

Yet, automated control can also reduce innovation and other valuable variations. Overly restrictive systems can prevent employees from giving special perks to their best customers. Tight controls in supply chain systems can force store managers to live with what headquarters tells them, rather than finding the right product mix for their local customers.

As with the previous paradox, the first place to look for opportunities along the controlling-versus-innovating dimension is control. New technologies such as mobile and embedded devices are creating new ways to improve process efficiency, increase product quality, and prevent fraud. But while some companies tend to focus only on control, others are breaking the paradox to control and innovate at the same time.

Controlling Process Quality

Although Asian Paints managed both sides of the standardizing-versus-empowering paradox in its selling processes, it chose to focus on one side—controlling—in manufacturing.[26] Paint manufacturing is a low-margin business with many opportunities to make mistakes. The biggest driver of cost is raw materials, which constitute 60 percent of costs. Chemicals must be mixed in the right quantities at the right times, and materials can cause environmental damage if not managed properly.

High growth in paint demand created the need to set up new manufacturing plants every three years. According to Manish Choksi, CIO and head of strategy, building world-class manufacturing plants "calls for a high degree of automation to deliver labor efficiency but also better quality and less waste."[27] Seeing the potential of technology to improve manufacturing, executives opened a 200,000-ton plant in 2010 that was almost wholly automated, followed by a fully automated 300,000-ton plant in 2013. The new plants are completely integrated from an information management perspective. Data from shop floor control systems and warehouses is linked seamlessly to the ERP.

This has helped to further sustain the firm's operational efficiencies. Raw materials flow in from storage tanks, where machines mix the materials and place the finished product into containers in a continuous process. Technicians monitor progress and maintain the machinery, but computers control everything else.

To the company's executives, the benefits of automation extend well beyond reducing labor costs. Automation has led to greater scalability, better quality, and stronger safety and environmental protections. Fewer workplace accidents occur. The company needs to hire fewer workers for high-turnover factory jobs. Product quality improves because there is less process variation. And with full telemetry on process steps, engineers can troubleshoot production problems faster than before.

Controlling Fraud

New technologies are creating new ways to control fraud. Financial services companies have systems and compliance organizations to detect and prevent unauthorized trading. Credit card companies have real-time automated fraud management operations. But digital technology is opening possibilities in other industries, too.

Employee theft and fraud are widespread problems in firms. The Association of Certified Fraud Examiners reported that the typical organization loses 5 percent of its revenues to fraud each year.[28] According to the National Restaurant Association, theft for its members accounted for 4 percent of annual food sales, or more than $8.5 billion in 2007. These numbers are significant because pretax profit margins often range between 2 and 6 percent for restaurants.[29]

For example, in restaurants, opportunities abound for servers to supplement their income through fraud. They can use multiple techniques to steal from their employers and customers, including voiding and "comping" sales after pocketing cash payment from customers and transferring food items from customers' bills after the bills have been paid. These activities have occurred largely outside management's eyes, as servers become practiced at varying their techniques to avoid detection.

Recently, a large US-based restaurant chain implemented software to address the problem. The system examines the whole universe of cash register transactions to identify cases of fraud that are so obvious as to be indefensible by servers. Managers can then confront the servers about the activity, armed with specific information about when and where it happened. Corrective actions vary from letting servers know they are being watched to fining or firing them.

A study of the system's impact in a chain of 392 casual dining restaurants found an average 21 percent decrease in the most egregious forms of theft after implementation.[30] Even more interesting, researchers found that total revenue at each restaurant increased by an average of 7 percent, suggesting either a considerable increase in employee productivity or that much more theft is being prevented than the system can detect. Furthermore, drink sales (the primary source of theft in restaurants) increased by about 10.5 percent. This increase is particularly important because the profit margins on drinks in casual dining are between 60 and 90 percent, representing approximately half of all restaurant profits. For restaurant owners, this type of digital control represents an immediate opportunity to increase profits without major investment or process change. For servers, it may represent something else.

The possibilities extend to other contexts as well. For years, governments have used computers to detect signs of fraud in tax returns or equity trading. Now, they are looking in other areas. For example, recent research has identified signals of fraud in automotive emissions inspections.[31] Governments can use these signals to target their enforcement operations and reduce corruption.

Breaking the Controlling-Versus-Innovating Paradox

While the benefits of using technology to control process variation and reduce fraud are enormous, technology can also spur innovation. Measuring tightly controlled processes gives companies like Asian Paints, Caesars, and Codelco the opportunity to identify problem areas and improve processes. They can conduct controlled experiments, accurately measuring differences between treated and nontreated groups. Caesars CEO Gary Loveman was once quoted as saying, "There are three sure ways to get fired at Caesars. The first is to steal from the company. The second is to harass someone. And the third is to conduct an experiment without a control group."[32]

A restaurant firm is actively conducting experiments in pricing and promotion across a set of franchised booths in sporting and entertainment pavilions. Using digital signage, the company can experiment with bundling and pricing to increase sales. Sellers can change their menus according to whether a baseball game, football game, or concert is happening nearby. Now the company is experimenting with dynamically adjusting prices to shift demand as a result of weather, time of day, and inventory levels. The company shares what it learns in each location so that others can benefit. But the company retests each idea in each new venue to ensure that ideas from Milwaukee will really sell in Miami, and vice versa.

Even more powerful is the experience of Seven-Eleven Japan (SEJ), whose strong, central process controls increase efficiency while also enabling innovation.[33] The company has built an information and process platform that connects every store to headquarters and distribution centers in real time. Store managers have the status of every order they have placed, whether it is for hot foods, delivered twice daily; cold food, delivered daily; or hard goods, delivered less frequently. A dashboard in each store shows real-time performance relative to similar periods in the past. Managers know what is selling and what is not, and they can vary their orders accordingly. The managers can even adjust orders on a daily basis, such as ordering more hot foods on days that are expected to be cold and rainy.

SEJ's strong process controls also enable innovation. The company routinely launches new products and tests them in a sample of stores, getting rapid feedback on product performance. Good products stay, and poor products drop. SEJ also experiments with services such as banking and bill paying that can use the firm's many retail locations to provide customer convenience.

The company has begun to foster new innovation opportunities at the local level. Store managers are encouraged to make hypotheses about what will sell, and order accordingly. They might see children wearing a certain color, and order accessories in that color. Or they might suggest a new product in light of what customers have been requesting lately. Successful experiments turn into innovations that the company can share across all of its stores. In a company where more than 50 percent of products are new each year, the opportunities afforded by local innovation capability are very valuable.

Seven-Eleven Japan shows clearly how technology can break the paradox between controlling and innovating. The standards and processes that reduce variation can also provide opportunities to conduct experiments that improve the company's performance. This kind of experimentation on tightly controlled processes is a well-known innovation technique for digital firms such as Amazon and Google.[34] Now it is moving rapidly from the digital world to the physical one. It would not be possible without the integrated real-time data that today's digital technologies can provide. But only companies that take active steps to use information differently can unlock the innovative potential that digital operations provide.

Orchestrating and Unleashing

New digital technologies are unleashing people from the constraints that once bound them. People can increasingly work where they want, at the hours they choose. They can communicate as they wish, with a few friends or hundreds of "friends," sharing sensitive information easily with people inside and outside their organizations. To many workers, this sounds like freedom. To many managers, it sounds like chaos.

On the other hand, digital technology can synchronize processes more closely. Mobile scanners in warehouses and stores link directly to inventory systems and financial systems, launching requests that span your company and reach into other companies. GPS and mobile phones allow you to track field workers, so that you can schedule them and monitor their performance more closely than ever before. Radio-frequency identification (RFID) tags and sensors on devices provide mountains of information to track devices or monitor processes in real time.

In using these new technologies and data, many companies focus only on the benefits of orchestration. But more is possible. Some companies envision how to break the paradox, unleashing people and processes from constraints while simultaneously orchestrating activities closer together.

Digitally Orchestrating Supply Chains

Digital technologies create many opportunities to orchestrate supply chains better. Channel partners—suppliers, intermediaries, third-party service providers, or customers—can share information on a real-time basis. Proactive supplier collaboration and visibility of raw material flow can improve order quality and reduce sourcing costs. Companies that have digitally transformed their supply chains are racing ahead and reaping huge benefits.

Kimberly-Clark Corporation, a US-based personal and health-care products supplier, built a demand-driven supply chain using data analytics to gain better visibility into real-time demand trends. This capability enabled the company to make and store only the inventory needed to replace what consumers actually purchased, instead of basing its manufacturing on forecasts from historical data. Kimberly-Clark utilized point-of-sales data from retailers such as Walmart to generate forecasts that triggered shipments to stores and guided internal deployment decisions and tactical planning. It also helped the company create a new metric for tracking and improving supply-chain performance. The metric, defined as the absolute difference between shipments and forecast and reported as a percentage of shipments, effectively tracks stock-keeping units and shipping locations. Using this metric, Kimberly-Clark has reduced its forecast errors by as much as 35 percent for a one-week planning horizon and 20 percent for a two-week horizon. Improvements over an eighteen-month period translated to one to three days less safety stock and 19 percent lower finished-goods inventory, with direct impacts for the company's bottom line.[35]

Apparel retailer Zara is another example. Zara supports its "fast-fashion" business model through unique buyer-driven supply-chain capabilities.[36] Designers and others at company headquarters monitor real-time information on customer purchases to create new designs and price points. Through standardized product information, Zara can quickly prepare computer-aided designs with clear manufacturing instructions.

In manufacturing, cut pieces are tracked with the help of bar codes as they flow further down the supply chain. The company's distribution facility functions with minimal manual operations as optical readers sort and distribute more than sixty thousand items of clothing every hour. Zara also leverages the close proximity of production to the central distribution facility to reduce supply-chain risk and lead time.

Complete control over its value chain helps the company to design, produce, and deliver new apparel to stores in around fourteen days, where other industry players typically spend about nine months. Zara's smaller batch sizes lead to higher short-term forecast accuracy and lower inventory cost and rate of obsolescence. This reduces markdowns and increases profit margins. For example, unsold items at Zara account for 10 percent of stock, compared with the industry average of 17 to 20 percent.

Orchestrating and Unleashing at Air France

Companies like Kimberly-Clark and Zara have created substantial benefits by digitally linking every element of their supply chains more closely. While orchestration-focused approaches like these can be very valuable, other opportunities exist in breaking the orchestrating-versus-unleashing paradox. Operations become better orchestrated while workers gain freedom to do some tasks outside the leashes of paper, desks, and office hours.

Air France found that it could break the paradox by moving from paper to electronic materials in its flight operations.[37] The company's documentation challenges extend to four thousand pilots and hundreds of flights per day around the globe. Previously, each pilot, aircraft, and flight route required a unique set of documentation on board, collectively adding sixty pounds of paper to each flight.

Additionally, paper was a poor technology base for orchestrating operations. Critical decisions about safety or scheduling waited as typists entered information from forms into systems. Truly time-critical processes required employees to coordinate manually by phone or radio, and they often had to fill out forms after the process finished.

The logistics of coordinating documentation for each flight is no small task. In the past, each plane carried reference documents and pilots kept separate copies at home. Dedicated rooms in two Paris airports—Orly and Roissy—held racks of information cards on each destination Air France served. Each aircraft required specific manuals and performance calculators, with variations depending on the plane's specific engine system. Back-office personnel prepared a flight folder for each flight that included weather information, airport details, and flight itineraries. This mountain of paper documentation helped maintain the safety and security of Air France's flights, but also created a lot of operational complexity. Sebastien Veigneau, first officer at Air France, explained: "In the past, we used to receive our planning every month on printed paper. Planning documents were dispatched individually to all four thousand pilots and all fifteen thousand stewards, stewardesses, and pursers."[38]

In 2006, Air France managers realized that technology could unleash employees from paper forms and manual coordination, while orchestrating processes more closely. The firm could reduce cost and risk, improve pilot training, and make critical processes faster. Air France started by digitizing most reference and flight documentation and then issuing laptops to all pilots. The pilots could use laptops to do tasks they formerly did on paper. Meanwhile, by installing tablets called Electronic Flight Bags on its aircraft, the company paved the way to reducing paper in flight operations. Air France benefited because all notes were legible and available in real time and in the same place. Digital documentation was easier to maintain and update than paper-based documentation. Pilots could have the most up-to-date documents with a single tap. And passengers benefited by not having to wait so long because operations were more efficient.

Although the initial process showed promise, it also encountered difficulties. Application design issues and pilot reticence led to some dissatisfaction. In 2009, the company paired IT personnel with active pilots to develop a solution that was faster, simpler, and more modern. In just a few months, the team developed an iPad-based solution dubbed Pilot Pad that pilots found more useful than the original laptop-based approach.

Air France's operational changes were largely invisible to customers, but the efforts affected customers through greater safety, better coordination of flight crews and airplanes, and reduced waiting time.

Digital orchestration enabled Air France to improve its processes substantially. However, the benefits extended beyond the tarmac. The transformation also unleashed pilots from tasks that had created frustration and extra effort in the past. Using their PilotPads, pilots could access the company's online scheduling platform from anywhere in the world. Now, whenever Air France updates a document in the library, 60 percent of affected pilots review it within twenty-four hours, which allows the pilots to stay informed, wherever they are. The pilots can also do required training courses more conveniently. Previously, pilots were required to attend in-classroom presentations to keep up-to-date with the latest aircraft and practices—a challenge, given the typical pilot's busy travel schedule. New e-learning modules enable pilots to complete training whenever and wherever they wish.

To date, the Pilot Pad program has been a success. By unleashing itself from paper, Air France his orchestrated its processes better than ever before. Plus, the tablet device has unleashed pilots to do their nonflying duties wherever and whenever they want. As Veigneau told us, "When Pilot Pad was rolled out, it turned flight operations into an efficient and user-friendly process. The only question we have from pilots now is, 'When will I get my Pilot Pad?'" Air France expanded the program to all of its pilots in 2013. Now, seeing the solution's potential for pilot engagement, the flight operations group plans to continue pushing its boundaries through new digital capabilities. For example, cabin crew are being equipped with iPads in 2014.

BUILDING YOUR OPERATIONAL ADVANTAGE

The digital transformation of operations began in the 1960s and 1970s with basic transactional systems. It accelerated in the 1980s and 1990s with the introduction of PCs, e-mail, and online systems. It leaped forward in the 2000s with mobile phones, ubiquitous internet, and cheap global communications. Now it is poised to accelerate even faster through technologies such as flexible robotics, advanced analytics, voice and translation technologies, and 3-D printing.

So, how can you think about opportunities to transform your operations? The digital operations advantage is about more than great tools. It's a combination of people, processes, and technology connected in a unique way to help you outperform your competitors. None of the examples in this chapter were only about adding new technology to a process. They were actually about using digital technology as an opportunity to rethink the way your company's processes work. If you grasp the power of transformed operations, you can create an operational advantage that few others can copy.

In looking for opportunities to transform operations, don't think about mobile or analytics or embedded devices. Think about constraints that you've lived with for years—constraints you don't even consider constraints because they're just common knowledge. Are the assumptions behind those constraints still true? Or can new technologies allow you to work radically differently? That is where you can find the best opportunities.

Look for ways to apply each of the six levers to your operations. And figure out how you can use technology to break paradoxes. But don't stop there. The Digital Masters we studied used multiple levers—alone and in combination—to transform their operations. One change led to another and then another.

Companies have unleashed their product design and production processes from paper, opening up possibilities to orchestrate their processes in new ways. Codelco used automation to control and then innovate its processes. Asian Paints rethought assumptions from a legacy of history, standardizing its sales processes while empowering frontline salespeople to perform more-strategic tasks. Caesars controls its processes digitally, while empowering workers to make decisions independently and actively working to find innovations that improve each process.

Digitally transforming operations requires vision that extends beyond incremental tweaks. But it also requires something more. Transformation requires good data, available in real time, to the people and machines that need it. For many companies, true operations transformation starts by overhauling legacy systems and information to provide a unified view of processes and data. This is no small task, but it is well worth the effort. As we discuss in chapter 8, improving your technology platform is the foundation upon which all other elements are built.

LEADING DIGITAL CHECKLIST: OPERATIONS

✓ Free yourself from old assumptions of the predigital age.

✓ Look for bottlenecks and inefficiencies in your processes, and consider whether new digital technologies can help you rethink your operations.

✓ Consider how each of the six levers may help you improve operations.

✓ If you can't address both sides of a paradox at once, start with standardization or control. This may open up possibilities to address other levers.

✓ Consider examples from inside and outside your industry.

✓ As with customer experience, a strong digital platform is essential for operational transformation. We'll discuss this more in chapter 8.

CHAPTER 4

REINVENTING
BUSINESS MODELS

Do not quench your inspiration and your imagination;
do not become the slave of your model.

—VINCENT VAN GOGH

We have shown how Digital Masters, such as Burberry, can create value from transforming customer experience. They can also, like Codelco, achieve huge operational efficiencies from transforming operations. But some companies transform even further. They rethink customer experience, internal operations, and economic formulas to reinvent their business models.

As we described in the introduction to this book, waves of digital change are occurring closer and closer together. Competitive landscapes are in perpetual motion. Many of the barriers to entry that once protected incumbent companies and sectors have fallen. Competition is global, and digital technologies have provided resources to go after new opportunities. The shelf life of existing business models is becoming shorter, questioning the very notion of lasting competitive advantage.

Executives in every industry must be awake to the opportunities and threats of rapid digital evolution and be ready to reinvent business models as needed.

Business model reinvention sometimes involves radically shifting what you sell, how you sell it, or how you make money from it. Reinvention may involve reimagining the nature of competition in your industry or reconfiguring your value chain to deliver at a substantial efficiency advantage against your competitors. It can also be about making the transition from multinational to truly global operations, moving from products to value-added services, or moving into brand-new markets. It may also entail creating new digital businesses or services, either to augment your current business model or to replace it.

Executives see the value-creation potential in business model reinvention, for at least three reasons. First, reinvention can reorder value chains and create big shifts in the competitive landscape. It has already created or redistributed billions of dollars of value in sectors ranging from retail to air transport.[1] Second, well-executed business model reinvention and its operational underpinnings can be difficult to replicate. And third, today's exponential technological innovation is continually challenging companies with opportunities (and threats) to fundamentally rethink the way they do business. For example, 3-D printing is already generating new models of manufacturing as well as new customer propositions in ways unimaginable a few years back.

But despite the buzz, business model reinvention remains elusive. In our survey, a mere 7 percent of respondents stated that their company's digital initiatives were helping to launch new businesses. Only 15 percent said that new business models were emerging thanks to digital technology.[2] Many executives may not be looking for business model reinvention opportunities. Others may consider them too risky to attempt.

So why would you want to worry about business model reinvention? Because not paying attention is an even bigger risk. Executives in music, newspapers, and equity trading have already seen the radical upheavals that digital business model reinvention can bring to their industries. Industries ranging from insurance to education are starting to experience the same thing. Whatever your industry, you need to be on the forefront of challenging your current business model. Otherwise, someone else will.

INCUMBENTS BEWARE

The business model that operates the London taxi market had been stable for many years. Companies were mediating supply and demand through expensive infrastructure: 24/7 call centers and GPS equipment fitted in the vehicles. Despite this technology, getting a cab in London was still not an easy experience. Something was bound to happen.

When three business entrepreneurs and three taxi drivers (all cofounders of a start-up called Hailo) met in a Soho café in London in 2010, business model transformation was the last thing on their minds. Terry Runham, Russell Hall, and Gary Jackson—the three taxi drivers—had previously tried to get an e-taxi business off the ground, with mixed results. Ron Zeghibe, Jay Bregman, and Caspar Woolley—the three businessmen—had an algorithm, built originally for an e-courier business, which was looking for a new life. All six hit it off instantly. They all agreed that the current inefficiencies in the London taxi market could be turned into an opportunity.

The key insight from the taxi drivers was counterintuitive. Don't worry about the customer experience at this stage. Worry about creating a system that works for the drivers. The rest will follow. The entrepreneurs saw the potential. They could create differentiation on the supply side, where they could erect barriers to entry. Every competitor wanted to lock in customers, and the competitors were fighting a me-too race with similar customer mobile apps. A different approach was needed.

Early on, the team focused on fixing two fundamental pain points that are core to taxi drivers' lives—maximization of occupancy, and isolation. Most taxi drivers spent between 30 and 60 percent of their time with an empty cab. So offering a job in exchange for a small fee made sense. In addition, although taxi drivers form a small, close-knit community, they often feel isolated. So offering a social community, something that would engage drivers and tie them together, made sense. With this, Hailo created a precise value proposition for the supply side of this two-sided market.

Hailo uses analytics extensively to provide drivers with a better view of available jobs, how to get to those jobs efficiently, and how to track performance over time. The app also gives drivers real-time traffic updates. Drivers can send a burst alert when multiple jobs are available in a given area, such as at the end of a theater show. Hailo went even further by providing a complete logbook for individual drivers on the app. Drivers can measure the percentage of time they are occupied, the amount of diesel fuel they burn each day, their earnings per hour, and a realm of other management data. They can set daily personal targets and can compare their performance against their historical profiles.

To remedy isolation, the app provides a newsfeed where drivers can update their status and share information with other cabbies—a taxi-driver Facebook. Drivers can designate a group of their best friends, whom the cabbies can track in the city and chat with throughout the day.

Only a few months after the introduction of Hailo, average occupancy had gone up significantly. These dramatic results amazed the taxi community. Drivers claim that the use of Hailo has led to an average 30 percent spike in business.[3] As a result, by 2013, over 60 percent of the London cab population had joined the network.

But what about the end customers in all this? Hailo developed a very simple and intuitive customer smartphone app. Once a customer locates a cab, he or she receives its registration number and the name, photo, and mobile number of the driver. On average, a Hailo cab is four minutes away, wherever a customer is in the city. Unlike their competitors, Hailo drivers also give customers a five-minute wait time before starting their meters. Up until early 2012, 99 percent of payments were in cash. Two-thirds of the taxis could not even process a credit card, and there was a customer surcharge of 12.5 percent. With Hailo, customers can register their cards and pay with a single tap directly from their phones. As of 2013, there were close to half a million registered customers in London alone.

How does Hailo make money out of all this? The profit model is simple; Hailo provides jobs in exchange for a 10 percent flat fee on the ride. There is no subscription fee. As one of Hailo's founders noted, "Once you cover you costs, it's geared towards profit."[4]

Digital technologies have also enabled Hailo to have extremely low-cost operations. Hailo does not provide hardware, so there is no cost of installing expensive GPS-tracked mobile display units—the cabbies' smartphones do that. Through bulk negotiation, the company helps drivers get great deals from phone companies. Unlike competitors, Hailo has no need for the expense of manning 24/7 call centers, because the algorithm in the software does a better job at scheduling each cabbie's jobs than people could.

The firm has gone global, covering several cities around the world—often adapting its economic model to suit local conditions. The firm has built a very successful business model in eighteen months. Hailo founder Ron Zeghibe explained: "We understood that if we wanted to apply technology to this industry, we needed people who knew the industry inside-out. Listening and using their insights to build the DNA of the business is paying huge dividends for us. We are now in a position to go into any market against incumbents with a fair chance of overshadowing them."[5]

What Hailo shows is that using digital technologies to combine excellence in both operations and customer experience, weaved into a differentiated business model, pays dividends. Transformative business models such as Hailo, or its San Francisco–based equivalent, Uber, are rarely just a technology story. Digital technology is, of course, core to the success, but it is wrapped in many other elements that together make a great business model: supply-side control, economic model, customer experience, and efficiency in execution.

FIVE ARCHETYPES OF BUSINESS
MODEL REINVENTION

Although it has become part of today's management lexicon, business model reinvention is still an emerging field with several interpretations and definitions.[6] In the last few years, several books have contributed to a better understanding of business model development or innovation at the firm and industry levels.[7] Some have also focused on the specific role of technology in business model reinvention. These books have looked either specifically at information-systems-driven business models, or at disruptions brought about by business applications of new digital technologies mainly from innovative start-ups.[8]

In this book, we have focused on how businesses conduct their digital transformations from the lenses of large global organizations. Leaders in large firms, looking to reinvent their business models, must put their wide-angle lenses on. Emerging technologies, start-ups, small new entrants, and firms in adjacent industries all warrant consideration. Not all technologies are individually disruptive, but in combination, they can have a substantial impact on your business over time.

In our research, we have seen all the models described in the literature at play. Some are more common than others, some are more radical than others, and some are more applicable across industries than others. All options present opportunities to create substantial business value. All have different risk profiles.

We've observed five broad archetypes of business model reinvention driven by digital technology. The first, *reinventing industries*, involves a substantial reshaping of an industry structure, as Hailo did for the taxi market, or responding to fundamentally new consumer behaviors. The second category is about *substituting products or services*—when your core products or services become directly substitutable by a new digital format. The third category, *creating new digital businesses*, involves the creation of new products and services that generate additional revenues. The fourth category, *reconfiguring value delivery models*, means recombining products, services, and data to change the way a firm plays in the value chain. The fifth is about *rethinking value propositions*—using new digital capabilities to target unmet needs for existing or new customers.

It is worth paying attention to all varieties. Business model reinvention drives opportunities to create new value. Both defense and offense are important. Assume both your competitors and potential new entrants—often from outside your industry—are already hard at it. So how do you look at reinvention? Let's examine the models we've seen at play in our research.

REINVENTING INDUSTRIES

Reinventing an industry is a tall order for any firm. It does not happen every day, and it is a complex and risky endeavor to pull off. Companies often need to venture outside the comfort zone of the core business to deliver new forms of value. Reinvention can also require new competencies, new modes of operations, and new economic models.

Firms used to focus on developing competitive advantage from delivering a superior customer experience, optimizing internal operations, and developing access to wider distribution channels. With the power of the internet and new digital technologies, companies are now able to connect many participants with one another and create new platforms for them to interact and transact.[9] Firms can also leverage assets they don't own, and reconfigure their value chains—from buying IT services à la carte from cloud-based infrastructure providers like Amazon.com, to crowdsourcing their R&D with platforms like InnoCentive, to staffing key roles from global online job marketplaces such as oDesk.

Platform economics does not apply only at industry level; we will see later how Nike and Volvo, for instance, have used platform thinking to create new sources of revenue or new connections to customers. But all the business models we observed for reinventing an industry through digital technology involved some form of platform play.

A well-documented example of a company that succeeded in building an industry-changing platform is Apple. With the iPod, Apple delivered a convenient and user-friendly way of downloading music onto a brilliantly designed player. But the magic came later, when Apple launched its iTunes store—a service that created a tight link between hardware, software, digital music, and videos in one user-friendly package. The rest is history. Not only did Apple ensure that the iPod became a high-margin product of choice, but the iTunes store also allowed the firm to become a major distribution platform and establish a base price for single-track music. Such industry reinventions are rare, but when they occur, they fundamentally change the rules of competition.

Multisided platforms are not new. American Express, PayPal, and Square successfully linked merchants to consumers. Video-game console makers, like Sony's PlayStation and Microsoft's Xbox, linked game developers and users. More recently, Google Android linked handset manufacturers, application developers, and users.

What's new is that the power of digital technology has substantially opened up the scope of opportunities for platform business models. Industries ranging from automotives to education to health care and even legal services are becoming ripe for transformation. In a 2013 article, Geoffrey Parker and Marshall Van Alstyne paraphrased entrepreneur and venture capitalist Marc Andreessen's quote from our introduction chapter to say: "Platforms are eating the world."[10] They argue that we are in the middle of a significant shift in business models—a shift powered by the internet and a generation of connected users.

Companies in what is commonly called the *sharing economy* are rethinking the nature of large, asset-heavy industries, with implications for the business models of large firms. Rather than allow all revenues to go to a few big companies that create specialized assets for rental, new companies are brokering connections between customers and people who may want to share their assets for a time. From car-sharing to accommodation and vacation rental to temporary workers to collaborative financing and even dog sitters, collaborative consumption is making steady progress as an alternative consumer choice.

Think about hotels. Chains such as Marriott, Hilton, and others invest tremendous amounts of capital to build specialized properties that they rent to customers by the night or month. But other people have similar assets that they would happily rent out to make some additional income: a beach house, a spare bedroom, or a house in town while they're on vacation. Why can't a company make money by taking advantage of these private individuals' desires to rent out their properties, and profit from the relative immaturity of such a market?

In 2008, Airbnb saw a vacuum in the traditional room-rental model. Airbnb is a trusted online and mobile-phone-based community marketplace for people to list or book accommodations around the world. The company started small, but grew very quickly. It went from 100,000 guest-nights booked in 2009 to 750,000 the following year and passed two million the year after. As of 2013, Airbnb was present in thirty-three thousand cities in 192 countries around the world.[11] Every night, it helped approximately 150,000 people stay in rooms rented through its service—a significant number compared with Hilton's 600,000 rooms worldwide.[12] The business model is based on brokerage. Airbnb takes a 3 percent cut from the renter and 6 to 12 percent from the traveler, depending on the price and quality of the property. For this charge, Airbnb provides customer service, payment handling, and $1 million in damage insurance coverage for its hosts. Renters and hosts can rate each other, thus increasing the trust and the quality of the service.

Large corporations took notice. In 2013, Marriott, in collaboration with mobile and web app company LiquidSpace, started renting meeting spaces in its hotels, on demand, challenging the notion that you have to be a hotel guest to use its facilities.[13] Large hotel chains around the world are now considering how to extend concepts of the sharing economy to other parts of their business models.

The sharing economy is making inroads into many other rental industries. Car-sharing start-up Zipcar was founded in 2000. Zipcar customers can rent cars for an hour or a day, using their phones or credit cards to reserve and gain entry to the car. Insurance and parking are part of the business model. Cars are conveniently located in parking lots distributed around town, rather than in a few rental facilities. Drivers can access a car quickly, without wasting time on rental paperwork and check-in processes. For drivers who need only occasional use of a car, the convenience and price advantage of Zipcar over traditional car rental or car ownership allowed the company to grow rapidly. It is now the world's leading car-sharing network. By mid-2013, Zipcar had 810,000 members and offered ten thousand vehicles in several countries in North America and Europe.[14]

As in the accommodations industry, large firms got into the act. In 2009, automaker Daimler/Mercedes Benz started its Car2go service, renting Smart Fortwo cars on a per-minute charge, regardless of distance traveled or fuel consumed. As of 2013, Car2go operated over eight thousand vehicles in eight countries, with over four hundred thousand customers signed.[15] Meanwhile, in 2013, car-rental giant Avis acquired Zipcar.[16]

Although it is unclear today whether such business models create extra value or just replace existing business, there is no question that over time, these types of digitally enabled asset-sharing models will become significant. They will certainly appear in more industries over time. If you can identify underutilized assets, find a way to optimize their usage through a time-sensitive access model, and find the right economic formula, you may be sitting on a valuable new source of revenue.

Reinventing industries through multisided-platform business models has gained significant attention from business leaders in the last few years. Understanding the underlying economics of such platforms is a prerequisite to exploring industry reinvention. Recent academic research has also advanced our understanding of platform economics.[17] Multisided platforms can efficiently aggregate disconnected participants in fragmented industries—helping to reduce what economists call search and transaction costs, as Hailo did for taxis or Airbnb did for rooms.

Well-executed platforms can create significant barriers to entry through network effects. For instance, the more buyers eBay gets, the more it will attract sellers, which in turn attracts more buyers.

The value to customers on one side of the platform typically increases with the number of participating customers on the other. In addition, the power of the crowd can displace traditional gatekeeping, for instance, when advice from fellow travelers replaces advice from travel agents.

Platform opportunities that reinvent entire industries do not pop up every day. But they do exist in many industries. Crafting a new industry-changing business model requires vision, creativity, careful planning, experimentation, and investment. Few succeed, but those who do gain a significant advantage.

SUBSTITUTING PRODUCTS AND SERVICES

In some cases, transforming the business model becomes essential, because the fundamental product or service that you are providing is being substituted by new digital technology. In such instances, you need to replace yourself. To do so, you may have to cannibalize your own revenues. But if the shift from your old offering to a new digital offering is real, there is no other way.

After digital photography replaced film, and smartphones replaced cameras, both Kodak's and Fujifilm's traditional business models became obsolete. Both companies saw change coming. But Kodak didn't survive and Fujifilm did. Kodak stuck to its core for too long. Fujifilm managed the digital onslaught by diversifying. It used its expertise in chemical compounds to move into cosmetics, and in films to make optical films for LCD flat-panel screens.[18]

In looking at your business models, if you see steady declines in customers or profits, start rethinking quickly. You can experiment with new models that use your brand, while your existing business still makes enough money to subsidize the experiment. Your experimentation may scare away start-ups or give you an advantage over competitors who try to threaten you. But these fundamental shifts are better addressed early.

Beginning some two decades ago, individuals and businesses have enjoyed access to multiple new forms of delivering and receiving document and text communications—from e-mail to social media. But the experience has not been positive for all. Postal operators have experienced, at best, a slow decline in their core businesses—the physical delivery of letters. In Australia, for instance, the number of addressed letters mailed declined 17 percent from 2009 to 2012—a 20 percent revenue hole for Australia Post.[19] The company has moved from 100 percent market share of written or text-based communications to less than 1 percent within one generation. For this radical case of digital substitution, a rethink of the postal services business model was clearly in order.[20]

In response to the shift to digital communication, a number of postal companies around the world have pursued electronic-to-electronic (E2E) services. Accelerating the cannibalization of the existing business might seem counterintuitive. But these postal companies believe that the integration of physical and electronic channels could create a new platform that allows them to retain the role of intermediary and facilitator in communications and commerce.

The Nordic Posts of Denmark and Sweden were among the first to explore diversification into e-services in the 1990s. One of the most established and successful postal digital mailbox examples is e-Boks, in which Post Danmark holds a partial ownership, along with Nets, the Nordic banking payment system.

e-Boks started as a closed, one-way system supporting transactional business-to-consumer and government-to-consumer communications. The company intended to provide an authenticated, universal archive for consolidated household document administration. e-Boks enabled large business and government senders to fully digitize their transactional communications processes with consumers. e-Boks also made organizations' preferences for digital or physical communications simpler to manage. To consumers, e-Boks offered convenience, security, and choice in a familiar online system (similar to online banking). The service integrated payment options, enabled media preferences by sender, and offered a lifetime online archive for important personal business documents.

e-Boks can be accessed on the web or via an app used by several hundred thousand individuals. Two-way communication in e-Boks now provides a secure channel for communication containing sensitive information, like social security numbers. Receivers' replies can be downloaded directly into the sending company's business applications. Similarly, contracts and agreements requiring a signature can be handled within e-Boks, generating an electronic record of acceptance or rejection that is legally binding under Danish law. At the same time, the portal solutions still provide consumers with a choice of channels.

e-Boks' growth is closely linked to strong e-government policies establishing the legal status of digital communications, and active government support and adoption. State, regional, and local government agencies in Denmark are linked into e-Boks, as are most banks, utilities, and other major commercial organizations. As e-Boks added new areas of service, the number of people using the service increased, and network effects led to people's increasing acceptance of the service. As of 2013, about 80 percent of the Danish adult population has signed up for e-Boks.[21]

Since processing steps like printing, folding, and envelope-stuffing make up most of the total expense involved in sending a normal letter, large organizations generally can reduce their distribution costs by up to 80 percent by switching to digital mailings.[22] The digital mailbox has initially focused on personal business communications—account statements, bills and invoices, salary slips, tax correspondence, and health communications such as lab results. However, once the secure, permission-based platform for connecting senders and receivers is established, it creates further opportunities. New revenue streams from business senders can be created: new consumer-centric applications, permission-based marketing applications, and database management solutions.

Most postal companies around the world consider a "sender-pays" model—as with physical mail—the most viable pricing strategy in the near term. But they are exploring opportunities around click-through pricing, value pricing, and building modular subscription services for consumers.

When your core product or service is being replaced by new digital formats, there's no going back. You have to choose the right way and time to disengage. Squeezing the old to fuel the new model is good practice and will allow you to defend your core business for a while. But proactively managing the transition is ultimately the only viable strategy.

CREATING NEW DIGITAL BUSINESSES

Large firms can find it hard to create new sources of growth with business model reinvention. The focus on growing the current business incrementally and protecting existing assets can curtail radical thinking. More often than not, start-ups and new entrants are the catalysts for creating new digital businesses. But it is not always the case.

Nike has traditionally built its business through a combination of strong innovative products, intensive brand building through multiple media platforms, and efficient operations. As the possibilities of new digital technologies emerged, Nike quickly capitalized on all three areas. The company transformed both its customer experience, by introducing new selling processes and connecting athletes worldwide, and its operations with new design and manufacturing methods.

Nike did not start by strategizing on its business model, but rather looked at ways it could provide even more value to its connected customers. Beyond its presence in public social sites, Nike decided to weave its technology and information together into a new business model. The Nike+ concept was born.[23]

Nike+ includes multiple connected components: a shoe, a sensor, an internet platform, and a device such as an iPod, an iPhone, an Xbox, a GPS watch, or a FuelBand. The FuelBand, a product of this new concept, can geo-track a person throughout the day, giving users real-time updates on how many calories they have burned, or steps they have taken, providing real motivation for athletes. Nike+ provides NikeFuel points, a proprietary metric for tracking fitness activity that you can share online. Runners can also share their routes and performance online with their friends on Twitter or Facebook. They can even get training plans from a digital coach.

At the same time, Nike gathers valuable data about how customers use its products, which allows the company to improve its brand marketing and, in the process, create a highly engaged community of users. As early as 2008, Nike was able to learn things that it never knew before: "In the winter, people in the US run more often than those in Europe and Africa, but shorter distances. The average duration of a run worldwide is 35 minutes, and the most popular Nike+ Powersong, is 'Pump It' by the Black Eyed Peas."[24]

Through Nike+, the company has extended its business model from providing only apparel to providing new hardware, technology, rich data and useful add-on services for its customers. The company is now attracting external partners to continually enhance the services on the Nike+ platform. Not bad for an already successful company of some forty-four thousand people. Mark Parker, Nike's CEO, colorfully explains, "One of my fears is being this big, slow, constipated, bureaucratic company that's happy with its success. Companies fall apart when their model is so successful that it stifles thinking that challenges it. It's like the Joker said—'this town needs an enema.'"[25]

Nike has increased its market share and developed new revenue streams with a range of add-on products and services.[26] It understood the nature of its customers' needs for engagement and asked, "How do we provide even more value?" In this way, Nike engineered a coherent digital platform that interconnects its products and services to the benefit of athletes worldwide.

RECONFIGURING VALUE DELIVERY MODELS

Often, reinventing your business model will not be about changing the rules of an industry, replacing your products or services, or creating a new digital business, but will be about reconfiguring your value delivery model. Using technology to connect all your products, services, and information in a different way can build stickiness with customers and competitive advantage. When done well, it creates switching costs and incentives for customers to favor transacting with you.

Many companies want to reconnect with their customers without endangering the third-party distribution model that has been successful for years. This is a dilemma that many traditional business-to-business (B2B) companies are trying to crack. It requires rethinking the traditional vertically integrated model.

Insurance companies, for instance, have built profitable businesses using agents to distribute their products and services to their end customers. But what happens when the percentage of the population that wants to work with agents drops? Or when you have become so disconnected from your end customers that you find it hard to understand their detailed needs? You need a new business model.

Many automakers are B2B companies. They produce cars and sell them to dealers. The dealers then sell the cars to customers. The carmakers are completely dependent on dealers to sell their products, yet dealers are costly and can be difficult to manage. Even worse, dealers own the customer relationship, and auto makers have very little contact with these end customers.

Swedish car corporation Volvo decided to do something about this traditional model. In 2012, the company relied on a network of twenty-three hundred dealers in one hundred countries worldwide to sell its products. Dealers managed all sales and after-sales services. Because they controlled the selling process, local dealers traditionally owned customer knowledge. The company conducted traditional market research, but had little or no direct knowledge of its end customers.

Volvo was facing increased competition. The nature of demand was also changing—cars were no longer sold as a single product but were sold as a transportation solution changing the nature of the customer experience. Packed with advanced IT and communications technologies, connected cars promised to provide customers with more effective and safer transportation with less harm to the environment.

How could Volvo develop a more direct relationship with end customers without disrupting its dealers' relationships? The company decided to undertake a deep transformation of its business model from a B2B model to a "B2B2C" model, where Volvo would provide some services directly to end customers.[27] These services were designed not to compete with dealers. In fact, the services reinforced the attraction of Volvo cars, thereby benefiting dealers. To evolve to this new B2B2C model, the company relied heavily on digital technologies—mobility, social media, analytics, and smart embedded devices.

To increase engagement, the company started making active use of social media platforms such as Facebook, Twitter, and YouTube in addition to its web presence. The purpose when interacting on social media was not to sell—and compete with dealers—but to reinforce proximity with existing customers, open a two-way conversation, build trust, and increase loyalty.

Then Volvo did more. Addressing the need to add a push-to-talk button to its cars, Volvo is developing its connected-car concept. Volvo on Call, the company's roadside assistance service, is delivered through local call centers operating under global framework agreements. A driver in a newer Volvo car can push a button to talk directly with an operator in the call center. Through GPS, the call center provides services such as finding the closest retailer, dispatching a tow truck, or calling the police. In addition, the On Call service triggers automatic alerts during an accident. The service is also available through a mobile app, which opens commercialization to customers owning an older car with no GPS or GSM (global system for mobile communications) technology embedded. The On Call service is included for several years after the purchase of a new vehicle and then is renewable, for a fee.

Of course, Volvo was not the first company to provide such a service. The US company OnStar was a precursor, which other companies then followed. What Volvo did was use the push-to-talk requirement to reconfigure its value-delivery model with dealers and customers. Volvo could get closer to customers without encountering strong resistance from dealers. Call centers are too costly for any dealership to do on its own, but are useful for selling cars. Dealers were happy to have Volvo corporation handle call center activities, so they did not have to do so.

Having incorporated connected-car functionality throughout the car, Volvo started releasing new digital services such as stolen vehicle tracking, door control, heater starting, remote dashboard, and car locator services.

Rather than bypassing dealers, Volvo is using its new customer contact methods to provide information and services to dealers. The company created a central customer database and implemented a global CRM solution. Volvo now has integrated existing data from dealers with a constant feed of information from the car itself. New analytic capabilities allow Volvo to move closer to one-to-one marketing while also providing dealers with information about their customers. In addition, Volvo can launch new services such as maintenance reminders that tell customers when dealers have openings in their service schedules. It's a win-win dual business model enabled by digital technology.

RETHINKING VALUE PROPOSITIONS

There is a lot of media excitement today around big disruptions created by new digital business models. While they are important, not all business model changes have to be disruptive to create value. Similarly, the changes don't always have to take you into brand-new markets. In creating a new business model, you don't even need to wait until your current model is threatened.

Business model transformations can also allow you to reinforce your presence in your current market. But these transformations can be no less dramatic. They can be about combining products and services in innovative ways: making better use of analytics, designing new economic models, or repackaging your offering. Of course, not all of these approaches are mutually exclusive, and some companies have combined these models to generate even more value.

A puzzling insight about customers was bothering Japanese property and casualty insurer Tokio Marine Holdings. Many of its customers needed insurance not on a yearly basis but for very specific activities in narrowly defined periods. The company decided to augment its traditional business model to address this unserved need.

Mobile and location-based technology gave company executives a way to make the firm's product more relevant to customers for specific lifestyle situations. In 2011, the company partnered with mobile carrier Docomo to offer customers a series of innovative insurance products under the banner One-Time Insurance. These products were available through a specialized mobile app. The app provides users with targeted recommendations for certain lifestyle insurance products such as skiing, golf, and travel-related insurance. Through the app, the company can proactively send relevant and customized insurance packages to consumers on the spot.[28] In January 2012, the company also launched One Day Auto Insurance—a new kind of auto insurance that can be purchased on mobile phones. The product offers consumers the ability to insure a vehicle for a required number of days when they use a car borrowed from friends or family members.[29]

While some companies, like Tokio Marine, have used new technology and data to enhance their value propositions, others have used the data they already possess to create new value propositions based on the data itself.

Entravision Communications Corporation is a Spanish-language media company with significant reach in the US Latino audience, a market that collectively has over a trillion dollars in purchasing power.[30] The company, started in 1996, operates over a hundred radio and television stations and digital platforms. The company was unique in its ability to offer highly localized marketing in different geographies. As Entravision processed a growing amount of both internal data and data resulting from licensing agreements with its partners, it began to see the potential value of mastering this new currency. Using advanced analytics, the company started to obtain fine-grained behavioral insights, which were highly sought after by companies selling products and services to the Latino population.[31]

The demand for deep insights into Latino markets began to grow beyond traditional media buyers, moving Entravision's client conversations into analytics and predictive modeling. Thus, in 2012, Luminar was born. Luminar is a dedicated business unit that shifted from delivering internal analytics to offering big data as a service to external clients. The company has since gained clients ranging from Nestlé and General Mills to Target, among others.[32] In 2013, the business expanded further by launching the Luminar Audience Platform for buying targeted online audiences. The company now collects and analyzes data for fifteen million US Latino adults, representing around 70 percent of the US Latino adult population's transactions in brick-and-mortar, online, and catalog.[33] The company that traditionally saw itself as a broadcasting group now sees itself as an integrated media and information technology company serving the Latino market.

MAKING SENSE OF BUSINESS MODEL TRANSFORMATION

Successful business models do not last forever. Sometimes, the creation of new value requires you to venture into the unchartered territory of new business models. Business opportunities or competitive threats can be the catalyst for such change. Digital Masters are not paranoid. But they do assume that competitors, and new entrants, may use the potential of digital technologies to go after their business. You should make the same assumption.

First, you need a good grasp of your current business model (or models). You should also constantly be on the lookout for symptoms of business model change that should ring alarm bells in your organization. Are you experiencing a gradual decline in traditional revenue streams or margin erosion due to commoditization? Are new competitors emerging from unexpected places or adjacent industries? Are cheaper digital substitutes for your products or services making inroads in your market? Are traditional barriers to entry coming down in your industry?

You may choose to operate defensively or offensively. When in defensive mode, companies often use data and any other advantage they can muster to slow the decline of the old model. In addition, aggressive operational cost cutting can release cash and investment capacity to support the transition. But you can also decide to play offense. You can be a first mover in rethinking the business model of your industry. You can disrupt competitors, or other industries, by substituting a traditional product or service with a new digital offering. You can use new digital business models to create new sources of revenue. You can reconfigure your value-delivery model and play a different role in the value chain. Or you can look at opportunities to rethink your value propositions, serving your existing customers in new ways. The scope can be daunting, but the exercise is strategically worthwhile.

Don't start with the technology. Start with how you can deliver greater value to customers, and think about how to deliver this value operationally at a profit. Then exploit the possibilities offered by digital technology to help you get there smarter, cheaper, and faster. Learn how other industries have solved similar problems or taken advantage of similar opportunities.

Multiple avenues will be possible. You will need to prioritize options that generate the greatest value to customers, that are operationally hard to copy, and that can provide you with a profitable economic model. You will also have to lower your risk by running controlled experiments on your new model. At the same time, gather the data that will help you learn and revise your assumptions. Often, the technology shifts that create new opportunities for business model change are the same ones that can disrupt your existing model.

Designing, experimenting, and implementing new business models is a task for top business leaders. It is a strategic activity. Functional heads will not have sufficient authority to drive new business model experimentation across business silos. The implementation of a new model requires vision, leadership, and governance. If the new model is ultimately designed to replace the old, you need to know when to shift resources and at what rate; the transition won't happen overnight. If the old and the new are designed to coexist, you need to carefully manage potential conflicts and resource allocation between the two.

We've now reviewed the three investment areas that constitute the *what* of digital transformation—creating compelling customer experiences, exploiting the power of core operations, and reinventing business models. Let's now turn our attention to the *how*—the committed leadership required to successfully conduct a digital transformation.

LEADING DIGITAL CHECKLIST: BUSINESS MODEL

✓ Constantly challenge your business model with your top team.

✓ Monitor the symptoms that drive business model change in your industry—for example, commoditization, new entrants, and technology substitution.

✓ Consider how you might transform your industry before others do it.

✓ Consider whether it is time to replace products and services with newer versions if your present offerings are under digital threats.

✓ Consider creating brand-new digital businesses using your core skills and assets.

✓ Consider reconfiguring your delivery model by connecting your products, services, and data in innovative ways to create extra value.

✓ Consider reinforcing your presence in your current market by rethinking your value proposition to meet new needs.

✓ Experiment and iterate your new business model ideas.

PART II

BUILDING LEADERSHIP CAPABILITIES

Having discussed the *what* of digital capabilities, we now turn to the *how* of driving transformation. Not all companies are able to get started on the digital journey. However, for the vast majority of firms, the problem is not getting people started—it's getting everyone moving in the same direction. Both challenges are the domain of leadership. Leadership capabilities are essential to achieving true digital transformation; they turn digital investment into digital advantage.

In part II, we describe the four key elements of leadership capability. Digital transformation starts when you create a transformative vision of how your firm will be different in the digital world, and then engage your employees to make the vision a reality. Establishing the right digital governance model is critical, since it acts as the rudder to steer your digital initiatives in the right direction. Finally, technology leadership capabilities—strong relationships between IT and businesspeople and the right digital skills—will help you build and continuously reap benefits from a well-designed digital platform.

CHAPTER 5

CRAFTING YOUR DIGITAL VISION

We do not need magic to transform our world. We carry
all the power we need inside ourselves already.
We have the power to imagine better.

—J. K. ROWLING

When Jean-Pierre Remy became the CEO of Pages Jaunes in 2009, the company was in trouble. As the market leader in the fast-dying French Yellow Pages industry, the company saw its print revenues declining by more than 10 percent every year.[1] After all, in an age of Google, Craigslist, and Yelp, who would look for companies in a thick yellow book? Pages Jaunes needed to adapt to the world of digital search, and it needed to do so quickly.

Remy tried to convince his employees that digital directory services were an opportunity. The company still had a trusted brand, strong relationships with its advertisers, and a small foothold in digital services. But employees in the hundred-year-old company were skeptical; Pages Jaunes had always been the industry leader, and there was little need to change the business. Many employees saw digital as a sideshow that was irrelevant to selling ads in thick paper books. The workers had lived through the creation of Minitel—France's revolutionary online networking system of the 1980s and 1990s—with no impact on the company's competitive position.[2] They had lived through the dot-com bubble and bust of 1997 to 2002, and Pages Jaunes remained the industry leader. Even as revenues declined, some employees blamed poor management instead of a major industry shift. Very few saw digital as the danger and opportunity it truly was.

What the Pages Jaunes employees needed was clear: a transformative vision of the future that was more compelling than their current view of the business. Remy found one such vision: Pages Jaunes was not in the business of producing heavy yellow books. It never had been. It was in the business of connecting small businesses to local customers. Books were just an outdated technology; digital technology could do the job better.[3] This vision was clear and compelling. It painted a distinct picture of the future while linking to the company's current capabilities. The vision made it plain that digital was the future and that paper books would disappear. It gave employees an idea about how their jobs and skills might fit in the new world, and how they might play a role in the digital future.

Remy also announced an audacious goal: Pages Jaunes would shift its business mix from having less than 30 percent digital revenues to more than 75 percent within five years.[4] This explicit goal stopped employees from debating about how much and how fast they needed to change. It also provided a clear way—digital revenues as a share of total revenues—to measure progress. Anything that increased digital revenues was good. Anything that increased paper revenues was less important.

Remy spent the next two years helping everyone—from employees to customers to investors—understand the promise that digital could hold for the future of the business. He communicated honestly and repeatedly with his employees. Some of what had made the company great would still be valuable in the future. Other things would slowly need to disappear. The company's brand could still be strong in the digital world. The customer relationships that salespeople had built up over years were still valuable, but salespeople would need to learn to sell digital services instead of paper ads. Some book-oriented skills, such as printing and delivery, would be less useful in the future. But Pages Jaunes would remain in the paper business for several years longer—time enough for people in the paper end to retire, retrain, or move to another company.

Pages Jaunes senior executives moved fast to realign the company's investments and skills. They hired senior people who had digital skills and the mind-set to work in the digital economy. They retrained salespeople to sell digital services, and retrained designers to create digital ads and webpages. They invested in prototypes for digital services, such as web page design and mobile apps, to show clients how they could reach their customers in new ways. They even inked a deal to partner with Google instead of competing with it. Finally, Remy sent a strong signal by freezing all nonessential investment in the traditional book business.

The transition was neither smooth nor immediate. In a country where firing employees is very difficult, some employees resisted the change. Remy convinced some to join in the transformation, while he found ways to work around those who did not. When digital revenue grew more slowly than planned and physical-book revenue declined faster because of the worldwide recession, executives had to restructure the company's debt. But customers began to see the value of digital services, and salespeople learned how to sell them.

By 2013, four years after Remy announced his new digital vision, and despite Europe's economic woes, Pages Jaunes had nearly met its transformation goals. Annual digital revenues were growing fast enough to replace most of the company's annual losses in the paper-based business. For the first time since he had joined the company, Remy projected overall revenue growth by 2015. While Yellow Pages companies around the world struggled to handle digital competition, Pages Jaunes has now become a company powered by digital, not paper, technology.

VISION MATTERS; TRANSFORMATIVE
VISION MATTERS EVEN MORE

The changes being wrought through digital transformation are real. Yet, even when leaders see the digital threat and opportunity, employees may need to be convinced. Many employees feel they are paid to do a job, not to change that job. And they have lived through big initiatives in the past that failed to turn into reality. To many, digital transformation is either irrelevant or just another passing fad. Still other people may not understand how the change affects their jobs or how they might make the transition.

Our research shows that successful digital transformation starts at the top of the company. Only the senior-most executives can create a compelling vision of the future and communicate it throughout the organization. Then people in middle and lower levels can make the vision a reality. Managers can redesign processes, workers can start to work differently, and everyone can identify new ways to meet the vision. This kind of change doesn't happen through simple mandate. It must be led.

Among the companies we studied, none have created true digital transformation through a bottom-up approach. Some executives have changed their parts of the business—for example, product design and supply chain at Nike—but the executives stopped at the boundaries of their business units. Changing part of your business is not enough. Often, the real benefits of transformation come from seeing potential synergies across silos and then creating conditions through which everyone can unlock that value. Only senior executives are positioned to drive this kind of boundary-spanning change.

So how prevalent is digital vision? In our global survey of 431 executives in 391 companies, only 42 percent said that their senior executives had a digital vision. Only 34 percent said the vision was shared among senior and middle managers. These numbers are surprisingly low, given the rapid rate at which digital transformation is reshaping companies and industries. But the low overall numbers mask an important distinction: Digital Masters have a shared digital vision, while others do not. Among the Digital Masters that we surveyed, 82 percent agreed that their senior leaders shared a common vision of digital transformation, and 71 percent said it was shared between senior and middle managers.[5] The picture is quite different for firms outside our Digital Masters category, where less than 30 percent said their senior leaders had a shared digital vision and only 17 percent said the shared vision extended to middle management.

But having a shared digital vision is not quite enough. Many organizations fail to capture the full potential of digital technologies because their leaders lack a truly transformative vision of the digital future. On average, only 31 percent of our respondents said they had a vision which represented radical change, and 41 percent said their vision crossed internal organizational units.[6] Digital Masters were far more transformative in their visions, with two-thirds agreeing they had a radical vision, and 82 percent agreeing their vision crossed organizational silos. Meanwhile, nonmasters were far less transformative in their visions.

WHAT DO DIGITAL VISIONS LOOK LIKE?

Where should you focus your digital vision? Digital visions usually take one of three perspectives: reenvisioning the customer experience, reenvisioning operational processes, or combining the previous two approaches to reenvision business models. The approach you take should reflect your organization's capabilities, your customers' needs, and the nature of competition in your industry.

Reenvisioning the Customer Experience

Many organizations start by reenvisioning the way they interact with customers. They want to make themselves easier to work with, and they want to be smarter in how they sell to (and serve) customers. Companies start from different places when reenvisioning the customer experience.

Some companies aim to transform their relationships with their customers. Adam Brotman, chief digital officer of Starbucks, shared this vision: "Digital has to help our store partners and help the company be the way we can . . . tell our story, build our brand, and have a relationship with our customers."[7] Burberry's CEO Angela Ahrendts focused on multichannel coherence: "We had a vision, and the vision was to be the first company who was fully digital end-to-end . . . A customer will have total access to Burberry across any device, anywhere."[8] Marc Menesguen, managing director of strategic marketing at cosmetics giant L'Oréal, said, "The digital world multiplies the ways our brands can create an emotion-filled relationship with their customers."[9]

Other companies envision how they can be smarter in serving (and selling to) their customers through analytics. Caesars started with a vision of using real-time customer information to deliver a personalized experience to each customer. The company was able to increase customer satisfaction and profits per customer using traditional technologies. Then, as new technologies arose, it extended the vision to include a mobile, location-based concierge in the palm of every customer's hand.[10]

Another approach is to envision how digital tools might help the company to learn from customer behavior. Commonwealth Bank of Australia sees new technologies as a key way of integrating customer inputs in its co-creation efforts. According to CIO Ian Narev, "We are progressively applying new technology to enable customers to play a greater part in product design. That helps us create more intuitive products and services, readily understandable to our customers and more tailored to their individual needs."[11]

Finally, some companies are extending their visions beyond influencing customer experience to actually changing customers' lives.[12] For instance, Novartis CEO Joseph Jimenez wrote of this potential: "The technologies we use in our daily lives, such as smart phones and tablet devices, could make a real difference in helping patients to manage their own health. We are exploring ways to use these tools to improve compliance rates and enable health-care professionals to monitor patient progress remotely."[13]

Reenvisioning Operations

Organizations whose fortunes are closely tied to the performance of their core operations and supply chains often start with reenvisioning their operations. The business drivers of operational visions include efficiency and the need to integrate disparate operations. Executives may want to increase process visibility and decision-making speed or to collaborate across silos. For instance, in 2011, Procter & Gamble put operational excellence at the center of its digital vision: "Digitizing P&G will enable us to manage the business in real time and on a demand-driven basis. We'll be able to collaborate more effectively and efficiently, inside and outside the company."[14] Other companies, in industries from banking to manufacturing, have transformed themselves through similar operationally focused visions.

Operational visions are especially useful for businesses that sell largely to other businesses. When Codelco first launched its Codelco Digital initiative, the aim was to improve mining operations radically through automation and data integration. As we described in chapter 3, Codelco continued to extend this vision to include new mining automation and an integrated operations-control capability. Now, executives are envisioning radical new ways to redefine the mining process and possibly the industry itself.

The operational visions of some companies go beyond an internal perspective to consider how the company might change operations in its industry or even with its customers. For example, aircraft manufacturer Boeing envisions how changes to its products may enable customers to change their own operations. "Boeing believes the future of the aviation industry lies in 'the digital airline,'" the company explained on its website. "To succeed in the marketplace, airlines and their engineering and IT teams must take advantage of the increasing amount of data coming off of airplanes, using advanced analytics and airplane technology to take operational efficiency to the next level."[15] The manufacturer goes on to paint a clear picture of what a digital airline means in practice: "The key to the digital airline is delivering secure, detailed operational and maintenance information to the people who need it most, when they need it most. That means that engineering will share data with IT, but also with the finance, accounting, operational and executive functions."[16] The vision will improve operations at Boeing's customers, but will also help Boeing's operations, as the information from airplanes should help the company identify new ways to improve its product designs and services. The data may also lead to new business models as Boeing uses the information to provide new services to customers.

Reenvisioning Business Models

Some executives combine ideas around operational processes and the customer experience to envision new business models. The new vision may extend the current business model or may depart from it substantially. There are many resources and frameworks that can help you envision new business models.[17] And in chapter 4, we shared examples of companies that digitally transformed their business models. In our research, we have seen two broad ways to form a new business model vision: defensively or offensively.

Some companies take a defensive approach to reenvisioning the model. Often, these companies are under threat and need to focus on their long-term survival. For example, information-based industries such as books, music, and travel are now going through fundamental structural changes. The rapid pace of change in these industries is forcing companies to redesign their business models. The defensive approach is where Pages Jaunes started. Facing a burning platform, the company's executive team needed to create a vision that could drive rapid change.

On the other hand, some companies are lucky enough not to face a crisis; they can take a more offensive approach. Executives in these companies can focus on the potential opportunity of new, digitally powered business models, rather than overcoming a crisis situation. However, lack of crisis can be both a blessing and a curse. It's a blessing because companies in this situation have time to experiment with new digital approaches. But it can be a curse if employees—or their leaders—see little reason to change. Banco Santander is taking an opportunity-based approach to its business model, highlighting a vision for how digital technologies can help it break into new market segments: "Our objective for the coming years is to exploit the growth opportunities in segments where the bank has a low presence, such as companies, insurance, and cards. Specifically, we are making significant investments in IT systems and staff to be able to take advantage of these opportunities."[18]

A few companies go beyond the challenges and opportunities of today. They create visions to prepare for—or even drive—the next long-term shift in their industries. General Electric, for instance, focuses its vision on the coming wave of smart connected devices. In 2011, CEO Jeffrey Immelt stated, "We will lead in the productivity of our installed products and their ecosystems. This will require leadership of the 'Industrial Internet,' making infrastructure systems more intelligent."[19]

Progressive Insurance has, for decades, had a vision to be smarter than competitors at assessing risk and pricing policies. In 1956, the company set an industry standard by reducing rates for low-risk drivers with its Safe Driver Plan.[20] The company then started to use proprietary analytics to identify which high-risk drivers were less risky than they appeared on paper. It could price its policies so that it got the customers it wanted, while making other customers want to choose Progressive's competitors.[21]

Later, Progressive went a step farther, envisioning what would be possible if it had information on customers' actual driving behaviors. For more than fifteen years, the company has experimented with gathering telemetry from customers, offering discounts and pay-as-you-drive policies as an incentive. In 1998, it launched a pilot in Texas using specialized GPS-based devices.[22] In 2004, it piloted TripSense, which used an inexpensive sensor that drivers could easily install on a port in their cars. The information obtained from these pilots led to the Snapshot program, which is based on a similar device and which Progressive launched nation-wide in 2011.[23]

Progressive's Snapshot box is not a simple gimmick that separates drivers who think they are good from those who think they are bad. Through its telemetry boxes and analytics capabilities, Progressive can link actual driving behaviors—speed, distance, acceleration, and braking—to risk. Because company executives have been willing to invest in gathering and using new information, Progressive can offer services that its competitors cannot. Through its vision of being smarter than competitors at assessing and pricing risk, Progressive continually strives to find ways that it can serve good drivers at lower prices, offer lower-cost options to less-affluent customers, and encourage poorer drivers to choose other insurance providers.

HOW CAN YOU FRAME A TRANSFORMATIVE DIGITAL VISION?

There is no single best way to express a vision for digital transformation. It's not a formulaic process. You need to craft a vision that builds on your strengths, engages employees, and can evolve over time. You'll need to identify the benefits you want, what the end point looks like, and how you will engage your customers, employees, and investors. Here are some steps you can take.

Identifying Strategic Assets

In crafting your digital vision, you need to identify some strategic assets that will help you win. If the new vision can't build on some of your company's strengths, then there is no sense trying to implement it. Another company—one that is faster, more nimble, and less burdened with legacy issues—will execute better and win the game.

But how can you identify your strategic assets? Start by looking at what kinds of assets you have. Physical assets like retail stores or manufacturing plants may or may not be valuable in a new digital, globally interconnected world. Competence-based assets, such as product design expertise, flexible and efficient operations, and excellent frontline staff, can be very useful as long as the processes they support remain valuable. Intangible assets, such as brand, reputation, and company culture, are more difficult to judge; they can be very helpful to reach a future state, but can also inhibit your transformation. Data assets can provide you an analytic advantage over your competitors or become products you can sell to others.

Once you have identified potential strategic assets, you'll need to assess whether those assets will remain strategic in the new world. In the 1990s, management researchers developed a simple yet powerful tool for making this assessment.[24] Strategic assets are VRIN: valuable, rare, inimitable, and nonsubstitutable. Valuable assets are those you can use to exploit opportunities or neutralize threats. Assets must be rare, and not available to most competitors. They must be inimitable (or, to be more precise, imperfectly imitable), since otherwise, competitors can copy them and beat you at your own game. And strategic assets must be nonsubstitutable; otherwise, someone may find a different way to do what you do, but better and at a lower price.

During the dot-com bubble, many internet firms found that customer eyeballs were not rare enough to support advertising revenues; paying customers were valuable but also far more difficult to obtain. Newspaper firms thought their classified advertising operations were strategic assets, only to find that companies such as Craigslist and eBay could imitate what newspapers do, but could do it better and at a lower price. Executives at film-rental company Blockbuster may have been correct when they believed the firm's network of stores was an inimitable asset. Unfortunately, Netflix beat Blockbuster when the start-up found a simple way to substitute for what Blockbuster stores did.

When Jean-Pierre Remy crafted a new digital vision for Pages Jaunes, he didn't start from scratch. Instead, he and his senior team systematically examined the company's core assets. Some, such as printing and distribution capabilities, would have little value in the digital world. Others, such as money and information about customers, could be used with little change, but were easily copied by competitors. However, two assets—the Pages Jaunes brand and the relationships between sales-people and their customers, could be strategic. These assets were valu-able, rare, and difficult to copy. And with some change, they could become their own substitutes. That's why Remy chose to build a new vision around these assets. Pages Jaunes would continue to be a trusted brand in the local marketing business, and its salespeople would help its customers make their own way into the digital future.

Creating Transformative Ambitions

Having a vision is not enough. The vision needs to be transformative. Incremental visions will limit the benefits that you can attain in your digital transformation. Even if you succeed, the most you'll get is incre-mental payoff. If digital is leading to radical changes in every industry, you can help your company by defining what a radically different digital future looks like.

You can liken the situation to caterpillars and butterflies. Competitors with the vision to transform into digital butterflies can fly to new heights. Meanwhile, an incremental vision will only turn you into a faster-moving caterpillar. Companies using analytics to improve targeting in their physical or electronic mail campaigns are making caterpillars faster. The real-time, location-based customer-engagement process employed at Caesars transforms the caterpillar into a butterfly.

Your digital aspirations can be divided into three categories: substi-tution, extension, and transformation.[25]

Substitution is the use of new technology as an alternative or a replacement for substantially the same function that the enterprise already performs. For example, if you use mobile phones simply to do what people already do from their PCs, or if your version of analytics is simply a better way to do basic reports, then you're in substitution mode. Substitution sometimes generates incremental cost or flexibility improvement, but it doesn't really fix inefficient processes. It can also be a way to experiment with new technologies before you do something bigger. But something bigger is required.

Extension significantly improves the performance or functionality of a product or process, without radically changing it. Many manufacturers and resellers now enable field workers to access information through mobile devices, reducing the workers' need to visit the office at the start and end of shifts. In another example, a pharmaceutical company has created a social-media physician community so that it can learn about issues and opportunities by allowing doctors to talk with one another. While regulators put severe restrictions and audit requirements on any corporate communication with physicians, there are far fewer restrictions on monitoring what physicians say to each other. Extensions like these improve on existing processes or extend the company's existing capabilities, but still focus on doing the same activities as before.

Transformation is the fundamental redefinition of a process or product through technology. When executives at Asian Paints used embedded devices and analytics to create fully automated factories, they changed the nature of their manufacturing processes, delivering higher levels of efficiency, quality, and environmental sustainability than were found at manually tended factories. Codelco's digital mines, the mobile concierge apps at Caesars, and Nike's FuelBand are similarly transformative. Each digital transformation reinvented the nature of an offering, allowing the firm and its customers to do things radically better than they could before.

Unfortunately, the previous examples notwithstanding, we found few companies doing transformative things with digital technologies. Figure 5.1 tallies the most transformative efforts for each firm we interviewed during the first year of our study in 2011.[26] Although many firms were investing in new technologies, few were doing more than substitution or extension. Only 18 percent of firms—fewer than one in five—were investing in analytics to drive breakthrough change in customer experience. Meanwhile, fewer than one in six firms were transforming their products or practices using other technologies.

FIGURE 5.1

How transformative is your digital vision?

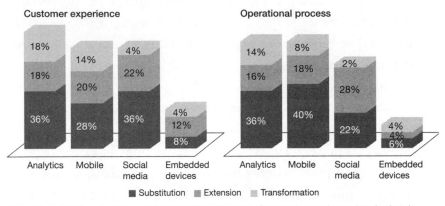

Note: Charts plot how the firms we interviewed in the first year of our study are using each technology in customer experience or operational process initiatives. For each firm, only the most transformative usage is counted.

Source: Adapted from George Westerman, Claire Calmejane, Didier Bonnet, Patrick Ferraris, and Andrew McAfee, "Digital Transformation: A Roadmap for Billion-Dollar Organizations," Capgemini Consulting and MIT Center for Digital Business, November 2011.

Consider your digital vision. Are you aspiring to do more of the same? Or do you see an opportunity to radically reshape your business—to unchain it from the shackles of old technologies and business practices? Is your vision focused on only a single part of the company, or are you envisioning a change that crosses silos? Executives with an incremental vision get what they aim for—incremental improvement. Those who realize the transformative power of digital can achieve much more.

Defining a Clear Intent and Outcome

One constant among the companies we interviewed is that people are busier than ever. Employees have to work harder and harder just to meet their current objectives. Few workers have time to work on a broad, softly defined vision of the future. The vision may never become reality. Or it may be very different when it does. Meanwhile, there are more important tasks to handle right now.

If you want people to engage with a vision, you need to make it real for them. What does "good" look like once the vision is realized? How will people know they've achieved it? Why should they care?

Great digital visions include both *intent* and *outcome*. Intent is a picture of what needs to change. Outcome is a measurable benefit to the company, its customers, or its employees. Together, intent and outcome help employees visualize the future of the organization and help motivate them to start realizing the outcome.

The CEO of Pages Jaunes clearly stated his intent to move beyond thick paper directories while retaining the company's valuable role in connecting small to medium-sized businesses with local customers. He shared examples of new digital services that the company could provide. He then coupled intent with a concrete outcome: the company would earn 75 percent of its revenues from digital services within five years.[27] This combination of intent and outcome gave everyone in the organization a clear set of guidelines to envision new ways of working. It also ensured that the transformative vision focused not on technology but on finding new ways to improve performance and customer satisfaction through digital services.

Similarly, Hispanic media conglomerate PRISA painted a clear picture of how a digitally transformed media company would operate across its wide range of media properties, from newspaper to satellite TV to educational publishing. Video of a soccer star recorded in Africa could be immediately available to PRISA's media properties in Spain, Brazil, and other parts of the world. Or the company could coordinate social media and digital marketing with traditional media advertising in global campaigns across media outlets. PRISA's CEO, Juan Luis Cebrian, gave a clear target: 20 percent of the company's revenues would be digital within five years.[28]

Evolving the Vision over Time

If you create a compelling vision and help employees believe in it, then the broader organization can fill in the details. Aim to make your digital vision specific enough to give employees a clear direction, while giving them the flexibility to innovate and build on it.

Asian Paints started in the early 2000s with a vision to move from a regional company to an integrated one.[29] This vision combined operational efficiency with new ways to serve customers.[30] The vision provided a clear mandate for change while enabling people throughout the company to refine the details over time.

Since then, Asian Paints executives have led three successive waves of digital change—each building on top of the other. The first wave focused on industrialization, the second on creating a customer-centric organization, and the third on automation. It is moving to a fourth wave, which will link structured and unstructured data—such as internal and external social media—to further improve customer engagement and internal employee collaboration.[31] The company's original vision remains a key inspiration behind improvements in operations and the customer experience, even as the company has extended its vision through successive waves of capability.

Meanwhile, digital technologies are a moving target. They continually change as some technologies die, others improve, and new ones are invented. Nobody can reliably predict the next new technology blockbuster. And it's impossible to make specific long-term predictions of how companies and individuals will use technology. Your organization's digital vision will evolve as technical advances and your new capabilities create new opportunities.

The vision of using analytics to deliver personalized customer service at Caesars started by providing better information in real time to employees and evolved to self-service personalization through the website. Then the vision evolved again to include a real-time concierge on every customer's mobile phone. At Progressive Insurance, the vision of making smarter decisions based on available data about customers evolved into new ways to gather data about actual driving behavior. That change in vision led to radically new products and decision-making processes.

HOW TO GET STARTED

An inspiring digital vision is the cornerstone of successful digital transformation. Though many executives are waking up to digital technology's potential impact, few have created a compelling vision of the digital future. Digital Masters have a transformative digital vision. Other companies need to create one.

As you craft your digital vision, focus on your business, not the technology. Technology can remove obstacles and extend your capabilities, but it is not an end in itself. Focus on how you can enhance the experience of your customers, streamline your operations, or transform your business models.

Aim to be transformative, not incremental. Make your digital vision specific enough to give employees a clear direction, while giving them the flexibility to innovate upon it. Dream big, and then ask your employees to help you make the dream a reality. This is no small task. Crafting a vision for digital transformation is a journey. You need to plant the seed at the top, and then engage people at all levels to make the vision live and grow. In chapter 6, we'll show how you can engage your employees to make the vision a reality.

LEADING DIGITAL CHECKLIST: DIGITAL VISION

✓ Familiarize yourself with new digital practices that can be an opportunity or a threat to your industry and company.

✓ Identify bottlenecks or headaches—in your company and in your customers—that resulted from the limits of old technologies, and consider how you might resolve these problems digitally.

✓ Consider which of your strategic assets will remain valuable in the digital era.

✓ Craft a compelling and transformative digital vision.

✓ Ensure that the vision specifies both intent and outcome.

✓ Make your digital vision specific enough to give employees a clear direction, while giving them the flexibility to build on it.

✓ Constantly be looking to extend your vision using the capabilities you have created.

CHAPTER 6

ENGAGING THE ORGANIZATION AT SCALE

If my mind can conceive it, and my heart
can believe it, I know I can achieve it.

—JESSE JACKSON

Ask any executive who has led an organization through a large transformation, and he or she will tell you that a company's strategic vision is only as good as the people behind it. This remains true for digital transformation. As we showed with the example of Pages Jaunes in the previous chapter, creating a compelling digital vision is only the beginning of the journey.

Unlike incremental change, which can be achieved by a few people working on their own, transformation can only be achieved through the engagement of many. It is a commitment first made by leaders, then by a few champions, and finally by the critical mass needed to make the radical change happen. But what does it mean to be engaged? In our definition, when employees are energized to make the vision a reality, they are engaged.

Business transformation involves making important, some-times disruptive, changes in how organizations get things done. Core organizational processes are redesigned, new technology tools replace old ones, new skills are developed, and new ways of working are introduced. Winning people's hearts and minds through that process isn't easy. As Sir Richard Branson once said, "Loyal employees in any company create loyal customers, who in turn create happy shareholders. The process sounds easy, but it's not, and it has defeated some of the biggest organizations of the twentieth century."[1] Employee engagement matters. And it matters even more to succeed at transformation.

Fortunately, engaging employees in organizational change is not uncharted territory. There is a wide body of research that explains how you can use the power of engagement to successfully transform your organization.[2] Some of this work puts people's hopes and fears and other feelings at the center of the engagement strategy.[3] Other work focuses on individual and team renewal as a key step in the transformation, or on achieving a psychological alignment and developing a capacity for collective learning.[4] But all work points to one thing: engagement is foremost a task of leadership.

Digital technology brings another dimension: real-time employee engagement on a global scale. Blogs, Twitter, and digital video are helping leaders connect with their organizations in ways that mass e-mails or town hall meetings cannot. Executive bloggers can share a frequent, candid perspective on the state of the transformation, and digital videos help put a personal face on executive communications. Additionally, enterprise social platforms create a new breed of open, two-way organizational communication, where leaders and employees can discuss, share, and collaborate in real time.[5] With digital technology, leaders have new powers to engage their employees in making change happen.

CONVIVIALITY GOES DIGITAL
AT PERNOD RICARD

Pernod Ricard is a world leader in wines and spirits, with sales exceeding $10 billion in 2012–2013.[6] It employs some nineteen thousand people in globally decentralized operations organized within six brand companies and eighty market units. The company is home to prestigious global brands such as Absolut Vodka, Chivas Regal Scotch whisky, Jameson Irish whiskey, Perrier-Jouet Champagne, and Ricard Pastis, the anise-flavored liqueur.

Created from the merger of Pernod and Ricard in 1975, the company has grown its brand portfolio with three transformative acquisitions—Seagram, Allied Domecq, and Absolut Vodka. Already leading the premium segment, the company has the ambition to become the global leader in wine and spirits. Pierre Pringuet, Pernod Ricard's CEO, explained: "We've now posted thirty-eight years of growth. Leadership is our goal. We want to be the company that leads industry growth. But we also want to be the one that changes the rules."[7]

For most companies, the combination of global complexity, a highly decentralized operating model, and rapid growth through multiple large acquisitions, is not generally conducive to building globally cohesive employee engagement. Yet employee engagement and culture at Pernod Ricard goes well beyond the corporate rallying cry. In 2013, an employee survey, carried out by an independent agency, showed that 94 percent of Pernod Ricard's employees are proud to work for the group, and 87 percent would recommend their company—a full 10 points above industry average.[8]

But employee surveys are lagging indicators. Such employee engagement and sense of belonging does not happen by chance. What really drove such results? In the last few years, Pernod Ricard has invested heavily in its people processes and in engaging the workforce around its strategy and digital vision. Alexandre Ricard, deputy CEO, explained: "Our vision is to use digital as a game-changer for Pernod Ricard. It will provide us with direct access to consumers. It will give us more influence and unleash new dynamics in our relationships with our trade partners. It will also allow the company to empower employees so they can play a full part in this growth journey. And, a data-driven approach will underpin all three pillars of this vision."[9]

To share this vision, the senior leaders used all available platforms—intranet, management seminars, and the company's own internal TV channel (PRTV). Digital transformation was part of the challenge, and the solution.

Wiring Pernod Ricard to Face the Digital Tsunami

As a global group with very strong consumer brands and multiple distribution models, Pernod Ricard was facing the impact of digital technology from all angles. Customers were talking about the company's products on social media and expecting more direct and engaging conversations with the brands. Retailers, wholesalers, and bars were experiencing their own digital transformations and facing new competition. Finally, employees, particularly those of the younger generation, were using more and more of their own digital tools in the workplace and expected the company to be more digital in its ways of working.

Acknowledging that digital technologies were transformative for the industry and the company, Pernod Ricard's entrepreneurial culture responded. Several units started their own transformation journeys with a wide range of consumer-driven initiatives, from digital advertising to social media to e-commerce. The units hired new digital talent and experimented with new business concepts.

At the group level, however, the first major digital initiative was focused internally: how to get the company to openly communicate at scale. The company decided to implement a companywide enterprise social network. In a company whose culture is as decentralized as Pernod Ricard's, wiring the organization was a prerequisite to share and scale successful initiatives across brands and markets. In addition, the most advanced digital units were able to support the less advanced ones, creating real "digital traction." The platform objectives became strongly rooted around entrepreneurship, innovation, and getting the organization to work in different ways. With this, the company's digital transformation started to accelerate. Alexandre Ricard explained: "Leadership is built on example. It is also built on an organization's ability to adapt to tomorrow's world. Digital has profoundly revolutionized . . . the way we act, live and work."[10]

In light of the historic corporate motto, "Make a friend every day," the company introduced its enterprise social network with the tagline "Share a new idea every day." The platform engages nineteen thousand employees in a continuous dialogue. The tool enables real-time data sharing, visual communication, mobile collaboration, and instant messaging on a global scale. From the initial decision through to test phase, the network took less than six months to implement. But the tool wasn't the most important. What mattered was engaging employees to act as a global team.

Key to success was vision, leadership, and business orientation. CEO Pierre Pringuet explained: "In a group that is highly decentralized, it is essential to promote the sharing of best practices, for instance when implementing marketing or sales initiatives. We needed to create new interactions where they did not previously exist. This networking of collective intelligence has been instrumental to speed up the group's digital transformation at every level of our organization."[11]

Pernod Ricard realized that without a strong top-down and bottom-up mobilization, change would not happen fast enough. The company started by engaging executives at both the global and local levels. After a period of training, more than 150 senior executives, including the senior leaders, became actively engaged on the platform. The project was reviewed regularly at the executive committee. But bottom-up involvement was also needed. To be successful and increase employee engagement, the enterprise network would need to be anchored in real business needs—helping people in their day-to-day work and making an impact on the company's performance. Alexandre Ricard emphasized: "You don't do digital because it's fashionable. You do digital because it has a real impact on business performance."[12]

To increase business focus, several use cases were defined at the outset—from innovation to brand marketing to business process improvement. The network has also enhanced internal communications and the deployment of new HR practices. Web conferences, or "coffee breaks," have increased participatory dialogues with employees to refine and improve the introduction of new HR projects or ways of working.

Employees have also found new and unexpected uses for the collaboration platform. As a group of Pernod Ricard employees perused an airport duty-free shop while waiting for a flight, they noticed something odd about the packaging on the store's Absolut Vodka display. They posted a picture of the display on the social network, tagged the company's compliance group, and asked if this was the standard packaging for the region. Within hours, the compliance group was able to confirm that the display was counterfeit. And within days, the display was removed and corrective actions were taken.

But to scale employee adoption, Pernod Ricard went further. Governance, communication, and training were deployed across the firm. A digital curriculum was developed with "Pernod Ricard University" to raise the company's digital IQ. The company leveraged its Millennial employees and identified early seeding-phase "champions" to evangelize other users. New roles, such as community managers, and new processes, such as content moderation, were created. Adoption was monitored through a scorecard with clear key performance indicators (KPIs) that measured both reach (the share of users who log in regularly) and engagement (the activity and contribution of users to the platform).

By 2014, Pernod Ricard's enterprise social network had connected 84 percent of its worldwide employees. A quarter of this population was actively contributing, with some thirteen thousand connections daily—well above industry benchmarks.

Alexandre Ricard explained: "Communities that are created on the network are free from geographical, functional or hierarchical boundaries. Immediacy and discussion are now at the heart of relations between our employees, and have become essential in our relationship with consumers."[13]

Accelerating Digital Transformation Through Co-creation

For Pernod Ricard, the implementation of a group-level enterprise social network created real value in itself by connecting employees and communities globally. But it was only a first foundational step to implement the company's digital vision.

"With the first phase of our digital transformation," Pringuet said, "we have connected the organization and transformed the way we communicate, work, and innovate. The second phase, the digital acceleration roadmap, will help us to expand and accelerate this process. It will make us go faster and further and become stronger in our quest for market leadership. And its success is highly dependent on bringing our people with us on this journey."[14]

To tackle the digital challenges facing its brands and markets—content, commerce, social media, consumer insights, and internal-process digitization—the company needed new digital capabilities, new ways of working, and other new behaviors. To achieve these desired changes and foster buy-in, the senior leaders decided to engage the employees in the co-creation of a digital acceleration roadmap.

The company mobilized a wide network of people called digital champions, who were driving digital change in the company's brands and market units. The digital champions engaged their teams locally and leveraged their local experience and customer knowledge. Pernod Ricard, through that process, managed to prioritize the initiatives that would have the biggest global impact on its brands and its business performance.

Today, the company is in full-speed implementation of its roadmap. Practices developed in corners of the world are being documented and readied for large-scale rollouts to other units. Individual brand units are developing and running strategic initiatives on behalf of the whole company. Headquarters is also playing its part, identifying synergies and providing the shared capabilities required by the local business units. This is engagement in action.

None of this could have happened without leadership. The digital vision is being driven and sponsored at the highest level in the organization. Nevertheless, transforming day-to-day business practices at scale remains a challenge. Digital-savvy top managers and digital champions at every level must continue acting as digital change agents to engage their nineteen thousand colleagues on this exciting journey.

Pringuet explained: "We have started a 'digital movement' that affects all aspects of our company and requires all of our people to be engaged in the program. Digital transformation will continue to be one of our key challenges in the coming years. We will only win together."[15]

ALL HANDS TO THE PUMP

As the Pernod Ricard story shows, and as we described in chapter 5, before you engage employees to make the vision a reality, you first need a compelling vision—one that energizes employees to do more than just show up at work in the morning. Leaders need to do their job of leading—setting clear expectations for what needs to change. But it doesn't stop there. Digital champions within an organization can have a great influence on showing employees what digital transformation means to the business. By setting clear expectations and engaging digital champions in your efforts to communicate a transformative vision for your company, you can reach a critical mass of believers that can shift the organization to a higher level of performance.

But as a leader, how do you practically engage the organization to take an active part in the larger digital transformation journey? Our research identified three critical managerial levers to engage the organization.

First, *connect the organization*—using digital technology to wire the organization so that everyone gets a voice and can collaborate. Second, actively *encourage open conversations* to facilitate strategic dialogue and create the opportunity for everyone to play a role in advancing the vision. Third, rather than design the solution and attempt to get buy-in afterward, *crowdsource your own employees* to co-create solutions. When done well, the combination of these levers can accelerate digital transformation.

Connecting the Many

Digital Masters understand how new digital channels can drive global employee engagement and transparent conversations to solve business problems. Communication goes beyond blast e-mails.

Wikis, micro-blogging tools, and enterprise social networks, also referred to as Enterprise 2.0 tools, have received much attention lately as key collaborative tools to wire up organizations.[16] Enterprise social platforms open strategic conversations to everyone in an organization. They foster cross-functional problem solving at global scale. Through these social platforms, business discussions become visible to everyone in the organization, driving greater transparency and accountability for what needs to be done. They also give leaders the opportunity to publicly recognize contributions and reward engagement. You need to find ways to connect your organization to make this global dialogue possible. Pernod Ricard decided to use an enterprise social network as the glue for a highly decentralized business model. Other companies have chosen different tools, like their existing intranets. The tool is not important. What matters is the open dialogue and the engaging of the organization to deliver the digital vision.

Consider the case of a large US-based medical technology company. Facing a major strategic shift, the company convened three hundred of its executives and top managers for a three-day workshop to develop its plan of action. Over the course of the session, video teams captured the discussion and the decision making. They also recorded short digital debriefs with executives at the end of each session to explain how the meeting was progressing. These digital clips were then streamed in near real time to the entire company. According to one attendee, the streaming produced a great sense of openness: "You're broadcasting, 'Here's what we're working on, day one' back to their organization. So when [executives] walk out of the meeting, people know that they were there and what they were working on. And all of a sudden, the organization has an expectation of follow-up." Reflecting on the transparency created by the new digital coverage of the event, the president said, "Last year, we walked out of the meeting and told the organization what the strategy was. This year, we're walking out of the meeting, and they already know."[17]

Engaging the Wider Conversation

To encourage open dialogue and increase adoption of new ways of working, executives have to both lead by example and engage a sufficient coalition of employees to get the change under way. Employees who are encouraged to contribute to the digital transformation will have a higher level of engagement and, in turn, will become better employees.

One of the best ways to lead an organization into embracing new technologies and new ways working is to act as a role model. Role models set expectations for the rest of the organization and give employees an opportunity to interact directly with senior leadership. For example, senior executives at Kraft record podcasts (dubbed Kraft casts) and make them available to employees with iPhones and iPads. These messages help keep employees in the loop on the latest corporate strategies and branding initiatives.[18]

Executive presence on digital platforms also helps create a pull effect for user adoption. Consider Coca-Cola. The iconic company is one of the top twenty brands on the planet for engaging customers through social media.[19] Coke's corporate website is now a digital magazine.[20] Customers can develop their own personalized blends of Coke products through the company's smart Freestyle vending machines. From the outside, Coke appears to be a leader in using digital channels to interact with its customers.

But Coca-Cola encountered challenges when it tried to use digital tools internally to improve collaboration among its employees. The company introduced an enterprise social platform in an effort to transform its self-described "secret formula" culture, but struggled to sustain user engagement. In a 2012 interview, global innovation director Anthony Newstead noted, "After an initial surge of activity, [user activity] slowly drifted back down." Newstead and his team investigated the cause and discovered that weekly posts from executive leaders were enough to attract other employees and sustain an active community. "With executive engagement, you don't have to mandate activity."[21]

But not all leaders feel comfortable going online and showing the way. In addition, sometimes the strongest ambassadors for digital transformation may not come from the company's most senior ranks. Employees on the front lines can be the most effective vehicles of promoting change in an organization. Influential supporters can help recruit others to your cause. Many Digital Masters proactively identify true believers within the organization and position the devotees to share their knowledge and enthusiasm with colleagues.

In some companies, these digital champions assume formal organizational roles. Nestlé, for example, introduced its Digital Acceleration Team (DAT) in 2012. The team, based in Vevey, Switzerland, serves a dual purpose as Nestlé's "center of excellence" for digital know-how, as well as an incubator for its digital champions. High performers from Nestlé's many brands around the world join the team for an eight-month assignment, where they work together to deliver targeted digital projects such as developing mobile strategies for emerging markets or developing recruiting strategies for digital talent. At the end of their rotation, the team members return to their home countries and brands to share their knowledge and skills. DAT alumni now form a global network within Nestlé, and individuals know where to go to leverage global practices in their home markets.[22]

Other organizations take a less formal—but no less effective—approach. To overcome the digital divide between generations of employees, several companies have established reverse-mentoring programs. L'Oréal, for example, launched its digital reverse-mentoring program as part of a campaign to raise the digital IQ of its employees and brands. The company paired 120 young, digital-savvy workers with more-senior management committee members. Each partner brought a different set of skills to the partnership. Younger workers shared their knowledge of digital channels and shopper behaviors, while senior managers shared insights from their years of experience in the company and industry. Together, the teams worked to identify key trends and understand the behaviors of new customers.[23] Individually, each partner walked away engaged from the experience with new skills and new insights.

Taking Advantage of the Crowd

Engaging the wider organization to chart the path to a company's digital future is healthy. The value of employees goes beyond their day-to-day jobs. Digitally savvy companies use crowdsourcing techniques to create solutions for their most strategic problems. Crowdsourcing gives employees a voice to actively engage in debates and share their views and ideas. With the rise of a more digitally aware working population, companies that don't learn how to engage with employees in a collaborative way will lose out.

Pernod Ricard, as we've seen earlier, took this step of employee collaboration to co-design and prioritize its entire digital transformation roadmap, to great effect. Other companies have crowdsourced employees to improve aspects of the customer experience, make operations more efficient, or co-create new ways of working. Still others have used crowdsourcing to institute a continuous flow of innovation. The potential applications are endless, as are the benefits when crowdsourcing is done right.

Crowdsourcing your employees can sometimes solve very pragmatic operational issues. French-based telecom provider Orange suffered from a common operational problem for operators: cable theft. The impact on operations was significant and costly, involving line downtime, field-force interventions, and other problems. Through its internal employee crowdsourcing platform, called idClic, Orange identified one employee who had developed a mobile app that enabled a much faster resolution of this problem—fast alarms to the police, clear process steps, and intervention management. The result was one million euros in savings per year for Orange on this idea alone.[24]

Engaging your employees can also be fruitful for collaborative innovation. Companies have traditionally been very specific about who engages in innovation, assigning responsibility according to an employee's skill or role. In a digital world, this sort of segregation is no longer desirable.

EMC, for example, harnesses the collective power of its global employee base to drive innovation in its products and operations.

The $21 billion company is a leader in enterprise storage, security, virtualization, and cloud technology. But staying on top of digital innovation in the fast-moving high-tech industry is a strategic imperative.

The company began running regional innovation contests in 2007, and their popularity quickly outpaced the small innovation team's ability to deal with the thousands of submissions received. The team needed a more scalable process for evaluating ideas. And it needed a way to ensure that good runner-up ideas didn't fall through the cracks.

A year later, the company launched an online platform to help manage the idea submission and review process.[25] Contest participants could post ideas that were visible to the entire global community. Community members around the world could then comment on each idea, provide feedback, and vote for their favorites. Since participation in the community wasn't limited to just those who had submitted ideas, anyone in EMC around the world had the opportunity to contribute.

The contest committee presents a People's Choice award to the idea that gets the highest popular vote each year. Senior EMC experts choose the other awards, but the social input helps the judges see potentially great ideas to consider and helps the innovators improve their idea submissions. In 2010, nearly four thousand EMC employees submitted ideas, commented, or voted in the company's annual innovation contest.[26]

Today EMC organizes the global innovation process on a calendar-year basis. But EMC's innovation process required more than a technology platform. Executive engagement was critical. The corporate chief technology officer (CTO) created a small internal unit to manage the contests, foster sharing across regions, and coach winning innovators in making their ideas a reality. In addition, the heads of major business units can sponsor tracks in the innovation contest. But to do so, they must agree to choose the winner from a list of finalists and provide seed money for winning teams.

Global employee engagement was also critical. EMC announces winners at an internal innovation conference. Each year, on a chosen day, employees in sites around the world gather for a day of activities that include executive speeches, videos, and guest speakers in addition to award announcements. Groups in Ireland, Israel, the United States, and other locations build their own schedules for the day, while attending global sessions remotely. The success of the corporate innovation contest has spawned local contests around the world. For example, people in China conduct their own award programs and share the winning concepts with the rest of the company. This engaging innovation process has now become part of EMC's ways of working.

The benefits are apparent, too. One winning idea was a consumer product that enables individuals to create a virtualized copy of their desktop that they can carry to any other PC. Another fostered a brand-new architecture for cloud-based and "internet-of-everything" product development. But the benefits extend beyond winning ideas. At a recent innovation conference, several sponsors stated, "I am funding the winner, but I'll be happy to champion the other finalists if you need me." And senior executives cite a palpable feeling that the process is creating more innovation, collaboration, and employee engagement across the company's business units. Employees feel part of a more unified global organization.[27]

Some companies even go beyond just crowdsourcing their own employees. They engage external partners and customers in an open innovation process.[28]

Procter & Gamble, for instance, has embraced an open innovation philosophy with strong drive from senior leadership. The aim was to bring a constant flow of outside innovations while internally developing the gating processes to manage ideas from inception to launch. Former CEO Bob McDonald explained: "People will innovate for financial gains or for competitive advantage, but this can be self-limiting. There needs to be an emotional component as well—a source of inspiration that motivates people."[29]

To support this effort, P&G developed its Connect + Develop portal several years ago. The portal's aim was to invite everybody—customers, suppliers, competitors, scientists, entrepreneurs, and others—to submit ideas. P&G not only publicizes what it knows and what it can do, but also highlights what it needs. In addition, the company doesn't restrict itself to product development; it's looking for new ideas in everything, from trademarks, packaging, and marketing models to engineering, business services, and design. Bruce Brown, P&G's CTO, said: "Connect + Develop has helped deliver some of P&G's leading innovations, and is critical in helping us deliver on our renewed growth strategy moving forward."[30]

In 2010, P&G extended its program to become the partner of choice for innovative collaboration and to triple the contribution of Connect + Drive to the company's innovation development. P&G has expanded the program to forge additional connections with government labs, universities, small and medium-sized entrepreneurs, consortia, and venture capital firms.[31]

Accepting the Sometimes-Rough Waters of Engagement

So are we facing a new engagement holy grail, thanks to digital technology? For all its merits, new technology also has its implementation challenges. Familiarity with digital technology varies widely across employees. Even digital-savvy employees don't always adopt new tools naturally. New ways of working can become a threat to the conventional way of doing things, for instance, taking responsibility away from middle management. Often, new digital practices create a more open, collaborative, and transparent work environment. But not everyone will be comfortable, especially those who owe their success in the company to the old way of doing things. One executive said, "We have a very tenured organization and an organization that has a whole lot of experience of doing things the way they have always been done. Trying to motivate people around changing that is a real challenge."[32]

Many companies face some version of these challenges when the conversation around digital transformation, itself, goes digital. We've seen many companies overcome these challenges effectively.

A gap is growing between workers who are familiar with digital tools and those who are not. A *digital divide* is opening up. Millennial employees are avid users of technology in their personal lives and are underwhelmed by the enterprise tools available to them at work. One executive commented, "These people coming into the company, mid-twenties, late twenties, even early thirties, they do everything electronically. They say 'Come on, I know the company is over a hundred years old, but our IT capabilities don't have to match the age of the company!'" Meanwhile, their more tenured counterparts still face a steep learning curve to adopt digital ways of working. This gap is leaving executives with the dilemma of alienating either group in the communication channels they choose. It needs to be actively managed. Business leaders need to work hard to use the best communication tools they have and encourage both groups to break their habits. For example, younger workers can be encouraged to pick up the telephone—or even walk to a colleague's office—when a serious misunderstanding is a distinct possibility. Similarly, older workers can be taught the benefits of participating in company blogs or other social media to get themselves out of a creative rut.

Digital tools can increase transparency in an organization. Generally, this is a good thing, but it can also increase *resistance to change*. Some managers may perceive increased transparency as an affront to their autonomy or a threat to their role in the company. Other managers engage in the conversation proactively. Some will eschew the conversation entirely, and others will openly challenge the use of digital platforms. Because managers are often on the front lines of introducing change into an organization, their level of engagement should be a serious concern for executives.

When a global company we studied implemented a new reporting platform as part of its transformation, many managers balked. Before the new platform, sales managers produced reports that were based on the managers' own internal systems. They controlled the numbers that were reported and the level of detail provided. The new system collected revenue and profitability data centrally and produced reports in a standard format. According to one executive, "That kind of transparency—they're not used to it, so there was an initial pushback."

Executives at the company made it clear that the new platform was reinforcing the idea of operating as a single company and that sales managers retained decision-making authority for their respective units. The leaders also made a conscious effort to frame benefits in terms that mattered to the managers. They showed the sales managers how the new information in the reports could help the managers sell more, minimize inventory holdings, and eliminate the hours spent building spreadsheets each month. Looking back, executives credit the new reporting platform with creating significant cultural change. "It's no longer a blame game," said one executive. "We live and we die together. The only way we're going to survive is if we're transparent and open to communication with each other."

ENGAGING TO MAKE YOUR DIGITAL VISION A REALITY

Digital Masters create a compelling vision of the future. They know where they want to go and what success will look like once they get there. But they also understand that digital transformation requires the concerted effort of the whole organization to turn that vision into reality. New processes, new business models, and new ways of working will affect people throughout the organization. Many leaders in these companies walk the talk. They embrace new digital channels not just to set a good example, but because these tools make these executives more effective leaders of change. Employees also use technology to stay more connected to each other. They make active contributions to the conversation around digital transformation and collaborate with their peers to solve its challenges.

Whatever leadership role you play in digital transformation, engaging your employees should be high on your agenda. Experiment with new ways of communicating, collaborating, and connecting with your colleagues, and engage them in a two-way conversation. Lead by example to champion new digital ways of working, and recruit other true believers to join you. Engage the critical mass of employees that is needed to move your organization to a new level. And focus on the conversations that are critical to solve business problems, not the tools themselves.

Some will remain skeptical about new technology and its role in the organization. But engaging the organization is not optional if you want to succeed with your digital transformation—it is necessary. Conversely, when used effectively, digital technology can help you engage employees at scale.

LEADING DIGITAL CHECKLIST: ENGAGING THE ORGANIZATION AT SCALE

✓ Lead the engagement effort to energize your employees to make the digital vision a reality.

✓ Use digital technology to engage employees at scale.

✓ Connect the organization to give a voice to your employees.

✓ Open up the conversations to give everyone a role in digital transformation.

✓ Crowdsource your employees to co-create solutions, and accelerate buy-in.

✓ Deal with the digital divide by raising the digital IQ of the company.

✓ Deal with resistance by being transparent and open about the goals.

CHAPTER 7

GOVERNING THE TRANSFORMATION

My fault, my failure, is not in the passions I have,
but in my lack of control of them.

—JACK KEROUAC

Even with a strong, engaging vision, it is extremely difficult to channel your organization's efforts in a single direction. Large, complex companies are full of entropy, constantly moving in the direction of less order rather than more. Once engaged in a compelling vision, managers throughout the company may move in their own directions to make the vision a reality. Other managers, not having bought into the vision, may try to ignore it. Some units may move too slowly, while others may introduce risk by moving before they have truly thought through regulatory, security, and organizational risks. Other units may waste resources on duplicative, uncoordinated, or incompatible efforts.

That's where digital governance comes in. Digital governance helps to steer the company's digital activities in the right direction. It turns the diverse energy of employees throughout the organization into a coherent engine that drives digital transformation forward.

DIGITAL GOVERNANCE AT P&G

Procter & Gamble (P&G) is a global consumer goods leader. Head-quartered in Cincinnati, Ohio, it has operations in about seventy countries and more than 120,000 employees. In 2013, the company had sales of more than $84 billion. P&G's ex-CEO Bob McDonald recognized the transformative potential of digital technologies for traditional industries. He set a clear goal: "We want Procter & Gamble to be the most digitally-enabled company in the world."[1] Achieving such a goal required a focus on digital throughout the company, which McDonald described in this way: "[We want] to digitize the work of the company from the creation of molecules all the way to running our factories off of the point of sale data of our retail partners."[2] P&G subsequently embarked on a multiyear digital transformation program to make that happen.

McDonald's vision was enough to set the transformation in motion, but more was needed to make the transformation successful. P&G needed very strong digital governance to turn the vision into reality across the company's many brands and regions. With the right governance mechanisms in place, P&G could allocate digital funding wisely, promote sharing across business units, provide centralized tools and skills to help business units innovate, and start to build a digital culture across P&G.

Foundations of Digital Governance

Fortunately, in building digital governance, P&G did not need to start from scratch. Although the idea of centralized governance can run counter to the culture of large diversified companies, P&G already had useful elements in place. In particular, Global Business Solutions (GBS), the company's shared services unit, is one of the four pillars of P&G's corporate structure. Originally an evolution of the company's IT unit, GBS today provides more than 170 shared services and solutions from six hubs to over three hundred P&G brands globally. In its thirteen years of operation, it has reduced the cost of shared services by 33 percent and halved the time to market for new products.[3] The unit is led by Filippo Passerini, group president of GBS, who also serves as P&G's CIO.

Establishing Digital Leadership

Passerini's dual role gives him a unique perspective on technology and its impact on business: "For us, technology is never the starting point. Technology is the enabling tool. The real driver for business transformation is a change in work processes, business processes or culture—in the way employees work and operate, rather than the technology per se. We prefer to be technology agnostic."[4] He proved himself as a leader of GBS not only by improving the unit's performance and increasing its scope of responsibilities, but also by elevating its strategic role in the organization. According to Passerini, "The mantra in our organization is that we wake up every morning with the idea that, today, we are working to become distinctive—and not become a commodity. If we become a commodity, then it would be all about cost."[5] To do this, he explained, "We think you need to start with the end in mind of what is the business value, and then work backwards into all the steps that unequivocally lead to that business value creation."[6]

When McDonald announced his new digital vision, Passerini was a natural choice as its leader. According to McDonald, "IT is the key enabling function in delivering our digitization strategy."[7] As head of IT and GBS, Passerini could mobilize the capabilities and relationships of GBS to meet the digital challenge. He became the company's de facto chief digital officer (CDO). As McDonald explained, "He is a group president of a business, not just a functional leader, a key member of our P&G leadership, and the one I hold accountable for the delivery of this all-important [digitization] strategy."[8]

Building a Digital Services Unit

GBS is responsible for leading the effort to digitize the company, providing governance, technology, processes, and tools to make P&G's

digital vision a reality. The aim is to help the company become simpler, flatter, faster, and more agile.[9]

Going digital for Passerini meant building an environment based on real-time operations. Digital governance was organized around three key principles: *standardize* systems, process, and information; *automate* to eliminate non-value-added interactions; and *accelerate* decision making via real-time information.[10] P&G started the journey by identifying the core processes that the company was running on—some one hundred processes. In conjunction with business units, the digital team's role is to identify transformational improvements and find combinations of process and technology to make them happen.[11]

In P&G's digital governance model, the centralized team provides end-to-end services to support the business needs of the operating units and brands. GBS focused its digital services on four main areas: consumer engagement, value chain innovation, business intelligence, and organization development.[12] "We manage it like we would the launch of a new brand, a new product," Passerini says. He tapped into the famous brand culture of P&G to structure the roles of the people in the central unit—naming individual roles as "service managers." The title came with clear responsibilities: set internal prices, monitor quality, and develop innovations. To create digital champions, Passerini also embedded IT people in various business units and made them accountable for delivering business results, from saving money to speeding products to market.[13]

Governing Technology Innovation

P&G has built a multilayered approach to stay abreast of the fast-changing digital technology market. New digital technologies can fuel innovation and improve company performance, but only if applied in the right places and with the right amount of investment. Every few years P&G looks at megatrends across the world. These megatrends are then distilled to identify those that impact P&G's business.

For those trends that will have an impact, the organization defines clear strategies to address them. Only then does the organization choose technologies to enable those strategies.[14] Such an approach closely ties with Passerini's management culture. According to Passerini, "I see myself as a business person who happens to have an interest in—and an understanding of—technology."[15]

For instance, consider how the company addressed a trend toward accelerating innovation cycles in several sectors. With virtual reality technology, P&G was not only able to prototype products but also to show how they would look on a store shelf, increasing the quality of consumer feedback. Retailers also offered early support for this type of digital modeling. The digital team provided not only virtual reality technology, but also any end-to-end services required to deliver an experiment. It even built a library containing images of products from both P&G and its competitors. Passerini says, "That is creating a lot of business value because we get much better quality feedback, and can go to market faster."[16]

Building a Digital Governance Culture

In addition to building the leadership and organizational structures for digital governance, GBS leaders realized they also needed to evolve the work culture across P&G. Transparency of data was a key aspect of competing in the digital age. P&G's high-tech physical environment, dubbed "business sphere," allows leaders to harness massive amounts of data to make real-time business decisions. The environment constantly displays data on how P&G is doing around the world. However, as Passerini admits, the data is not perfect. He says, "We intentionally put the cart before the horse, because it is a way to force change."[17] A key aspect of competing in the digital age is the ability of leaders to be comfortable with a certain level of ambiguity when it comes to digital initiatives.

That approach has been one of the hallmarks of how P&G governs its digital initiatives. For instance, Passerini took a risk when he introduced digital cockpits—a range of easy-to-read charts that contain the information that is most relevant to each P&G employee. The idea was that there would be one shared version of the facts, so people would stop debating what's happening and focus on solving problems. The initial versions failed and had to be re-architected over an eighteen-month period. However, by January 2012, P&G had 58,000 such cockpits operational with more than 80,000 planned by the end of 2013.[18] Such risk-taking was encouraged as an active means of driving change. Passerini explains, "We take a lot of risk. When there's a new idea, rather than talk about it philosophically, we do a pilot for free with one of the business operating units."[19]

Today, P&G is known as a leader in using digital technology to transform its businesses. McDonald backed his vision of making P&G the most digitally enabled company in the world by providing funding to make it happen. But with energy and funding around the vision, the company needed discipline and capabilities to make it a reality. In establishing digital governance, Passerini and the GBS team adapted successful practices where possible and built new capabilities where needed. Through its governance processes and its resources, GBS is now an integral part of digitally transforming P&G, from product development to manufacturing to marketing.

WHY DIGITAL GOVERNANCE IS NEEDED

The word *governance* derives from the Greek verb *kybernan*, which means "to steer."[20] Most companies have strong governance over finance and human resources. But companies vary in the extent to which they govern other aspects of their business, such as brand governance to ensure consistent and appropriate brand usage, IT governance to apply technology resources effectively, and vendor governance to ensure that purchasing is efficient and compliant with regulation.

New demands for digital capabilities, and new risks from digital activities, have made digital governance essential in all companies.

For example, social media reduces a firm's control over its global brand. A negative customer post on Facebook, Twitter, or YouTube can receive global attention immediately. Even as companies find new ways to work with customers through mobile and social channels, the companies are also paying close attention to their online reputations. But beyond social media, digital technology makes a firm's customer-focused activities more apparent to all, wherever they happen. That's why Burberry CEO Angela Ahrendts appointed a brand czar to synergize the use of the iconic company's brand around the world.[21]

New technologies can also have unwanted confidentiality and regulatory consequences. Lost phones and tablets can enable hackers to invade a network. Employees may post company secrets online or release information on mergers or company financials in inappropriate ways. Personal information about credit cards or patient health can find its way online. Customers may see employees' personal posts as corporate advice on investments or health. Any of these breaches can leave firms liable to reputational damage and millions of dollars in penalties or regulatory sanctions. As one executive told us, "The last thing we want to do is put the reputation that we've built for a hundred and fifty years on the line because of a security incident."

Digital Masters Govern Better

Our research shows that Digital Masters govern digital activities better than other companies do. Our 2012 survey measured governance capability as a composite of questions related to clear roles, strategic alignment of initiatives, cross-unit investment coordination, use of KPIs, and presence of a high-level transformation roadmap. According to this measure, Digital Masters govern 51 percent better than nonmasters.[22] The masters are far better at making decisions about what initiatives to pursue and at steering those initiatives to success.

Our qualitative and quantitative analysis shows that digital governance is one of the most important levers that senior executives can apply in driving digital transformation. Governance acts as a set of guiderails to keep everybody moving in the right direction. It provides both carrots and sticks to foster innovation and prevent inappropriate investment. It helps to manage the risks of transformation and to drive transformation forward efficiently.

Digital Governance as Opportunity

Digital Masters understand that governance not only prevents problems but also enables new digital capabilities. Mobile apps, collaboration networks, connected products, and social media create new opportunities, from marketing to manufacturing to customer service. Business cycles are getting faster and faster because of demands from both customers and employees.[23] Governance can help to implement new solutions faster than ever before, while also managing the challenges of security, regulatory compliance, and legacy system integration. It helps companies gain a more integrated view of customers and operations, collaborate more effectively, and make policy work better.

For example, as customers demand a more integrated experience and analytics demands more-integrated data, many companies struggle to unify their disparate data sources. "Data integration is the biggest challenge in setting up our digital services," explained an executive, echoing statements by many others. Digital Masters use governance to shape a unified platform for their digital initiatives, from new customer experiences to automated factories to advanced analytics.

In addition, as companies become more global, they are finding the need to *collaborate more effectively* across geographic locations, business units, and specialties. When employees find their own ways to collaborate outside the company's official sanctioned approaches, potential security, regulatory, and integration challenges can result. Many companies have used governance to establish official collaboration platforms for video conferencing, instant messaging, and knowledge sharing. Companies also use governance to *create and enforce policy,* stating which types of collaboration are (and are not) appropriate, and creating monitoring tools to detect policy violations.

Making Digital Governance Work

When designing governance for your digital activities, focus on how you will achieve two key goals:

- *Coordination:* Prioritizing, synchronizing, and aligning initiatives across the enterprise

- *Sharing:* Using common capabilities and resources (including people, technology, and data) across the enterprise

In many big companies, coordination and sharing tend to be unnatural acts. To a manager in a business unit or region, coordination means endless meetings and unwanted restrictions. Building on shared resources can make you dependent on the goodwill and delivery capability of people you do not control. It's no wonder that organizational antibodies rise up to defeat new corporate-level governance activities whenever possible.

Yet, the biggest benefits of digital transformation come exactly from engaging in unnatural cross-silo acts of coordination and sharing. According to a senior executive in an international banking group, "Digital impacts firms globally, across traditional silos. It requires more coordination when [we are] making decisions and conducting actions, compared to the way we do business usually. Questions are not local but global, and so the choices we make engage the company as a whole, in all countries and business units."

This is why executives at Nike created a strong digital unit to work across the firm's major business units. It's why Nestlé built its digital acceleration team. And it's why you need some mechanisms to ensure the same benefits. Governance makes up for issues that arise from the way your company is structured. It encourages employees to follow certain practices that they wouldn't do if left to their own devices.

KEY MECHANISMS FOR
DIGITAL GOVERNANCE

In building your digital governance, think about how you will use three major governance mechanisms: committees, leadership roles, and shared digital units. Each mechanism has strengths and weaknesses in terms of delivering sharing and coordination. And each may be more or less appropriate to your company's culture. One of your jobs as an executive is to choose mechanisms that give the right levels of coordination and sharing for specific resources, while managing any cultural conflicts that the new mechanisms create.

Governance Committees

If your company has been paying attention to the rapid pace of technology change, you have probably already established executive-level committees to govern some digital activities. Committees are a relatively easy way to get started on coordination. Unfortunately, they rarely provide enough governance—especially in companies where not all units are on board with the digital vision.

Steering committees are most common. These groups, consisting of some of the most senior executives in the company, make decisions such as ratifying policies, prioritizing competing interests, and killing low-value projects. Through their power to set policy and allocate resources, steering committees can help the enterprise to act in a unified way. Volvo, for example, has a strong committee to steer the launch of its connected-cars concept. The committee helps to align activities across engineering and manufacturing units and to set policy to address dealers' concerns that the corporation is starting to talk directly with customers.[24]

Steering committees can also make the case for investments that business units might not undertake on their own. An example is a manufacturing company's investment in a global customer platform: "This investment was primarily based on what I would call an 'art business case,' rather than the 'science business case,' and this was the right thing to do," explained a senior executive. "We did it big enough to be successful, but small enough to not be stupid."

Some companies also create *innovation committees* to govern emerging technology. The committees don't do the work of innovation; they play a policy and oversight role. Innovation committees identify challenges that can be resolved through innovation, fund experiments and pilots, and consider how to adopt useful innovations.

Northwestern Mutual established an innovation committee to stay ahead of and respond to constantly changing demands from the firm's independent financial representatives. As representatives started to use tablets and social media, the committee investigated how to use this technology in a way that was efficient, secure, and aligned with regulatory requirements. The goal of the committee is not to prevent unwanted action, but rather to help the company innovate safely with new technologies and processes. According to an executive, "We cannot be slow to think about these technologies because our field force adopts them quickly. We have regulatory concerns that we have to deal with, and we have training and education challenges. We need people with different perspectives talking together about these emerging technologies."[25]

The innovation committee helps to choose technology standards and set policy before investing in capabilities that will be shared across the company. An executive explained: "We are bringing together all the people who can say, 'Wow, we could do this. It's not a problem.' That's our IT architects. And then we've got everybody else saying, 'Well, if we do this, how do we protect confidentiality? How do we retain data? How do we train? What's it going to take to make this usable before we officially condone its use in the field?' So, it brings all of the right levels of perspective to the table."[26]

Digital Leadership Roles

Committees can make decisions, but they cannot drive change. Leaders do that. New leadership roles include chief digital officers (CDOs), who lead digital transformation at the enterprise or business level, and less senior liaison roles.

Chief Digital Officers

In March 2012, Starbucks appointed Adam Brotman as its first CDO, reporting directly to the CEO. According to Brotman, digital "has been an essential part of how we build our brand and connect with our customers . . . [T]here's been such a seismic shift [in our interactions with customers] that we needed to pull it all together and make it a priority."[27]

The CDO's job is to turn a digital cacophony into a symphony. He or she creates a unifying digital vision, energizes the company around digital possibilities, coordinates digital activities, helps to rethink products and processes for the digital age, and sometimes provides critical tools or resources. Such a leader may do this alone or with help from committees or digital units.

Some CDOs have responsibility only to establish a vision and coordinate digital activities. These tasks are relatively workable in most companies, since they offer little threat to autonomous managers. We often see more-junior people in this type of CDO role. They make suggestions and create energy, but often must rely on others to drive real change.

However, many CDOs are also charged with creating synergies and driving transformation. These tasks can be much more difficult in companies that have a history of decentralization and autonomy. When this type of CDO role is created, organizational antibodies rise up to attack it. Local unit chiefs may reject what they see as unnecessary interference from a role they consider illegitimate. That's why a strong CDO role requires a respected leader. And it requires strong communication from the top of the firm that the CDO role—and its authority—is real.

At Starbucks, Brotman has responsibility for web and mobile communications, including social media; Starbucks cards and loyalty programs; in-store Wi-Fi and the Starbucks Digital Network; and the company's in-store digital and entertainment teams. He earned respect from his prior positions in the company, and he has the CEO as his chief supporter.

At Volvo, the firm hired a seasoned senior executive to take responsibility for its connected-cars concept. With the support of a strong senior executive steering committee, he drives coordination and sharing across silos such as product design, manufacturing, marketing, and after-sales service.

You may or may not want to appoint a new C-level executive to manage digital transformation. But the responsibilities of the CDO will be required. You may appoint a temporary CDO to get your house in order, or you may develop other ways to get the job done. Whatever approach you choose, you need to create appropriate levels of digital technology synergy, brand integration, investment coordination, skill development, vendor management, and innovation over the long term.

Digital Liaisons

Official liaison roles, such as the digital champions we mentioned in the previous chapter, can steer digital transformation at a local level. Members of Nestlé's digital acceleration team play an informal governance role by being part of the conversation in their units and sharing practices across units.[28] But large companies often require a stronger liaison role—one that acts as a mini-CDO for each business unit.

When the CEO of PRISA decided to establish digital governance, he hired a group-level CDO. This CDO built the company's shared digital unit, led the development and rollout of a global content management system, and set direction for most digitally related questions. In PRISA's highly decentralized corporate culture, the group CDO had limited authority to drive change in each of the company's media properties around the world. Instead, the CEO mandated that each property appoint its own CDO. These local CDOs, who were typically very senior managers from the unit, had the mandate to lead digital transformation in their divisions while coordinating with the group CDO and each other.[29]

Shared Digital Units

Committees can decide, and leaders can drive change. But implementing change sometimes requires a centralized set of expertise and resources. Digital units, like those developed by P&G, Nike, and PRISA, are a very effective way to govern and drive digital transformation. Digital units vary in size and role, but all have a common goal to drive synergy across the firm. Some digital units help business units conduct digital initiatives, while others conduct all digital initiatives for the business units. All have resources such as skills, infrastructure, and financing that can be shared across the firm.

Digital units can do what committees and leaders can't do on their own. They can create shared infrastructure such as unified customer databases, an enterprise wireless platform, advanced analytics teams, and innovation labs. A senior executive in a global insurance group explained: "It would not make sense for the different entities of the group to develop all the digital stuff themselves. It costs time and money and requires coordination. And by doing it themselves, they would not benefit from the experience gained across the company."

Building some digital infrastructure and skills centrally creates an incentive for local units to go along with the new standard. The decision moves from "How much would it cost us to do this on our own?" to "How can we get the most out of the central platform?" "How can we leverage these capabilities as much as possible?" At PRISA, for example, the digital unit was essential in creating a global content-management system. The leaders of each media outlet did not have incentives to invest in the system, but the enterprise-level effort created a system that all outlets can use. Through the new system, journalists in each media outlet can store, track, and share media such as text, audio interviews, and video clips with other PRISA outlets around the world.

Some digital units provide specialized digital expertise to the rest of the company. When we interviewed 150 executives about digital transformation, the most important barrier they identified was missing skills. Among the companies we studied, 77 percent cited skill challenges in areas such as mobility, analytics, and social media.[30] The companies are actively recruiting experts in these areas, with varying degrees of success. Hosting these skills in the digital unit allows the company to recruit the right experts and use them across the firm. Many units also build skills through training and knowledge sharing, as we discuss in chapter 12.

Digital units can exercise power and influence beyond what more-lightweight committees and leadership roles can do. But don't go into them lightly. Digital units require significant investment in resources and management attention. For example, Nike's digital unit plays a role in digital activities across the firm. It cooperates in marketing and other initiatives and provides key skills. It contains a set of innovation groups to clarify the future vision, identify new technological opportunities, and build new capabilities. It also serves as the home for digital products. Doing all of this in a company as fast-moving and entrepreneurial as Nike required a strong mandate from the top, hiring seasoned leaders to run different functions, and many millions of dollars per year. But its impact has made the investment worthwhile.

FINDING THE BEST GOVERNANCE MECHANISMS FOR YOUR ORGANIZATION

To design governance for your organization, start with the behaviors you want to encourage. What do you need to coordinate? What sharing do you want to encourage? Consider how well your organization will do these on its own, or how you might foster any "unnatural acts" you need.

Highly decentralized organizations may need strong central governance to ensure sharing and coordination, but may be able to use less stringent governance to oversee local innovation. Highly bureaucratic or centralized organizations may find coordination and sharing to be more natural, but may need some extra help to innovate or to transform their processes.

Each governance mechanism has its strengths and weaknesses (table 7.1). Additionally, some mechanisms may fit naturally with your organization's culture, while others will require strong top-down effort to implement.

Shared digital units can create strong synergies around infrastructure, tools, standards, and capabilities. When digital units work, they accelerate innovation and drive efficiency. They can pool together funding, digital tools, and people with specific skills to develop digital services for all units in the company. Some coordination also comes naturally as the units develop technology standards and implement

TABLE 7.1

Digital governance mechanisms have their strengths and weaknesses

	Role in coordination and sharing	Typical benefits and challenges
Shared digital units	*Sharing* is the main objective, by pooling specialized resources and providing infrastructure. Standards and policies created by the unit provide some *coordination* and *sharing*. However, stronger *coordination* of digital initiatives requires additional mechanisms.	*Benefits:* new digital skills, shared digital services, economies of scale. *Challenges:* structure and positioning in the organization, coordination difficulties with local unit leaders, definition of the service catalog.
Governance committees	*Coordination* is the primary goal. However, some decisions and policies may mandate *sharing* of specific resources and capabilities.	*Benefits:* digital standards and policies, resource optimization, adoption of new digital trends. *Challenges:* additional mechanisms often required to lead transformation or to enforce standards and policies.
Digital leadership roles	These roles drive *sharing* by encouraging the use of key digital resources. They also assist *coordination* across different initiatives and organizational units.	*Benefits:* shared digital vision, culture change, stronger policy compliance. *Challenges:* responsibility and authority, relationship between corporate and local units, coordination between levels.

Source: Adapted from Maël Tannou and George Westerman, "Governance: A Central Component of Successful Digital Transformation," Capgemini Consulting and MIT Center for Digital Business, August 2012.

policies governing use of their services. However, challenges exist in defining the right structure and positioning in the organization. Even if positioned correctly, the unit can adopt an inward focus, losing touch with the needs of different business units. In addition, there can be funding and coordination difficulties, especially if executives in some part of the organization see the unit as a threat to their autonomy.

Governance committees aim for coordination: making investment decisions, prioritizing resources, and establishing policies and standards. The goal is to synchronize activities across the firm without adding a lot of bureaucracy. When they work, these committees can keep everyone moving in the same direction. However, they tend to be limited to decision making, not doing. Lacking a staff, they have a limited ability to manage activities closely, or to create new things. Additional mechanisms are often required to lead transformation or to enforce standards and policies.

Digital leadership roles can drive sharing by helping local units know when (and how) to adopt firm-level solutions or use centralized resources. These roles also coordinate across different initiatives and organizational units. When they work, the roles can ensure that the digital vision is shared across the enterprise. They can foster culture change, improve policy enforcement, and ease the transition to new ways of working. However, these roles have challenges too. If senior executives do not take the roles seriously, they may staff them with people who do not have the seniority or influence to be successful. Another challenge is inherent in the role itself. Liaisons need to balance the interests of both the enterprise and the business unit. This can be very difficult to do consistently and without bias, especially if you physically sit in one area or the other.

TAKE STEPS NOW TO BUILD DIGITAL GOVERNANCE

Digital governance should not be left to chance. Ineffective governance creates waste and missed opportunities, making digital transformation riskier and costlier than it needs to be. Governance requires conscious design and engagement by the company's most senior executives. The right governance model provides appropriate levels of coordination and sharing for digital initiatives, in line with the company's structure, culture, and strategic priorities. No single governance model is optimal for all companies, but lack of governance is never optimal.

Your digital governance model will use combinations of the three mechanisms for different activities and at different levels of the organization. Executives at Nike chose to build governance around a new digital unit, along with a steering committee and new roles. Asian Paints used a steering committee, but considered the IT unit its digital unit, with the CIO playing the role of CDO. Nestlé built a digital acceleration team and digital champion roles, but not a steering committee. Northwestern Mutual built committees but not a digital unit or new roles.

Whatever you choose, remember one thing: governance models should not be static. You will need to adjust your governance arrangements as your digital capabilities grow and your competitive situation changes. You can understand when it is time to revisit your governance models by paying attention to the behaviors governance is intended to enhance and by adjusting governance to encourage new behaviors. You may find you need to create more centralized control over your digital activities or may need to build additional capabilities in your digital unit. Or, as coordination and sharing become part of the culture, you may devolve much of your governance to business units.

LEADING DIGITAL CHECKLIST: DIGITAL GOVERNANCE

- ✓ Look internally (e.g., IT, finance, HR, and capital budgeting) for effective governance practices.

- ✓ Consider which digital decisions must be governed at the highest levels of the company, and which can be delegated to lower levels.

✓ Place somebody in charge of leading digital transformation, whether that is a chief digital officer or another leader.

✓ Identify governance mechanisms, such as committees and liaisons, to assist in governance.

✓ Examine whether you need a shared digital unit, including the resources it would have and the roles it would play.

✓ Adjust your governance models as your company's governance needs change.

CHAPTER 8

BUILDING TECHNOLOGY LEADERSHIP CAPABILITIES

We are stronger when we listen,
and smarter when we share.

—RANIA AL-ABDULLAH

If, before you had read this book, we asked you to think about what makes leadership work, you would probably have thought of vision, governance, and engagement (among other things). These three tools are essential to guide any kind of major transformation.[1] But another essential element of digital leadership capabilities is not necessarily something you might think of as leadership. It's the strong relationship that Digital Masters encourage between their IT and business leaders, and the way these companies use that relationship to drive change in their internal platforms and digital skills. These are what we call technology leadership capabilities, and they are essential for driving transformation that is based on digital technology.

TECHNOLOGY LEADERSHIP AT
LLOYDS BANKING GROUP

Lloyds Banking Group (LBG), based in London, is one of the world's largest banks, with more than $1 trillion in assets. In 2006, LBG executives began to understand that their existing online retail platform, while working well, could not scale to the new demands that the company was going to place on it in the future. Soon after, a merger with Halifax Bank of Scotland made the situation more pressing, as it would add millions more customers to the strained system.

The executive team asked a senior business executive, Ashley Machin, and a senior IT executive, Zak Mian, to rethink the company's approach to digital retail banking. The pair knew each other only in passing, but soon developed a strong working relationship. Starting small, they put together a plan to replace the old platform with a new, more scalable one—a true foundational investment for the company's future digital strategy. This first step was the start of a partnership that began to transform nearly all of the bank's digital customer engagements, and then more.

Machin described how the transformation began:

> The senior-most leadership of the bank did something pretty courageous, which you cannot traditionally do. We looked at what we wanted to achieve, and we looked at the infrastructure we currently had. And our recommendation was, "Do you know what? We're going to spend the first couple of years just building and completing new infrastructure." And the only customer benefits at the end of that new infrastructure will be a fundamentally redesigned user interface and hence user experience. And we will have a state-of-the-art platform, which will enable us to respond far more quickly to customers.
>
> We did the pitch, and the bank supported a program that said, "Let's build a foundation that will last us for decades to come."

That's a huge up-front investment with no real return in a traditional sense. The only return was that it puts you in a position to be able to roll out customer processes and offers in a way the competition can't.[2]

In addition to rethinking the platform, the two leaders also rethought the way IT and business worked together. Understanding that their team needed to work faster than traditional IT development processes could, they created a new unit that merged both IT and business talents. Instead of business providing the requirements and IT delivering the technology, people from both sides of the house worked together to innovate the company's processes. The team took responsibility not only for delivering technology, but also for ensuring the business changes that would be necessary to deliver the expected benefits. Machin and Mian hired staff from inside and outside the company, built a team with system development consultants in India and the UK, and went to work.

Once the basic platform was in place, the team started to take on new challenges such as credit card processing. Mian explained: "We had extended the platform for retail and also commercial, and then it was absolutely time to reenergize the transformation agenda rather than the re-platforming agenda." Demand took off, and leaders of many units—from credit cards to mortgages to commercial products—asked for help in digitally transforming their businesses.

Looking back, Machin said, "One of the regular questions I get is, 'How have you managed to get such an integrated and symbiotic relationship between IT and business?' And quite simply, I think the answer is, you need to have a shared passion for the outcomes you want, and to have a highly trusting relationship that you are both determined to do the right thing for the customers and [to] be slightly agnostic, for want of a better word, about how you get there."

The strong IT–business partnership and the ability to deliver great digital customer experiences, ROI, and flexible technology has paid off for the team and the company. In 2013, CEO António Horta-Osório recognized that the group had a further opportunity to strengthen and accelerate the company's plans and to develop digital propositions across all customer-facing divisions in the group. In September 2013, Horta-Osório made "head of digital" a group executive-committee-level appointment, reporting directly to him, creating a new digital division under Miguel-Ángel Rodríguez-Sola, the director for digital, marketing, and customer development. This digital unit, now more than a thousand people strong, moved into a new dedicated location. Commenting on future plans, Mian added, "What gives me confidence is that although we know we need to continue to adapt and learn, the shared agenda and integration of business and IT teams is now in our DNA."

THREE ELEMENTS OF TECHNOLOGY LEADERSHIP CAPABILITY

As the Lloyds story shows, technology leadership is not just about IT leaders, although they are part it. It's not just about technical skills, although they're essential. It's about merging the skills and perspectives of business and IT leaders so that they drive transformation together.

When the IT–business relationship is strong, IT people can suggest new opportunities, and businesspeople listen. Businesspeople have an instinct for the problems that poor technical decisions can create, so they make better decisions, with no need for the CIO to lecture them on standards and procedures. IT and business groups are able to move faster together than they could separately, so they can conduct experiments, launch new capabilities, and transform outdated platforms better than other companies can.

In talking about technology leadership, therefore, we won't just focus on the leaders' relationship. We'll also look at what they do with that relationship—building digital skills and transforming the technology platform that underpins all digital processes, from customer engagement to operations to business models.

THE IMPORTANCE OF STRONG
IT-BUSINESS RELATIONSHIPS

Many executives told us that, given their IT units' poor performance, they were going to find a different way to conduct their digital transformations. The business executives were going to move forward despite their IT units, not with them. We did not find this to be true with Digital Masters, which have much stronger IT–business relationships than nonmasters do. In our research, the precise measure we used was a well-known concept from the IT research literature: *shared understanding*.[3] The concept is a composite of four survey items that assess the extent to which IT and business executives share a view of the role of IT in the organization, including its potential in improving productivity and serving as a competitive weapon, as well as a common view of prioritization. Digital Masters averaged a statistically significant (32 percent) higher level of shared understanding than nonmasters did.[4]

Shared understanding is the starting point for larger changes in the IT–business relationship and the nature of IT itself. In Digital Masters, IT and business executives have deep trust and respect for each other. They are also very clear on their roles as they work together to make digital transformation happen. This translates to what they can do. Digital Masters reported feeling 21 percent higher control over their destiny than nonmasters, a difference that is also statistically significant.[5] By working together, these leaders can do what they need, and they can get more done. Their companies' digital skills are higher, and the state of their digital platform is better than in nonmaster firms.

When the relationship is strong, the IT–business partnership merges customer and product knowledge, technical knowledge, organizational change capabilities, and IT capabilities into a single, continuous collaboration. Unfortunately, in many companies, the relationship seems to be more like a troubled marriage than a smoothly functioning partnership.[6] Conversations are full of conflict, and little collaboration takes place. The poor relationship serves as a handicap that can slow action and increase the risk of change.

The Causes of Poor IT–Business Relationships

Poor relationships between IT and business leaders can have many causes. Sometimes it's the personality of the IT leader. A common complaint among senior executives is that their CIO seems to speak a different language from the business. Another is that the CIO doesn't seem to understand what's really important. For example, a chemical company CIO we interviewed described how he communicates regularly with business executives about the innovative possibilities of digital technologies. Yet none of his business executive peers (whom we interviewed separately) seemed to find the discussions credible.

Sometimes the issue arises from IT's delivery capability. According to Bud Mathaisel, who has served as CIO in several large companies, "It starts with competence in delivering services reliably, economically, and at very high quality. It is the absolute essential to be even invited into meaningful dialog about how you then build on that competence to do something very interesting with it."[7] Unfortunately, some IT units today do not have this competence. One business executive we interviewed said, "IT is a mess. Its costs are not acceptable. It proposes things in nine or ten months, where external firms could do them in three to nine weeks. We started offshoring our IT, and now our IT guys are trying to change." A legacy of poor communication, byzantine decision processes, and broken commitments is no foundation on which to build a strong IT–business relationship.

However, the fault doesn't always rest only with IT leaders. In many cases, business executives share some of the blame. As we'll show later in this chapter, high-performing IT requires a good digital platform, and good platforms require discipline. If your approach to working with IT can be characterized by impatience, unreasonable expectations, or insisting on doing things your way, then you'll need to think about how to change your side of the relationship.

Regardless of the cause, if your IT–business relationships are poor, it's essential to fix the problem. A bank executive stated, "IT has been brought closer to business during the last five years. It is very important to success because many of the important transformations in our business are enabled by technology." With strong relationships, IT executives can help business executives meet their goals, and business executives listen when IT people suggest innovations. Executives on both sides are willing to be flexible in creating new governance mechanisms or shared digital units. At Codelco, Asian Paints, and P&G, the CIO even leads digital transformation for the company.

Improving the IT–Business Relationship

So, how can you start to improve your IT–business relationship? Angela Ahrendts, CEO of Burberry, told her CIO he needed to help drive the bus with the executive team.[8] However, leadership changes or top down mandates are only the start of the change. Few CIOs can change the business by themselves, and not all business executives will climb on the bus with the CIO, even if the CEO demands it.

Fixing the IT–business relationship can take time, as people learn how to trust each other and redefine the way they work together. As with any struggling relationship, the best starting point is to fix the way you communicate. Does IT really cost too much, or are costs reasonable, given what IT has to do? Is the IT unit really too bureaucratic, or do all of those procedures actually serve a useful purpose? Are you a good partner to IT or a difficult one? How can IT make it easier for you to get what you need, while still making sure things are done correctly? What investments can help IT improve its technology, internal processes, cost-effectiveness, quality, or speed?[9]

MIT research into IT turnarounds has identified a series of steps that can change IT from a poorly respected cost center to a high-functioning business partner.[10] The key change mechanism is transparency—around performance, roles, and value. The first step is to help IT employees think, and talk, differently about what they do. The second step proceeds to showing very clearly how well (or how poorly) IT delivers value for money—the right services at the right quality and right price, and where problems still exist. And then the third step moves to changing the way IT and business leaders make investment decisions and assess the returns that projects deliver. Through transparency around roles, performance, and investments, both sides can make smoother decisions and work together to identify and deliver innovations.

Creating Dual-Speed IT

Changing the IT–business relationship is well worth the effort, but doing so takes time. Your company may not have the time to wait before starting your digital transformation. Rather than improving the IT unit, some companies try to build digital skills into another unit, such as marketing. They try to work around IT rather than with it.

Although building digital skills is useful, trying to work around IT can be fraught with challenges, especially if people do not understand the reasons for IT's systematic, if sometimes ponderous, processes. This kind of flanking action can waste money, make the digital platform more complex, and, even worse, open the company to security and regulatory risks.

A better approach is to create a dual-speed IT structure, where one part of the IT unit continues to support traditional IT needs, while another takes on the challenge of operating at digital speed with the business. Digital activities—especially in customer engagement—move faster than many traditional IT ones. They look at design processes differently. Where IT projects have traditionally depended on clear designs and well-structured project plans, digital activities often engage in test-and-learn strategies, trying features in real-life experiments and quickly adding or dropping them based on what they find.

In a dual-speed approach, the digital unit can develop processes and methods at clock-speeds more closely aligned with the digital world, without losing sight of the reasons that the old IT processes existed. IT leaders can draw on informal relationships within the IT department to get access to legacy systems or make other changes happen. Business leaders can use their networks to get input and resources. Business and

IT leaders can even start to work together in the kind of two-in-a-box leadership method that LBG and other companies have adopted.

Building dual-speed IT units requires choosing the right leaders on both sides of the relationship. Business executives need to be comfortable with technology and with being challenged by their IT counterparts. IT leaders need to have a mind-set that extends beyond technology to encompass the processes and drivers of business performance. Leaders from both sides need to be strong communicators who can slide easily between conversations with either business- or IT-focused people.

Dual-speed IT also requires perspective about the value of speed. Not all digital efforts need the kind of fast-moving, constantly changing processes that digital customer-engagement processes can need In fact, the underlying technology elements that powered LBG's new platform, Asian Paints' operational excellence, and Nike's digital supply chain enhancements required the careful, systematic thinking that underpins traditional IT practices. Doing these big implementations in a loose learning-by-doing method could be dangerous. It could increase rework, waste money, and introduce security risks. But once the strong digital platform is there, building new digital capabilities can be fast, agile, and innovative. The key is to understand what you need in each type of project and how much room any project has to be flexible and agile. Great IT leaders know how to do this. If teamed with the right business leaders, they can make progress quickly and safely.

Dual-speed IT also takes new processes inside IT. Few digital businesses have the luxury to wait for monthly software release cycles for all of their applications. Digital-image hosting business Flickr, for example, aims for up to ten deployments per day, while some businesses require even more.[11] This continuous-deployment approach requires very tight discipline and collaboration between development, test, and operations people. A bug in software, missed step in testing, or configuration problem in deployment can bring down a web site or affect thousands of customers.

A relatively new software-development method called DevOps aims to make this kind of disciplined speed possible. It breaks down silos between development, operations, and quality assurance groups, allowing them to collaborate more closely and be more agile. When done properly, DevOps improves the speed and reliability of application development and deployment by standardizing development environments. It uses strong methods and standards, including synchronizing the tools used by each group.[12]

DevOps relies heavily on automated tools to do tasks in testing, configuration control, and deployment—tasks that are both slow and error-prone when done manually. Companies that use DevOps need to foster a culture where different IT groups can work together and where workers accept the rules and methods that make the process effective.[13] The discipline, tools, and strong processes of DevOps can help IT release software more rapidly and with fewer errors, as well as monitor performance and resolve process issues more effectively, than before.[14]

Whether your CIO takes it upon himself or herself to improve the IT–business relationship, or you decide to help make it happen, forging a strong link between business and IT executives is an essential part of driving digital transformation. Strong IT–business relationships can transform the way IT works and the way the business works with it. Through trust and shared understanding, your technology and business experts can collaborate closely, like at LBG, to innovate your business at digital speeds. Without this kind of relationship, your company may become mired in endless requirements discussions, failing projects, and lackluster systems, while your competitors accelerate past you in the digital fast lane.

BUILDING DIGITAL SKILLS

Creating great customer experiences or market-leading operational capabilities is more than a technology challenge. It's also an organizational change challenge requiring new skills and new ways of working.

Yet, 77 percent of companies in our first year of research cited missing digital skills as a major hurdle to their digital transformation success.[15] To compound the problem, most companies are chasing after similar skills—social media analysts, mobile marketers, cloud architects, or data scientists, to name a few.

How Digital Masters Are Building Skills

So what are Digital Masters doing differently when it comes to skills? First, they are investing. Of the Digital Masters we surveyed, 82 percent are building the digital skills they need to support their digital transformation efforts. Only 40 percent of nonmasters are doing so.

Second, Digital Masters are accelerating and creating a gap. Our survey research shows that the masters had greater digital skills than nonmasters, reporting 31 percent higher social media skills, 38 percent higher mobile skills, and 19 percent higher analytics skills.[16]

But Digital Masters did not start with higher skills. Burberry did not become excellent at digital marketing and channels overnight. CEO Ahrendts hired a new, dynamic marketing team whose members mirrored the behaviors of the millennial customer.[17] Nor did Caesars excel at delivering personalized customer experience solely because its CEO, Gary Loveman, has a PhD in economics from MIT. Caesars' executives actively incorporated quantitative skills into the marketing area. In these companies, like other Digital Masters, top executives worked hard to build the digital skills they needed.

The skills difference extends beyond technology. Digital Masters report 36 percent higher skills in digital leadership than nonmasters.[18] Digital transformation requires changes to processes and thinking—changes that span your internal organizational silos. The clear delineation between technical skills and leadership skills is blurring fast.

The impact of digital technologies is now felt not only in the IT and technical departments, but also across the entire organization. Digital transformation's need for cross-functional collaboration creates a huge demand for hybrid digital skills—technical people who need to be more business savvy and businesspeople who need to be more technology savvy. A retail executive explained: "We are trying for the first time to work across the company. That implies going through a new level of complexity in the organization, and requires people to manage and network differently. That, I think, is the most important skill that needs to be developed."

The need for new skills can also result from the need to bridge the communication gap between digital and business competences. One executive said, "I need a charismatic quant—somebody who's an influencer and can carry his weight in a senior meeting, but at the same time, someone who can roll up his sleeves and look at data tables and build models and enjoy it."

These bridging roles may soon become the responsibility of every manager. "I believe," said Markus Nordlin, CIO of Zurich Insurance, "that the successful leaders of tomorrow, in any business or industry, are going to be true hybrid professionals who have spent some time in IT but have shifted to operations and vice-versa."[19]

A Two-Pronged Arms Race for Digital Skills

Aspiring Digital Masters are all chasing the same technical skills. The shortage of digital skills in the current marketplace is unprecedented. In Europe alone, forecasts point to nearly a million vacancies for IT-related roles by 2015.[20] And globally, out of the 4.4 million big-data jobs to be created by 2015, only a third will be filled.[21]

But by the same token, business professionals will increasingly need to be comfortable with digital tools and technologies to perform their core roles. By 2015, research firm IDC expects that 90 percent of all jobs will require IT skills.[22] Some business functions are already adding technology skills to their mix. Gartner reports that 70 percent of the companies they surveyed have a chief marketing technologist to support the digitization of the function.[23]

This skills race won't slow down anytime soon. Having the right digital skills is an important source of competitive advantage and a key enabler of digital transformation. Companies that build skills faster will get ahead.

To win at the digital skills race, you will need to tap into multiple approaches—hiring, partnering, incubating, and the like. It's not easy, as one executive explained: "Our recruiters don't know where to go to find these people, and people with the right skills don't look to our kind of company for opportunities." HR organizations will need to get up to speed quickly. A recent Capgemini Consulting survey found that only 30 percent of HR functions were actively involved in digital skills development.[24] This needs to change. Many Digital Masters have a carefully crafted plan to fight and win the talent race. In chapter 12, we'll show you how to do this.

THE DIGITAL PLATFORM AS A LEADERSHIP CHALLENGE

Our research confirms a wide body of research in the IT management field: the most fundamental technology foundation for digital transformation is a strong digital platform—well structured, well integrated, and only as complex as absolutely necessary.[25] We've seen this in case after case. Burberry fixed its IT backbone before it could transform customer engagement. Asian Paints created a unified platform before transforming operations. LBG reengineered its digital platform before expanding its digital services. The growth and innovativeness of Seven-Eleven Japan rides largely on the real-time visibility that its unified operational platform provides. Well-structured digital platforms are the foundation for new digital business models such as Nike+, Airbnb, and Hailo.

If this is true, then why do so many large companies have poorly designed technology platforms? Large companies often operate in silos, each with its own systems, data definitions, and business processes. The systems are confusing, sometimes duplicative, and often tied together in complex (and sometimes unknown) ways. Generating a common view of customers or products can be very difficult.

Every request for a nonstandard technology, every demand to do things your own way, every choice to go around corporate governance processes so you can move faster, and every integration meeting that your staff people miss will create more complexity. Sometimes that complexity is necessary, but often it is not. According to the head of the disability business for a major insurer, "We have, through the last fifty years, proliferated our IT systems and applications. We don't retire systems. We just add on top of them, which creates a tremendous amount of expense and complexity."[26]

Technologists have a term for this type of systems arrangement: *legacy spaghetti*. Companies mired in legacy spaghetti find it difficult to make sense of their information and even more difficult to make change happen.[27] Research shows that unnecessary complexity in the platform is the number one driver of IT risk in firms; it makes processes harder to change, harder to test, more prone to fail, and tougher to restore after it fails.[28] Spaghetti happens only because leaders let it happen. And removing spaghetti requires strong leadership.

The Power of a Strong Digital Platform

A well-designed digital platform is one reason that web-based companies are able to perform analytics and personalization much more readily than traditional firms.[29] Amazon.com, knowing everything you have purchased over many years, can make good recommendations for what you might buy next. Facebook and Google, knowing what you have written and read in the past, can target advertising to you much more effectively than can less informed firms.

But this capability is not limited to born-digital companies. The personalization and mobile capabilities at Caesars are built on its unified Total Rewards database, which records all interactions the company has with each customer. At Codelco, the unified digital view of its mines allows the firm to synchronize operations smoothly while identifying ways to innovate its processes.

To understand platform quality for the firms in our survey, we asked respondents the extent to which they had an integrated view of different aspects of their firms. Digital Masters average 17 percent higher than nonmasters for integrated views of operational performance and supply-chain status.[30] Beyond operations, the difference was even higher. Digital Masters average 25 percent higher than nonmasters for integrated views of customer data and 26 percent higher for integrated views of product or service performance.

If you don't have a common view of customers, it's extremely difficult to accomplish advanced customer-engagement techniques such as personalized service or location-based marketing. The challenge grows as you engage in multichannel operations. As a marketing executive said, "It's very difficult to get a good understanding of the customer when customer data is spread across so many systems."

For many traditional companies, the first step in preparing for digital transformation is to invest—sometimes heavily—in integrating data and processes across the enterprise. In this respect, firms that have already implemented ERP and CRM systems are a step ahead of others. Burberry's transformation required much more than digitally enabling stores or starting to do social media marketing. The company needed to invest millions into an ERP system that could help the company become digital end-to-end. Through unified systems and processes, Burberry could improve operations, understand sales patterns, and start to provide seamless service across channels.

Well-structured platforms can also to help manage the centralization-versus-decentralization challenge in globalization. At Caesars, for example, each hotel's website around the world is served by a single global platform. Each property's manager can customize the site's content and marketing campaigns locally, while headquarters supports the technology for all sites. Global media company PRISA's content management system means that a soccer video clip recorded in Barcelona can easily be used by a TV station in Madrid, a newspaper in France, and a radio station in Argentina on the same day.

The Scaling Power of Digital Platforms

Well-structured digital platforms have benefits beyond efficiency and agility. As we discussed in chapter 3, platforms can help leaders to drive unwanted variation out of key operations. But good platforms can also help a company scale volume faster than it needs to scale its labor. And they can help to roll out innovations quickly across a large and geographically distributed company.

US pharmacy retailer CVS is an example of how a well-structured platform can scale not only volume but also new practices. Customer service levels are a critical measurement in the retail pharmacy business. So when CVS experienced a decline in customer satisfaction in 2002, the drop got senior management's attention. Further analysis uncovered a key issue: 17 percent of prescription orders experienced delays from problems with the customers' insurance. Staff typically checked insurance after the customer had already left the store, meaning that problems could not be resolved until the customer returned to pick up a prescription. Moving the insurance check earlier in the process could resolve the problem.

CVS embedded the process change into its enterprise pharmacy fulfillment system, thereby ensuring 100 percent compliance. It was simply no longer possible to accept a prescription without doing the insurance check. Through its platform, CVS was able to replicate the new process throughout its 4,000-plus retail pharmacies within a year. Performance of the prescription processes improved sharply, driving customer satisfaction with it. During that year, overall customer satisfaction scores rose from 86 to 91 percent—a dramatic difference within the highly competitive retail pharmacy industry.[31]

Great Digital Platforms Won't Happen Without Leadership

Great platforms provide clear information to decision makers. They serve as the bases for advanced analytics capabilities and new digital services.

They are both efficient and agile. And they constantly provide new digital transformation options.

But great platforms don't just happen. In complex companies, platforms tend to grow in many directions at once, creating copies, customizations, and offshoots like so many weeds in a garden. Like good gardens, good platforms take constant attention to pull weeds, kill pests, and shape them into beautiful designs. You cannot get a single view of customers, or an integrated view of operations, without strong, top-down leadership.

IT leaders can help shape the platform. They can translate the digital vision into a vision of the technology platforms that will make it a reality. They can establish management tools such as architecture reviews to kill weeds and to move the platform in the right direction. They can adjust technology funding methods to support the right kind of growth. Intel's IT unit, for example, increases the priority of projects that align with the firm's architectural direction.[32] Business unit requests that that build on the company's standards are more likely to be funded than those that don't.

But IT leaders can have limited ability to force change in business practices. The typical CIO has little power, on his or her own, to change the actions of a strong business unit chief. That's where the company's senior-most executives need to play a role. Pages Jaunes CEO Jean-Pierre Remy did this when he stopped funding updates to the systems that supported paper-based books. P&G's digital czar, Filippo Passerini, uses a more positive approach. He promises business unit chiefs that his global services unit can reduce the cost of their purchasing, HR, and other processes by 10 to 30 percent—but only if they use his standard processes.[33]

Platform issues are not limited to big incumbent companies. Even Amazon.com—a company that was born digital—encountered platform issues. In the 2002 time frame, during a period of rapid growth and innovation, the firm's powerful platform began to suffer from a proliferation of spaghetti and nonstandard designs. It took top-down leadership from CEO Jeff Bezos to fix the problem. Bezos issued a strong mandate that all new development would follow a set of very clear design rules. The letter ended with this admonition: "Anyone who doesn't do this will be fired." Bezos then empowered a senior executive to make sure that the mandate was being followed.[34] Over the next several years, the company's culture of standardization evolved, and so did its platform. Now, more than ten years later, Amazon.com's well-structured digital platform continues to power the firm's ever-growing volume of online sales. It has also made possible new business models, such as Kindle books and streaming video. Amazon.com has also begun to sell cloud-based infrastructure services to other companies, transforming Amazon.com's internal platform into a product of its own.

The same can happen with your platform. Health insurance companies are already using their health claims platforms to create analytics-based products about trends in prescribing and medicine. A logistics company in China is able to sell forecasts of regional demand using the trends it has discovered in its historical sales platform.[35] And as Boeing makes its "airline of the future" a reality, it will have a rich platform, crossing the boundaries of many companies, which it can mine for new information-based services and products (see chapter 5). But all of these developments require leadership—to develop the right platform and skills, to keep them properly aligned, and to capitalize on the opportunities that they create.

TECHNOLOGY LEADERSHIP AND YOUR COMPANY, EVOLVING TOGETHER

Regardless of how you build your platform, our research highlights an important point. The real value of digital transformation comes not from the initial investment, but from continuously reenvisioning how you can extend your capabilities to increase revenue, cut costs, or gain other benefits. Initial investments become the foundation upon which you can make additional strategic investments. When Asian Paints first centralized its order-taking processes and implemented an ERP system, executives did not envision the many successful business model changes they would be able to make in the future. They just knew that the unified data and standardized processes would help the company reach a new level of performance.[36] Then, with unified data and a strong call center, they were able to envision new things. Mobile-equipped salespeople, armed with up-to-date sales and order information, could focus on growing the relationship with each retailer. Call center personnel could do outbound calling to serve retailers or let them know when a shipping truck would be in their neighborhood. By delivering to customer work sites instead of retail stores—a capability none of its competitors had—the company got closer to its end customers. Then, executives started exporting their processes to countries outside India.

The firm's digital foundation provided Asian Paints executives with options they'd never had before. But the leaders needed to be ready to seize the opportunity. The company started with business-savvy IT leadership paired with a business leadership team that understood the power of IT to change the business. The leaders worked closely together to make each change to the platform and then let platform changes create new opportunities. And they invested heavily in developing skills—from digitally enabling salespeople to growing internal analytics talent—that would help the company take each new step in the transformation journey.

The same pattern occurred at LBG, Codelco, Burberry, Caesars, and other companies. When your technology leadership capabilities are weak, everything is a risky struggle. When they are strong, you can do great things. And when you constantly pay attention to the link between IT–business relationships, skills, and your digital platform, you can constantly extend them to create valuable new digital transformation opportunities.

LEADING DIGITAL CHECKLIST: TECHNOLOGY LEADERSHIP CAPABILITIES

✓ Assess the state of your IT–business relationships: consider trust, shared understanding, and seamless partnership.

✓ Assess your IT unit's ability to meet the skill and speed requirements of the digital economy.

✓ Consider dual-speed IT approaches such as a unit within a unit or a separate digital unit that combines IT, business, and other roles.

✓ Focus your initial investments on getting a clean, well-structured digital platform; it's the foundation for everything else.

✓ Start building the right digital skills.

✓ Challenge yourself continually to find new things you can do with your IT–business relationships, digital skills, and digital platform.

WHAT'S NEXT

So far, we've shown you what it means to be a Digital Master and why you should care. We've walked you through the process of building each dimension of digital mastery: digital capabilities in chapters 2 through 4 and leadership capabilities in chapters 5 through 8.

Now it's time to put these ideas to work for your company. In chapters 9 through 12, we'll provide a playbook to help you get started on your own digital transformation journey.

PART III

BACK AT THE OFFICE:

A Leader's Playbook for Digital Transformation

You don't need the vision and leadership qualities of a Steve Jobs or Jeff Bezos to conduct your own digital transformation. As a successful executive, you already possess the basic skills to make your company an insurgent in your own market. As we showed in parts I and II, it takes some new thinking to set the course and committed leadership to drive the transformation. In part III, we have distilled the practices from Digital Masters to present a transformation compass to help you steer the course of this complex journey (figure III.1):

- *Framing the digital challenge:* Build awareness of digital opportunities and threats. Know your starting point, and assess your digital maturity. Craft a vision, and ensure that your top team is aligned around it.

- *Focusing investment:* Translate your vision into an actionable roadmap. Build cross-silo governance structures. Put in place the funding for your transformation.

- *Mobilizing the organization:* Send unambiguous signals about your ambitions and the change needed now. Build momentum

FIGURE III.1

The digital transformation compass

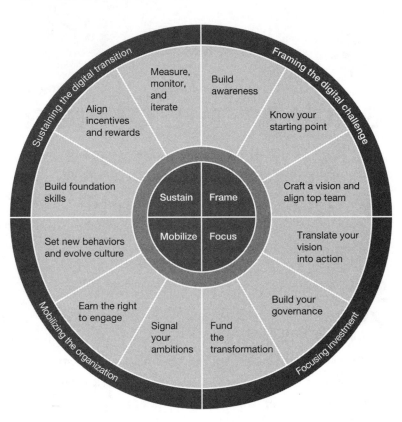

and engage the workforce. Set new behaviors and start evolving the organization toward a more innovative culture.

- *Sustaining the transition:* Build the necessary foundational skills. Align reward structures to overcome traditional organizational barriers. Monitor and measure the progress of the transformation, and iterate when necessary.

Digital transformation is anything but a linear process. You may have already started a number of digital initiatives. You may need to build skills in different areas and redirect your efforts from time to time. Use the digital transformation compass to guide you. The next chapters will steer you through the steps that Digital Masters have taken to maximize the success of their digital transformations.

CHAPTER 9

FRAMING THE DIGITAL CHALLENGE

As we showed in chapter 1, digital transformation has already hit every industry we've studied. Yet nearly 40 percent of the respondents we surveyed cite "lack of urgency" as a major obstacle to digital transformation.[1] Why is this? One of the key reasons organizations miss out is management inertia—failure to sense the need to change. They react to threats instead of shaping the future.

In industries such as publishing, digital technologies have already created such an upheaval that the context for transformation is clear; it's a burning platform. In other industries, such as manufacturing, the case for change is less obvious. One manager explained the reason for the skepticism: "There is too much hype. I can't push harder because of all the hype and the overselling from suppliers. I lose my credibility if I push too hard. So we take a slower approach just to make sure we don't give the naysayers their way."[2]

Combating inertia requires an awareness of the challenge, knowing where you're starting and deciding where you want to go. You know your industry. As a senior leader, you need to create the appropriate momentum around digital transformation. Do this by addressing three areas early in the process:

- *Building awareness:* Do top leaders in your organization understand the potential threats and opportunities from digital technologies and the need for transformation?

- *Defining your starting point:* How mature are your digital competencies, and which current strategic assets will help you to excel? Have you digitally challenged your current business model?

- *Creating a shared vision:* Have you aligned your top leadership team around a vision of the company's digital future?

FIGURE 9.1

The digital transformation compass: framing the digital challenge

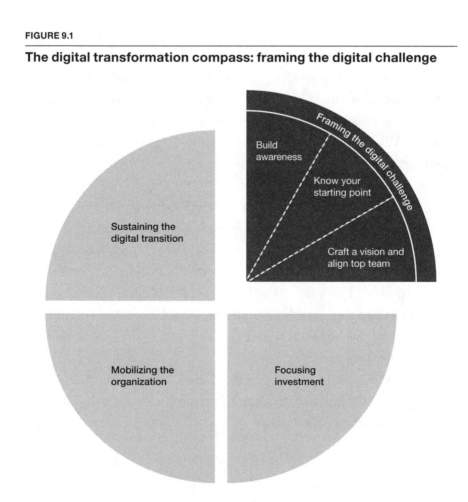

ARE YOU AWARE OF THE
DIGITAL CHALLENGE?

The first step in framing the challenge is to ensure that your top team understands the potential business impact of digital technologies. Only 37 percent of our survey respondents see digital transformation as a permanent fixture on their current executive agenda. By contrast, 61 percent of the same respondents believe that digital transformation will become critical to their business within the next two years.[3]

Put Digital Transformation at the Top of Your Agenda Now

Engage senior leaders in the debate about the implications of digital technologies for your current and future business. Ask, "How can those technologies potentially disrupt our competitive position?" and equally, "How can they help improve performance and delight our customers?"

As the most senior leader in the organization, the CEO is responsible for ensuring that this framing phase is successful. More often than not, motivational speeches and internal evangelization are not enough. You need to ensure that other leaders in your organization visualize the profound change at hand and understand the business possibilities that technology can already enable today. For good lessons, look to practical examples of companies and industries that have been helped or hurt by digital change.

Understand the Scale and Pace of the Digital Impact

The combination of the scale and pace of the digital impact, along with your own capabilities, will dictate your risk profile as a firm. Finding the right tempo for digital transformation in your organization is a managerial art form. Key aspects of your organization's culture will also play a role. Is decision making centralized or decentralized? What is the propensity of the organization to collaborate and share? You need to design digital transformation programs that protect profitable existing operations and assets, while making the transition to a new digital business or digitally enhancing part of it.

But be careful. As Andy Grove noted, "Only the paranoid survive."[4] Disruptive digital innovations often come from outside your industry. Events can sometimes dictate the pace of the change required. Competitive and industry analyses have become less useful than before. As we described in chapter 4, the London taxi market was not disrupted because incumbent companies failed to go online or develop mobile apps for hailing taxis. It was disrupted when Hailo saw the opportunity to bridge the inefficiencies of this two-sided market, winning the drivers first, then providing a great customer experience. Hailo's win-win business model allowed the company to sign more than 60 percent of London's twenty-three thousand licensed taxis in less than two years.[5]

Make the Awareness Process Experiential

Building awareness among the top team is a leadership challenge. Employees can be unforgiving. One of our respondents complained, "Management is composed of old people from fifty-five years and above. They know nothing about technology and its benefits and they don't want to learn."[6]

Conduct this awareness phase using sound, fact-based research, but also ensure that you make it a highly experiential exercise for your team. For example, presenting both a digital hall of fame and a digital hall of shame creates a balanced view of the risks and opportunities. We've also seen companies conduct a "digital hackathon," pairing senior executives with tech-savvy employees to understand and shape the potential impacts. Other formats and tools can help as well: analysis of disruptive innovation, war gaming, scenario planning, digital discovery expeditions, and external peer leaders' testimonies. All can help you to generate the right level of awareness in your executive team.

Consider the case of the CEO of a global manufacturing company. Although he had become convinced that digital technologies and online channels were going to have a profound effect on his company's operations and competitive position, the members of his management board were less enthusiastic. After a period of slow progress, he invited his board members to California for a weeklong program of intense digital immersion. He enlisted the advice of former CEOs who had failed to grasp the digital opportunity, highlighting the personal significance of what was at stake. He also showcased leading digital technology providers, industry visionaries, and companies that had transformed their businesses successfully, underlining the opportunities that digital technologies made possible. The week was an eye-opener for senior leaders. It elevated digital transformation to the top of the executive team's agenda.

Build a Coalition of Believers

Do you need everyone on board? Probably not. But we've seen many Digital Masters build an early coalition of senior leaders who play key roles in driving digital transformation inside the organization. Joe Gross of Allianz Group explained: "With digital meaning different things to different departments, it became critical to establish a common ground—a uniform understanding of what digital transformation meant."[7] Creating awareness helps to unite the core team around a common purpose and sets digital transformation off on the right foot.

The point is not to turn your senior team into technologists. The goal is to ensure that, collectively, they understand the potential threats and opportunities from digital technologies and the need for transformation.

DO YOU UNDERSTAND YOUR STARTING POINT?

Building a powerful coalition among your top leaders is essential, but it's not enough. Large companies survive major transitions not by radically replacing the old with the new, but by leveraging their existing resources and competencies in the new digital environment. You need to know your starting point. How digitally mature is your organization today? And what current strategic assets will be relevant in a digital world?

Assess Your Digital Mastery

To assess your digital mastery you need to take an unbiased view of your current digital initiatives and skills. Consider in detail both your *digital capabilities* and your *leadership capabilities*. They will point to one of the four levels of digital mastery we discussed earlier: Beginner, Conservative, Fashionista, or Digital Master. In chapter 1, we suggested that you assess your company's digital mastery by using the short maturity assessment tool included in the appendix. But, now that you have seen what Digital Masters do differently, it is time to take this assessment again. Using the Digital Masters described throughout the book as a benchmark, spend some time revisiting your company's position on the matrix. Consider not just what they do with the technology, but how they lead the change. Highlight strengths and weaknesses in your digital capabilities and your leadership capabilities. You now have an informed view of your company's transformation starting point.

Chart Your Transformation Journey

Now you can start charting the path and pace of your transformation. Every company is different. Your company might have the ambition of a Burberry—to move directly from Beginner to Digital Master. Doing so will mean simultaneously developing the leadership and digital capabilities to make your strategy a success. Or you might want a more Conservative approach—favoring prudence over innovation. This approach will involve building a foundation of strong leadership capabilities before experimenting too far with new digital technology. Or you might be like the Fashionistas—having already launched a multitude of uncoordinated digital initiatives. Your focus then becomes developing a coherent vision and a robust governance model and then streamlining or harmonizing digital initiatives across business units. If you are in a large global organization, digital mastery may also vary by divisions, lines of business, functions, or geographical locations. Understanding these differences is important as you craft a trajectory that will work for your organization.

Assess Your Strategic Assets

Next, we have seen how several Digital Masters conducted an early assessment of their strategic assets to define those that will be relevant in a digital world, and those that won't. As we showed in chapter 5, Pages Jaunes executives realized early that selling yellow books via its strong direct-sales force would not be a competitive advantage in the future. The company's paper-distribution model had no future. However, the company's direct-sales force and its strong relationships with local businesses were still key strategic assets. Retraining salespeople to sell digital services was a challenge, but gave the company the foothold it needed to move into the digital world.

It takes thoughtful analysis to identify which assets will help make digital transformation successful. You should view strategic assets through the lens of a digitally transformed world and identify those that have value. We showed in chapter 4 that rethinking assets, for instance, in the context of the sharing economy, can yield innovative business-model thinking. Several definitions exist about what constitutes strategic assets.[8] Beyond financial assets, which can be extremely useful to defend against new entrants, we have observed that four broad categories of assets can serve as the foundation for digital transformation: physical assets, competencies, intangible assets, and data.

Physical Assets. The most obvious assets, physical assets are retail stores, distribution networks, warehouses and depots, products, and so on. Some physical assets may be redundant in a digital world, but combining physical and digital assets in novel ways can often be a keen source of advantage. For example, 62 percent of banking customers in the United States today prefer to bank online.[9] Does this mean that all retail banks will eventually close their branches? It's unlikely. About 47 percent of US banking customers believe that a bank is not even legitimate unless it has physical branches.[10] But the industry's consensus is that a traditional homogeneous, full-service branch network, catering to customers across all segments, is no longer viable. Some branches will offer standardized banking needs, while others will be highly digitized, acting as physical extensions of online and mobile banking. Digital technologies are changing the role of physical branches, but they will not render branches extinct in the near future.

Competencies. This type of asset can also be essential to create a digital advantage. Competencies can reside within your functional skills (e.g., IT, sales) or core competencies—your unique know-how around products, processes, or technologies. For instance, your frontline employees and salespeople can be crucial assets in maintaining customer loyalty. They have amassed important knowledge about customer behaviors and preferences. Similarly, institutional competencies can be reinforced and augmented though the use of digital technologies. Nike has world-class product design and engineering talents. Digital technology helps the two groups work more closely together, speeding the product development process and enabling a radically transformed Flyknit manufacturing process.

Intangible Assets. By their very nature, intangible assets are often the most difficult to gauge. Examples of these assets include brand equity, company culture, patents, proprietary technologies, and an ecosystem of partners. Starbucks, for example, was able to leverage its brand as an asset and extend it online.

Data. This asset class has taken new prominence in the digital world and warrants significant executive attention. Data has become one of the most valuable digital assets for companies that have learned how to master analytics. But often, data is a hidden asset. Many companies still cannot extract value from the data they possess or cannot create new insights through the combination of their data with other sources. However, if you can use your data, you will create a new currency with huge value. Barclays Bank, for example, has started to monetize information on its thirteen million customers, selling aggregated spending habits and trends data to other companies.[11]

Start by looking at your strategic assets in a different light. Can they offer a competitive advantage in a digital world? Can you reconfigure or combine them to create something new and valuable? Do you have, or can you assemble, data-driven insights that no one else has? Use a broad ideation process to think outside the boundaries of what your firm and its competitors do today. But don't start with broadly defined brainstorming sessions. Start with known unmet customer needs or sources of complexity in your operations. Ask yourself, How can we use or combine assets differently to address these? And how can we use technology to deliver economically?

Digital Masters examine their strategic assets to align their initial investments with their core skills. Burberry started with its unique customer experience, Asian Paints with its culture of process excellence, and Caesars Entertainment with its strengths in analytics and customer data. It does not matter where you start. What matters is that you start in an area where you can leverage strategic assets early to establish your digital advantage.

Challenge Your Business Model

We showed in chapter 4 that business model innovation can be a huge source of value in digital transformation. But it can also be a threat to your business. As you gauge the scale and pace of the digital impact on your business and you reconsider your strategic assets, it is a good time also to challenge your business model.

Of course, you need first a good grasp of your current business model. Start thinking about how you could deliver greater value to customers. Then, figure out how this extra value can be operationally delivered at a profit. You can, at this point, exploit the possibilities offered by digital technology to look at creative and efficient options to get there. Also learn from how other industries have solved similar problems or taken advantage of similar opportunities.

Multiple avenues will be possible. You will need to prioritize options that generate the greatest value to customers, that are operationally hard to copy, and that can provide you with a profitable economic model. You will also have to de-risk the change by running controlled experiments on your new model. Then, gather data to learn and revise your assumptions.

How is it done? Several practical approaches can help you challenge your existing business model, explore new ones, or defend against a potentially disruptive one. We've seen companies conduct gaming sessions such as DYOB (Destroy Your Own Business) or WWAD (What Would Amazon Do?). Some practical frameworks also exist to help structure the thinking, such as the business-model canvas developed by Alexander Osterwalder and Yves Pigneur.[12] It is good practice to spend time going through this business model rethinking with your top team, even if your current business model is not under threat.

IS YOUR TOP TEAM ALIGNED AROUND A SHARED DIGITAL VISION?

You understand the business challenge posed by digitization. You know where you're starting and the range of possibilities before you. You and your team now need to decide where you want to go.

Craft Your Transformative Vision

Chapter 5 described how Digital Masters craft their visions. You need to do the same. Your vision needs to be focused on enhancing the customer experience, streamlining your operations, or combining both to transform your business model. Don't fall into the trap of the marketing slogan with no grounding in the reality of your situation. Authenticity matters. Your vision needs to recognize where you are starting from, taking stock of your existing competences and culture. It needs to be built around strategic assets—or a combination of strategic assets—that will be relevant in a digital future. And it needs to be transformative, not incremental.

As you craft a digital vision, focus on your business or your customers, not the technology. Design your vision with a clear intent—a picture of what needs to change—and clear business outcomes, that is, the resulting benefits for your customers, employees, and the company's performance. Remember, crafting a vision is a journey. So make it specific enough to give direction to the organization, but give yourself room to make the vision live and grow over time. Several processes and facilitated approaches exist to support the design of a good digital vision.[13]

Align Your Top Team

Having a great digital vision will get you part of the way, but not all the way—the vision needs to be shared. Many digital initiatives fail to capture potential value because the vision guiding them is not shared at the top. As Curt Garner, CIO of Starbucks, noted, "Our entire leadership team is very engaged and animated around digital and tech and what it can mean for the company. It is part of the shared goals we have as a leadership team to continue to lead in terms of innovation and customer-facing technology."[14] A shared digital vision is a prerequisite for successful digital transformation and a key component of Digital Masters' DNA.

But, of the executives we've surveyed, only 57 percent said their teams were aligned around a vision of a digital future.[15] Why is that? Senior leaders often confuse consensus with an aligned executive team. Avoid the trap of assuming that information means understanding and that lack of debate signals alignment. Digital transformation only works when your top team is actively engaged and owns the digital vision. You'll need to be a role model in this respect; test your vision by making it part of every speech and communication you deliver. Ask for feedback, crowdsource ideas, and iterate. Encourage other members of your top team to do the same, and compare notes.

Aligning executive teams is neither new nor specific to digital transformation. However, one thing is different with digital. Digital transformation will respect none of your traditional organizational boundaries. Digital transformation usually requires the collective talent and effort of cross-disciplinary teams to innovate and drive change. Joe Gross of Allianz Group explained: "The reason we involved marketing, sales and local entities, and not just IT or operations, in our digital transformation is because we needed everyone's active participation to drive change of this scale."[16]

Many management techniques can be useful to align your top team. Facilitated team-building exercises, individual and collective coaching, and 360-degree feedback are just a few examples. Incentives can also be useful. We've seen several companies give each senior leader a digital KPI relevant to the transformation goals. Whatever the technique, good dialogue matters in alignment. Carving out part of your regular management board meetings for a robust discussion on digital transformation is a good practice, as is conducting regular facilitated off-site sessions to steer the progress of your transformation.

How do you know when your team is truly aligned? A good litmus test is when all members of your senior team sense the urgency of transformation (awareness of the challenge), understand their strategic assets and level of digital mastery (starting point), and can articulate what the digital future looks like (shared vision) through words and specific goals. When all three conditions are met, it is time for execution.

So what's new with digital transformation? Technology adds another dimension to the traditional business challenges. You need to make sure your top team can articulate the new threats and opportunities created by digital technology. Rethinking your traditional assets through a digital lens creates new possibilities. Some assets will still be useful; some won't. New ones, such as data and insights, will be sources of new value in a digital world. Whereas a functional approach sometimes works in a traditional transformation, digital transformation respects no organizational boundaries. You need to have aligned executives who, as a team, have the authority to drive the change across silos.

HOW WELL HAS YOUR ORGANIZATION FRAMED THE DIGITAL CHALLENGE?

Table 9.1 (page 188) summarizes how to frame the digital challenge in three key steps. Look at the central questions at each step, and give an honest assessment of your company's progress on a scale from 1 to 7 (1 = strongly disagree; 4 = neutral; 7 = strongly agree). For each of the three steps, total your scores across the individual questions.

For each step, we have provided you with a target score that places you among the Digital Masters. We've also provided a threshold below which you should start taking action now to improve your situation. If your score is in the Digital Master range, you are ready to move on. If your score is in the middle range, reflect on why. Your team still needs to work out a few things in the framing phase. If your score is in the lower range, it is time for remedial actions. If it is well below, we recommend you conduct a full framing exercise with your top team.

TABLE 9.1

How well has your organization framed the digital challenge?

Answer each question, using a scale from 1 to 7, where 1 = strongly disagree; 4 = neutral; and 7 = strongly agree, and find the recommended action for your score.

Are you aware of the digital challenge?	Score
Our senior leaders are aligned around the strategic importance of digital transformation.	
Our senior leaders agree on the pace of digital transformation in our industry.	
Digital transformation is a permanent fixture on our executives' strategic agenda.	
Total score	

Scoring: **Over 15:** you understand the digital transformation challenge; **9–15:** isolate which part is not complete, and work with your team to remedy; **less than 9:** need to consider specific team awareness exercises and/or digital discovery programs.

Do you understand your starting point?	Score
We understand which strategic assets will be most important in digital transformation.	
We understand how our own digital capabilities compare with those of our competitors.	
We have a clear view of the most important first steps in our transformation.	
Total score	

Scoring: **Over 16:** you know where you are and what your transformation trajectory is; **7–16:** build alignment around a viable transformation path; **less than 7:** conduct a digital maturity assessment and a scan of best practices.

Is your top team aligned around a shared digital vision?	Score
Our senior leaders are aligned on a vision for the digital future of our company.	
Senior executives have a digital transformation vision that crosses internal organizational units.	
Our senior leaders have a digital transformation vision that involves radical changes compared with the way we have traditionally done business.	
Total score	

Scoring: **Over 16:** you believe your team is aligned; **7–16:** isolate the root causes of your concerns, and work with your team to remedy; **less than 7:** start a structured senior executive alignment initiative.

CHAPTER 10

FOCUSING INVESTMENT

Becoming a Fashionista is easy. Everywhere you look, there are opportunities to invest time, effort, and dollars into making your business more digital. It is all too easy to invest in them all. The siren song of digital technologies is a powerful one and can lead many companies astray. But Digital Masters know their own direction and they stay the course. They focus on the initiatives that will advance their vision and on which the Digital Masters can build existing skills and assets. These initiatives contribute new digital platforms and infrastructure and are the initiatives that Digital Masters can afford to invest in and see a return. Digital Masters have a keen focus on the things that are important and the discipline to disregard those that are not.

Focusing investment is where the rubber meets the road in digital transformation. You will need to commit real money to fund initiatives, you will have to engage real people in making things happen, and you will also need to keep everyone moving in the same direction. Our research shows that many companies struggle to turn vision into reality. In non-masters, 78 percent of respondents said that their senior executives agreed on the importance of digital transformation. But only 40 percent said that their leaders were aligned on how to execute it.[1] So, what does it take?

As you focus your early digital transformation investments, be sure to manage three areas carefully:

- *Translating vision into action:* Have you converted your digital vision into strategic goals? Have you translated your digital transformation priorities into a roadmap of initial activities?

- *Building governance:* Have you designed governance mechanisms to steer your transformation in the right direction?

- *Funding the transformation:* Have you designed a balanced portfolio of digital investments? Have you worked out the funding mechanisms for your transformation?

FIGURE 10.1

The digital transformation compass: focusing investment

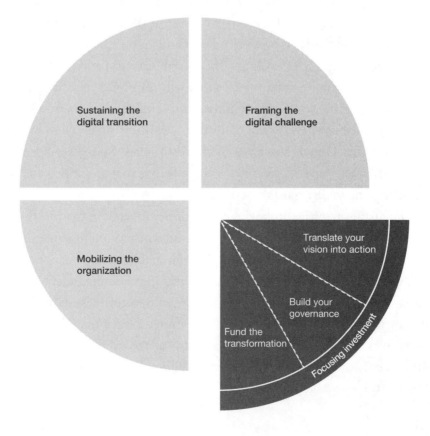

HAVE YOU TRANSLATED YOUR VISION INTO ACTION?

Translating your vision into a focused set of goals and initiatives is the key starting point for implementing your digital transformation. You and your team will have crafted a vision of your digitally transformed company: what your company will stand for, how it will operate, and what you need to do to get there—or partly there. That vision should start highlighting some of the major landmarks on your digital transformation journey—how you improve the customer experience, how you increase your operational performance, and how you adapt your business model. The astute investments in digital capabilities—the *what* of digital transformation—have already been described in part I of the book. But how do you turn vision into action?

Digital Masters first translate their vision into strategic goals that point to what an achieved vision would look like. Second, they build a roadmap of initiatives—a roadmap that starts guiding the organization toward the vision.

Define What Good Looks Like

Translate your digital vision into top-down strategic goals that point to what an achieved vision would look like. Articulate top-level goals only. Specific KPIs will come later, once you have a detailed program. For example, "By 2016, two-thirds of our customer contacts will come from digital channels." Or "Digital sales will represent 60 percent of our total revenue in four years." Or "In two years, we will have straight-through processing of our claims, without manual interventions."

Make sure your goals reflect what you are trying to achieve in a balanced way. Your goals should not just be about financials, but should also be expressed in terms of customer experience and operations as well as the organizational capabilities you need to build. This strategic scorecard will provide a basic template for your entire digital transformation efforts.

There are several tools and methods available to help you construct and manage this scorecard, such as the balanced scorecard methodology.[2] Many business management software tools can also help you automate the process. But the key is to create enough time with your top team to design and manage a scorecard that truly reflects what "good" will look like once your vision becomes reality. Of course, you will need to iterate and sometimes correct your course. But just like a traditional compass, the scorecard will provide a point of reference with which to navigate your digital transformation.

Build a Roadmap for Your Digital Journey

In a perfect world, your digital transformation would deliver an unmatched customer experience, enjoy the industry's most efficient operations, and spawn innovative, new business models. There are myriad opportunities for digital technology to improve your business, and no company can entertain them all at once. The reality of limited resources, limited attention spans, and limited capacity for change will force focused choices. This is the aim of your roadmap.

Find Your Entry Point

Many companies have come to realize that before they can create a wholesale change within their organization, they have to find an entry point that will begin shifting the needle. How? They start by building a roadmap that leverages existing assets and capabilities, as we discussed in chapter 9. Burberry, for example, enjoyed a globally recognized brand and a fleet of flagship retail locations around the world. The company started by revitalizing its brand and customer experience in stores and online. Others, like Codelco, began with the core operational processes of their business. Caesars Entertainment combined strong capabilities in analytics with a culture of customer service to deliver a highly personalized guest experience. There is no single right way to start your digital transformation. What matters is that you find the existing capability—your sweet spot—that will get your company off the starting blocks.

Once your initial focus is clear, you can start designing your transformation roadmap. Which investments and activities are necessary to close the gap to your vision? What is predictable, and what isn't? What is the timing and scheduling of each initiative? What are the dependencies between them? What organizational resources, such as analytics skills, are required?

Engage Practitioners Early in the Design

Designing your roadmap will require input from a broad set of stakeholders. Rather than limit the discussions to the top team, engage the operational specialists who bring an on-the-ground perspective. This will minimize the traditional vision-to-execution gap.[3] You can crowdsource the design, as we showed in chapter 6 with Pernod Ricard. Or you can use facilitated workshops, such as "digital days," as an effective way to capture and distill the priorities and information you will need to consider. We've seen several Digital Masters do both.

Make no mistake; designing your roadmap will take time, effort, and multiple iterations. But you will find it a valuable exercise. It forces agreement on priorities and helps align senior management and the people tasked to execute the program. Your roadmap will become more than just a document. If executed well, it can be the canvas of the transformation itself. Because your roadmap is a living document, it will evolve as your implementation progresses.

Design for Business Outcome, Not Technology

Technology for its own sake is a common trap. Don't build your roadmap as a series of technology projects. Technology is only part of the story in digital transformation and often the least challenging one. For example, we described in chapter 6 how the major hurdles for Enterprise 2.0 platforms are not technical. Deploying the platforms is relatively straightforward, and today's solutions are mature. The challenge lies in changing user behavior—encouraging adoption and sustaining engagement in the activities the platform is meant to enable.

Express your transformation roadmap in terms of business outcomes. For example, "Establish a 360-degree understanding of our customers." Build into your roadmap the many facets of organizational change that your transformation will require: customer experience, operational processes, employee ways of working, organization, culture, communication—the list goes on. This is why contributions from a wide variety of stakeholders are so critical.

Think a Series of Sprints, not Marathons

The digital world moves quickly. The rapid pace of technology innovation today does not lend itself to multiyear planning and waterfall development methods common in the ERP era. Markets change, new technologies become mainstream, and disruptive entrants begin courting your customers. Your roadmap will need to be nimble enough to recognize these changes, adapt for them, and course-correct.

To design an agile transformation, borrow an approach that has become common among today's leading software companies.[4] Keep people committed to the end goal, but pace your initiatives as short sprints of effort. Create prototype solutions, and experiment with new technologies or approaches. Evaluate the results, and incorporate the results into your evolving roadmap. Adam Brotman, Starbucks CDO, explained the iterative process: "We didn't have all the answers, but we started thinking about other things we could do . . . I think it worked to not go too far, too fast, but to keep a vision in mind and keep building on successes along the way."[5]

This test-and-learn approach will require some new ways of working in its own right, but it enjoys some distinct advantages. By market-testing ideas quickly before they go to scale, this approach saves time and money. Its short cycle times also make it more adaptive to external changes. Finally, it enables your transformation to sustain momentum through small, incremental successes, rather the big-bang approach of long-term programs. However, as we described in chapter 8, some efforts, such as your technology platform, are large enough that they need a more traditional approach to understanding requirements and delivering capabilities.

Put Dollar Signs on Your Journey

You need initiative-based business cases that establish a clear link from the operational changes in your roadmap to tangible business benefits. You will need to involve employees on the front lines to help validate how operational changes will contribute to strategic goals.

The basic building blocks of a business case for digital initiatives are the same as for any business case. Your team needs to work out the costs, the benefits, and the timing of the return. But digital transformation is still uncharted territory. The cost side of the equation is easier, but benefits can be difficult to quantify, even when, intuitively, they seem crystal clear.

Building a business case for digital initiatives is both an art and a science. With so many unknowns, you'll need to take a pragmatic approach to investments in light of what you know and what you don't know.

Start with what you know, where you have most of the information you need to support a robust cost-benefit analysis. A few lessons learned from our Digital Masters can be useful.

Don't build your business case solely as a series of technology investments. You will miss a big part of the costs. Cost the adoption efforts—digital skill building, organizational change, communication, and training—as well as the deployment of the technology. You won't realize the full benefits—or possibly any benefits—without them.

Frame the benefits in terms of the business outcomes you want to reach. These outcomes can be the achievement of goals or the fixing of problems—that is, outcomes that drive more customer value, higher revenue, or a better cost position. Then define the tangible business impact and work backward into the levers and metrics that will indicate what "good" looks like. For instance, if one of your investments is supposed to increase digital customer engagement, your outcome might be increasing engagement-to-sales conversion. Then work back into the main metrics that drive this outcome, for example, visits, likes, inquiries, ratings, reorders, and the like.

When the business impact of an initiative is not totally clear, look at companies that have already made similar investments. Your technology vendors can also be a rich, if somewhat biased, source of business cases for some digital investments.

But, whatever you do, some digital investment cases will be trickier to justify, be they investments in emerging technologies or cutting-edge practices. For example, what is the value of gamifying your brands' social communities? For these types of investment opportunities, experiment with a test-and-learn approach, as we discussed in chapter 8. State your measures of success, run small pilots, evaluate results, and refine your approach. Several useful tools and methods exist, such as hypotheses-driven experiments with control groups, or A/B testing.[6] The successes (and failures) of small experiments can then become the benefits rationale to invest at greater scale. Whatever the method, use an analytical approach; the quality of your estimated return depends on it.

Translating your vision into strategic goals and building an actionable roadmap is the first step in focusing your investment. It will galvanize the organization into action. But if you needed to be an architect to develop your vision, you need to become a plumber to develop your roadmap. Be prepared to get your hands dirty.

HAVE YOU CHOSEN THE RIGHT GOVERNANCE MODEL?

Defining your strategic goals and your implementation roadmap will help you get everyone focused on the digital priorities—the priorities you have selected for the positive impact they will have on your customer experience or operations. Roadmaps help with the *what* of digital transformation but not with the *how*—the way you conduct your transformation (discussed in part II). Earlier, we discussed in detail the need to craft a vision and how to do it. Later in the book, we will address how you can mobilize your organization effectively and the need to get IT and the business working in sync. But in this current stage, you need to figure out how you will ensure that everyone keeps moving in the right direction. This is where governance is useful.

Build the Right Governance

One of the major challenges of digital transformation is that there is no single obvious owner of the transformation. Marketing? IT? Operations? Your biggest business unit? In a complex company with many different functions, business units, and geographic areas, who owns the transformation can be a very difficult question to answer. But not answering it is a recipe for failure.

Digital transformation engages a broad, cross-functional set of stakeholders. Once those people are motivated (or once they see a big pot of money available for spending), they'll start moving in the direction they think is best. That direction may not be what's best for the company as a whole.

You need to steer the efforts of all of those people in a common direction. And that takes governance. In our research, we have seen that governance is an important driver of the profitability advantage enjoyed by Digital Masters. But our research also showed something else. No single governance model is right for every company. This is no surprise, because research over many years has failed to find the single best governance model for IT across all companies. Digital governance is, if anything, even more complex than IT governance.

As we discussed in chapter 7, digital governance focuses on two clear goals—coordination and sharing—whatever your company is. And there are some common mechanisms to help you make it work. In creating your digital governance model, you'll need to decide what you want to coordinate and share. Then you'll need to figure out how to make it happen in your company. Finally, you'll need ways to know when to adjust your governance over time.

Decide What You Need to Coordinate and Share

Start by identifying the behaviors you want to encourage or discourage. What do you want to coordinate across the company? What do you want to share? Consider all of the investments, resources, and activities in your roadmap.

First, ask yourself, "What *resources* should we be sharing or coordinating across groups?" Sharing resources like digital technology platforms, talent, data, or other digital assets can offer economies of scale. However, sharing requires extra effort to ensure that the resources meet the needs of the groups that are sharing them. You might choose instead to allow some resources to exist in each business unit, but coordinate their activities. And some may work perfectly well without coordination, at least in the short term.

A second question to ask is, "What *initiatives* should be shared or coordinated across the company?" Should you take on a single social media strategy for all your company's products or allow each brand to design its own? If each brand designs its own, should the brands coordinate their technologies or vendors? Should they work with common standards? Should they develop interfaces so they can work together?

Research shows that centralized control of a standardized platform can provide both efficiency and agility simultaneously.[7] Conversely, too much autonomy can lead to spaghetti, which reduces efficiency, creates risk, and decreases agility.[8]

Standardized systems and processes can provide economies of scale to all units, while allowing each unit to build extensions on top. For example, the Caesars online platform is standardized, allowing the company to manage it efficiently and to easily make changes that affect all units. But employees in each hotel can customize their websites' style, information, and marketing campaigns and can even build extensions on top of the platform to meet local needs.[9]

Also be sure that your choices of sharing and coordination do not stifle innovation. You want to build economies of scale and drive out unnecessary complexity, but you also want to allow business units some leeway to find new ways of working. Your processes can make exceptions to allow experiments to happen, or possibly even seed innovative activities.

Finally, consider whether sharing and coordination should be mandatory or optional and at what level of the firm. P&G prides itself on the entrepreneurial autonomy of its business units, but mandates strict coordination and sharing of processes such as finance and HR. Meanwhile, business unit leaders can opt in to other services such as innovation and brand management if they feel doing so would benefit them.[10]

Choose Mechanisms to Meet Those Goals

Some of the coordination and sharing you desire will occur naturally as part of the way your company works. But much of it won't. The design of your organization may lead to unwanted behaviors. Some units will optimize for their own needs instead of the company's needs. Others will follow the standard way of working without thinking about how to innovate it. Still others will shut down innovation in a too-intense desire to standardize.

If governance is not someone's job, it won't happen. For example, Adam Brotman of Starbucks, explained: "Before the CDO position was created, my job was web, mobile and social media . . . [I]t wasn't global digital marketing, it wasn't card [Starbucks Cards and mobile payments], and it wasn't loyalty. Those were in three different groups separately in the organization. We realized those were all one thing, they all work best together and if you listed the vision for where we wanted to go with digital, it was encompassing all those things."[11]

Chapter 7 highlighted in detail several mechanisms you can use to make governance happen. To design your digital governance model, select the mix of mechanisms that will encourage the right behaviors in your organization.

Governance Committees

These bodies are the simplest to implement. However, because they are no one's "day job," committees are limited in what they can accomplish.

Committees can be a useful starting point, but usually need to evolve to another mechanism.

Digital Leadership Roles

No major change effort happens without someone in charge. Many companies make digital transformation someone's day job by naming a chief digital officer (CDO) or an equivalent role. Unless you just want light coordination, you need to give teeth to the digital leader role by appointing a senior executive. Who that executive reports to, and what authority he or she has, matters a great deal. The executive's network of informal contacts can also be very helpful. Also consider how you can use formal liaison roles to help drive the change across your organization.

Shared Digital Units

These groups are effectively shared service units for the digital age. Rather than trying to bridge the gaps in the digital activities of IT, marketing, and other groups, shared digital units allow you to integrate their activities into a single group. These units are typically stand-alone and manage their own budget and resources. Shared units can act as a powerful accelerator for your transformation. But they are the most resource-intensive of all the mechanisms.

Plan to Evolve Your Governance Model

If no single governance model is right for every organization, another point holds true too. No governance model is right forever. As your digital capabilities improve, and as your governance models take hold, you'll find that you need to make some adjustments.

Pay attention to the coordination and sharing behaviors that you want to encourage. How well is your governance model making them happen? As business units learn that shared digital resources work well, you may be able to relax some of your more heavy-handed enforcement mechanisms. You might devolve centralized skills and initiatives to key business units. On the other hand, you might want to go the other way, expanding the role of your digital unit to drive even more sharing and coordination or launch new digital products.

Also pay attention to the negative consequences of your governance model. Are small business units getting enough attention? Are your governance processes too bureaucratic? Are your standards squeezing out innovative ideas that might be useful? Is a decentralized approach preventing you from sharing some practices developed by different business units?

Finally, think about your digital leaders. Do you need to augment your steering committee with a full-time CDO to drive changes in culture and governance process? If the organization is starting to adopt the right behaviors naturally, should you evolve the role of the CDO from strong governance toward something different—maybe driving innovation? Do you still need a strong enterprise-level CDO, or can unit-level CDOs work with a committee or shared unit to drive the coordination and synergy you need?

No governance model is perfect; they all need tuning. And over time, they will all need to evolve as you work to drive new behaviors and use your resources most effectively.

DO YOU HAVE THE FUNDING MODELS FOR YOUR TRANSFORMATION?

Digital transformation might be a strategic opportunity for your company or, sometimes, it may be a response to a burning platform. Regardless, the transformation will always need serious investment. You and your team have defined your strategic goals and the financial justification for your roadmap. Now, you need to build a balanced view between long-term capability building and short-term return. You also need clarity on the sources of funding. Finally, you need to ensure that the metrics used for your transformation make sense up and down the organization.

Manage Your Digital Investment Portfolio

You need to build an investment portfolio that balances the goals of your vision with the desired combination of short- and long-term pay off. A wide body of research covers IT portfolio management principles and classifies technology investments.[12] In our research, we have consistently observed four broad types of digital investments.

Foundational Investments

Foundational investments are the table stakes for the strategic success of your transformation. Without them, you may find it can become difficult to make any scalable progress at all. They are the core systems, platforms, or tools that you need to enable advances in digital customer experience or operations. Often, these investments are too costly, or their benefits too distributed, to be absorbed by one unit's P&L (profit and loss) alone.

A large global company, for example, invested in a global content-management platform to unify the flow of content between its diverse business units. None of the business units could justify the benefits on their own; the benefits were at the corporate level, including an aggregate of smaller returns in each business. The company's CEO understood that this investment was on the critical path of his company's transformation. Rather than build the business case for each unit separately, he made an executive decision to invest in the new platform.

Foundational investments do not lend themselves to detailed benefits cases. They require a leadership call. Hence, they are often funded centrally.

Maintenance Investments

Although maintenance investments do not help advance your digital capabilities, they are nevertheless essential to keeping the business running or minimizing risk. They may also be driven by external factors, such as regulatory and compliance requirements. Upgrading website functionalities, providing compliance analytics to regulators, or funding security applications would fall in this category.

ROI-Driven Investments

ROI-driven investments are tightly linked to your transformation roadmap. They are usually project-based with a clear line of sight to KPI improvements and ROI targets. These investments are generally managed within the normal financial planning cycle of your organization but may come from a separate digital fund or account.

Early-Stage Innovation Investments

By definition, early-stage investments are more speculative and their returns are highly variable. For example, these investments can fund incubators, digital labs, research partnerships, or specific experiments. Manage these as if you were a venture capitalist: select the most promising projects, kill losers early, and maximize the commercial value of winners.

Manage a portfolio that balances long-term capability building with short-term ROI. To start, map out the percentages that you currently allocate to each category. Then discuss with your team what the optimum balance needs to be to accelerate your digital transition. Often, investments in digital transformation are an easier sell when they are budget-neutral or generate at least as much value as they consume. Consider using cost savings from industrializing IT to fund other digital initiatives in the portfolio, such as those focused on building new capabilities or developing innovative new products. In other words, squeeze the old to fund the new.

Exploit Various Funding Mechanisms

Assuming your company is like most, you will have more demand for financing your digital transformation than funds available. The trick here is to diversify your sources of funding. There are many funding mechanisms available, but most fall into one of three basic models: central, local, and partner-supported.

Central Investments

Your company may need to make central investments when the services provided are owned by a central function or when you need to coordinate between entities, to leverage the investment. This will often be the case for your foundational digital investments. Central investments can also be used to fund your innovation—such as seed funds or incubators.

Local Investments

When projects within your roadmap are directly benefiting specific parts of the business, local investments work best. An example may be an e-commerce application for one of your brands. You need to ensure that, when possible, you leverage locally funded implementations across the wider business. If the potential for enterprise-wide leverage is substantial, you can offer a central subsidy for a local effort. Or, you can pay a royalty fee back to the unit in an app-store type of model when the application is used by others.

Partner-Supported Investments

Partner-supported investments come in several flavors. You can get a partner to support an initial investment in exchange for a minimum service volume and duration commitment. You can ask your partner for performance-based investments. You can sell or lease assets (physical or IP) to a partner to fund new investments. Or, if your partner is launching new technologies, you can act as a showcase pilot for their marketing in exchange for a substantially reduced investment.[13]

Don't Let Transformation Goals Get Lost in Translation

Executives speak the language of strategy, cost, and revenue. Employees on the front lines speak the language of product, work flow, and click-throughs. A survey by CFO Research Services found that only 36 percent of finance executives agree that the metrics they use to assess technology investment are commonly understood across the company.[14] Clearly, something is lost in translation between strategic measures of success and operational KPIs.

That translation also needs to work both ways. Senior leaders need to understand how operational improvements drive real business performance. As one high-tech executive said, "When the marketing guys came up with their click-through rate, cost-per-thousand impressions, and sentiment-analysis metrics to justify their investment, I could tell that the whole board had no clue what they were talking about. The outcome became obvious."

Strategic goals need to be understood in terms that make sense to on-the-ground employees. Likewise, operational and customer experience improvements must be translated into financial benefits that can be tracked and understood at senior levels. But as a senior leader, your role is to ensure that both groups speak a common language when developing the investment and funding case for your transformation.[15]

DO YOU HAVE A SHARP FOCUS?

Success in digital transformation is as much about what you don't do as what you do. In the context of so many opportunities to digitize your business, it's easy to become distracted by the latest shiny object. But when it comes to making real strategic commitments, investing real dollars, and involving real people, only a focused approach to digital transformation delivers real business value.

Play to your strengths. Leverage existing assets and capabilities to build your roadmap. Build governance mechanisms to steer the transformation and maximize its return. Be clear about your funding models. These steps are critical to turn your vision into action. The next step is to mobilize your organization to make it happen. In chapter 11, we'll show you how to do it.

So what's new about focusing investment in the digital world? You need to design an agile transformation roadmap to cope with the velocity of digital change. You may need to appoint a person to serve as chief digital officer. Since different units, such as marketing, may be more willing to fund digital efforts on their own, coordination is even more important than for other technology investments.

HOW WELL HAS YOUR ORGANIZATION FOCUSED ITS INVESTMENT?

Table 10.1 summarizes how you can focus investment in three key steps. Look at the central questions at each step, and give an honest assessment of your company's progress on a scale from 1 to 7 (1 = strongly disagree; 4 = neutral; 7 = strongly agree). For each of the three steps, total your scores across the individual questions.

For each step, we have provided you with a target that places you among the Digital Masters. We've also provided a threshold below which you should start taking action now to improve your situation. If your score is in the Digital Master range, you are ready to move on. If your score is in the middle range, reflect on why. Your team still needs to work out a few things in the investment-focusing phase. If your score is in the lower range, it is time for remedial actions. If it is well below, we recommend you start now to fundamentally rethink your investment process for digital transformation.

TABLE 10.1

How well has your organization focused its investment?

For each of the three questions, rate your company, using a scale from 1 to 7, where 1 = strongly disagree; 4 = neutral; and 7 = strongly agree, and find the recommended action for your score.

Have you translated your vision into action?	Score
We have a top-down strategic scorecard to guide our transformation.	
There is a high-level roadmap for digital transformation.	
Our roadmap encompasses all organizational changes required, not just technology changes.	
Total score	

Scoring: **Over 17:** your roadmap and scorecard are in good shape—focus on engaging your people in executing; **7–17:** review your roadmap and scorecard for content and alignment; **less than 7:** you need to conduct a full review of your scorecard and roadmap processes.

Have you chosen the right governance model?	Score
Digital initiatives are coordinated across silos such as functions or regions.	
We are clear on what needs to be coordinated and what needs to be shared across the enterprise.	
Roles and responsibilities for digital initiatives are clearly defined in the company.	
Total score	

Scoring: **Over 15:** your governance model is in good shape; **8–15:** check governance principles and/or program leadership; **less than 8:** you need to design or rework your governance principles.

Do you have the funding models for your transformation?	Score
Our business cases and key performance indicators are linked to our roadmap.	
We balance our portfolio of digital investments between long-term capability building, short-term return on investment, and experiments.	
We have a diversified funding model.	
Total score	

Scoring: **Over 16:** your digital funding process is strong; **8–16:** ensure that your portfolio, funding, and business case are aligned; **less than 8:** you need to rework your investment and funding case.

CHAPTER 11

MOBILIZING THE ORGANIZATION

Large, transformative change programs only succeed when leaders are able to earn employees' trust, engage them, and mobilize them into action. Digital transformation is no different. However, surprisingly, our survey shows that 64 percent of employees still do not feel that senior leaders have adequately shared a vision for digital transformation with everyone in the organization.[1] So, what can we learn from Digital Masters? To mobilize your organization and achieve high impact, ask yourself three fundamental questions:

- *Signaling:* Are you marketing the ambitions and the benefits of digital transformation sufficiently clearly to the organization?

- *Earning the right to engage:* Are you building sufficient momentum with employees by co-creating solutions and involving those who will have to make the change happen?

- *Setting new behaviors:* Are you actively encouraging a culture shift by using digital technologies to change the way people work and collaborate?

Crafting programs to answer these three questions will substantially increase the chances of success of your digital transformation efforts.

FIGURE 11.1

The digital transformation compass: mobilizing the organization

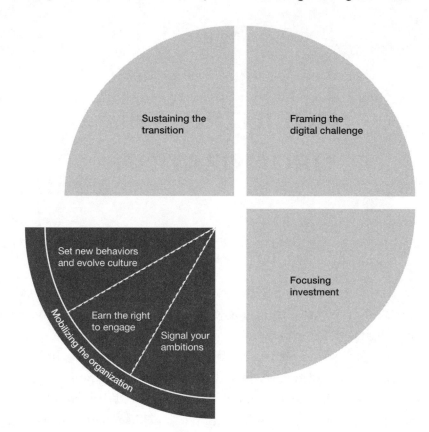

Of course, the effort is not just up to you. The entire leadership team should be on board for this journey.

ARE YOU SIGNALING YOUR AMBITIONS EFFECTIVELY?

In chapter 9, we discussed the need to both mobilize your top team on the impact of digital transformation and align around a future vision. But there is a tougher crowd to get on board—your entire organization. You need to become the marketing manager for your transformation ambitions. How? Send clear signals to the organization early. Make sure the value proposition you craft is clear and has meaning for individuals and functions. And then, market the ambitions at scale using all channels available.

Send Signals

Put your transformation process in motion early by sending unequivocal internal and external signals about the importance of the digital phenomenon and the resulting changes that are expected. The signals can take several forms. Some are metrics- or performance-driven, such as the CEO's declaration that Pages Jaunes would shift from having roughly 30 percent of its business online to more than 75 to 80 percent within four years.[2] Some signals can also be organizational. We've seen the COO of a large division within a global company be appointed for the CDO role within the same unit, sending a strong signal throughout the firm. Other signals relate to visible branding of the transformation to all the firm's stakeholders—as L'Oréal did when the CEO announced 2010 as the "digital year."[3] You can send signals in many ways; what matters is that you do it visibly to start mobilizing your organization.

Explain Benefits Clearly

But sending signals to employees is not enough. To market your ambitions effectively, you also need to explain the benefits and make digital transformation meaningful to key individual constituents. Put yourself in their shoes, and ask yourself, "What's in it for me?" Traditional financial and competitive logics are important but not sufficient to engage employees' hearts and minds. You need to articulate how digital transformation will improve the way people do their jobs—making their work easier, better, faster, or more fulfilling. You also need to adapt those messages for your different organizational communities. For example, explain to your finance department how digital tools will increase the visibility and accuracy of financial reporting; show your marketers how to get a more refined, data-rich view of their customer segmentation. Position the benefits of digital transformation in terms that make sense to the individuals who will be critical in making your vision a reality.

Facing a sharp decline in market share because of new competition, a global mobile operator redefined its vision: to become the first truly digital brand in the mobile market. To mobilize the organization, the company produced and distributed a video program on all its internal platforms. Board members and the top 150 executives then engaged in an open dialogue with employees and individual functions—using an internal social network—to explain the scale of change, the resulting customer benefits, and how work practices would improve and to solicit employee feedback and ideas.

Giving your digital transformation a meaning for each constituent and function will substantially increase people's engagement. As employees understand which part of the digital vision they can actively contribute to and how it can benefit their work, they will become advocates.

Use All Available Communication Channels

To mobilize at scale and ensure that the change is understood by all employees, use all available digital platforms within your organization—video, enterprise social networks, webcasts, intranets. Use your traditional channels as well. And encourage open feedback and dialogue. Reaching out to all employees in this way will create the scale, but remember, these tools are only carriers of the message. You also need to work on the message itself. What counts is authenticity. Show that you care about people's contribution to making the vision a reality and that you value the increased dialogue. Your internal communication and HR departments can be great allies to ensure the success of the mobilization. Enroll them in putting a two-way communication plan together. Then craft the right messages, and design a process to analyze the feedback.

HAVE YOU EARNED THE RIGHT TO ENGAGE?

Creating organizational momentum at scale is not a given management right; you need to earn it! How can it be done effectively? Do four things consistently. First, encourage the leadership of the company to become role models—actively promoting the behaviors that represent the new vision. Second, co-design a detailed implementation plan of the transformation with the people responsible for its success. Third, identify and engage early the true believers, those transformation champions who are willing to take risks in making the change a reality. Finally, find early quick wins of how digital can visibly improve the business, both internally and externally.

Walk the Talk

Mahatma Gandhi famously stated, "Be the change you wish to see in the world." This holds true for leading digital transformation. As a leader, you can influence the transition to digital by becoming a role model for the most important managerial decisions. An executive at Pfizer put it this way: "The way we are approaching it is to say 'Think digital first,' so everything we create, every piece of content, every piece of information we have, should be accessible digitally."[4] By acting as a role model for the desired change and encouraging your colleagues to do so, you take the first important step in earning the right to engage your employees. As described in chapter 6, Coca-Cola faced huge challenges when it deployed its internal social collaboration platform. Only when Coke's executives became engaged on the platform did the community become active. "With executive engagement, you don't have to mandate activity."[5]

For some tech-savvy business leaders, the act of being a role model will be obvious; for others, it might feel unnatural. But it is worth persevering. The benefits of executive engagement far outweigh the effort over the long run.

Co-create Your Transformation

Digital technologies allow you to co-create your transformation with people up and down the organization more easily than ever before. Pernod Ricard opened up the dialogue with its employees to co-create its entire digital roadmap. Not only is crowdsourcing a good way to generate new ideas and increase the quality of your transformation design, but it is also engaging.

In June 2013, Société Générale, the French-based global bank, mobilized sixteen thousand employees in nineteen countries to shape its detailed transformation plan.[6] The bank focused the exercise on the three core streams of its transformation roadmap, namely, improving customer experience, changing the way employees collaborate, and investing in the right IT systems to support the change. Using its internal social network, the bank gathered more than a thousand initiatives, which were reviewed and analyzed concurrently by thousands of employees. The most promising were presented to the CEO and the top team for final validation and integrated into the bank's transformation plan. Little buy-in was needed by the business after that. As Frederic Oudéa, Société Générale's CEO, explained, "There will be no overnight revolution in our digital transition; we must encourage business-led initiatives from the front line."[7]

Identify Your Digital Champions

Identifying your true believers within the organization will help scale your mobilization efforts and multiply their impact. Digital Masters leverage their digital champions through both formal and informal roles. These individuals have bought into the vision, the strategy, and the resulting need for transformation. They are essential to connect the top-down digital initiatives with the various dimensions of the organization—regional, functional, business lines, brands, and the like. They ensure that the part of the organization they champion remains engaged and that its specific needs and contributions are represented at the corporate level. No matter what their age or tenure in the company, digital champions are both technology savvy and business savvy. They network well and create horizontal influence to help you implement the transformation across silos. Look after your champions well. They will, most likely, be your organization's future digital leaders.

But why should middle management not lead the digital change? This is a tricky issue in many firms. As conversations move online and information is transparent and more freely available, middle-management roles in traditional hierarchical structures may need to evolve. Some middle managers may become great digital champions, but many others won't. This is particularly important in firms where the digital divide—the gap between digital-savvy managers and those who aren't—is important. You will have to tackle this leadership challenge early. Digital champions are essential to the success of your digital transformation.

Identify Quick Wins

Finally, earning the right to engage the organization is about getting results fast. You will need to stop telling, and start showing, early. Quick wins are a good way to motivate believers and to silence naysayers. But you need a formal process to identify the wins, to elevate their visibility, and to celebrate them.

This is where pilots and experiments can help. Luckily, digital technology allows for very effective and low-cost targeted experiments. Unlike celluloid films, digital photography allows you to take multiple shots and experiment with different angles and lighting conditions with next to zero risks. Similarly, digital technology allows you to experiment with the business and iterate more effectively. Find a pocket of efficiency gains in operations, make a better decision through an analytics pilot, or generate better sales results in a regional retail experiment. Quick wins like these will speak volumes and help mobilize your organization. And if you can scale those quick wins, it will also generate huge benefits to the organization.

ARE YOU SETTING NEW BEHAVIORS
FOR THE ORGANIZATION?

Digital technologies are transforming our traditional ways of working. New ways of collaborating, communicating, and otherwise interacting are changing the moral contract between companies and employees.

Michelle Pattison, global agile workplace director at Unilever, explained:

> *How employees receive communication and interact with their colleagues and employers, in a company like Unilever, has been changing fast, enabled by the technology we have at our finger tips today. In our traditional ways of working, as with so many businesses, time and attendance were the key measurement of employees. There was no argument about where you worked and when you worked. At Unilever, we have introduced our "Agile Working" program, which values the performance and output of our people. For us, time and attendance are artificial barriers that can be removed allowing employees to have a far greater say in how they work. It builds our capability around the world, it safeguards business continuity and keeps a far more diverse pool of talent in our business. It is a win–win all round.*[8]

The exact shape of the future digital organization is not yet clear. What is evident is that new ways of working, powered by digital technologies, are evolving the cultures and work practices within organizations. And over time, they will also change how organizations are structured and function. What are the drivers?

Digital technology is fostering a more transparent sharing of information up and down, but also across the organization. Forums, communities, and new data flows are improving collaboration and decision making. Online meetings, webcasts, and video communications are allowing employees from all functions, and regardless of location, to come together to solve problems or innovate. Traditional internal processes have gone self-service, giving flexibility to employees to arrange their work at will—whether people are booking a flight, filing expenses, or updating the weekly sales forecast.

We've seen many Digital Masters actively evolving their culture toward building such high-performing digital businesses. It does not happen randomly; it needs leadership. Your organization will have to adapt to these new ways of working and the resulting cultural evolution. How do you start? First, it's about driving new behaviors—what you reward and what you don't. Second, it's about encouraging adoption to ensure your technology investments benefit the business as intended. Third, it's about tolerating failure and learning from it. And finally, it's about making new ways of working become the routine.

Make Visible Changes to Work Practices

Adapting work practices and evolving culture involve a multitude of small changes in behavior from the top. Top-down communication, no matter how inspiring, is not enough. There is no silver bullet, but action and role modeling speaks louder than words.

Question your intuition—ensure that your most important managerial decisions are based on the power of data and analytics. Fight against organization fragmentation and silo-based thinking. Encourage the transparency, core process standardization, and operations efficiency that digital technologies provide.

Conversely, lead from behind, and adopt an encouraging style, to allow self-organizing teams to solve problems, innovate, and further your vision. This is management innovation powered by digital technologies and committed leadership. Do this successfully, and you will start to weave a new cultural signature within your organization.

Most CEOs talk about the need to be customer oriented. But Richard Branson, CEO of Virgin Group, was proactive about it. He invited his 2.3 million Twitter followers to pose questions about his company using the hashtag #AskRichard. By inviting the outside world into a dialogue, he sent strong signals externally but also internally.[9]

To advance your culture, sometimes you need to accept a level of risk. Peter Aceto, CEO of ING Direct in Canada, did just that. Using the company's internal social network, he encourages employees to vent their frustrations about the company directly with him. He explained: "We may not have solved major business issues by having this bitch session, but with my support, employees know that it is safe to be heard, and that dialogue is encouraged and feedback is actionable. And my senior team is reminded of the power that resides in having real conversations, honesty and open debate. Whether it is the Pandora's Box or a big can of worms you're opening, the point is the cans exist, the conversations take place and there's always room for improvement."[10]

Encourage Adoption, Not Deployment

A great way to fail in your digital transformation is to focus on the deployment of technology rather than its adoption by business users. Sound obvious? Yet how many millions of dollars have been spent on analytics technology with no visible improvements—or even any changes—to the way decisions are made within a business? How many companies have deployed internal social networks with great fanfare only to see a slow take-up or a huge slowdown after a few months?

The way some companies typically introduce these platforms to their organizations is partly to blame. Implementations that measure success in terms of live sites or licenses focus only on deployment, not adoption. They miss the true value of their digital investments: collaboration among actively engaged users, smarter decision making, increased sharing of best practices, and, over time, sustained behavior change. The result is often widely deployed internal applications that no one actually uses effectively. Why does that happen?

There are three main reasons. First, these kinds of digital programs are all too often treated as technology implementations. Poor technical leaders may measure success on deployment metrics, while considering true business adoption as someone else's job. Second, platform vendors often oversell the promise of instant change through digital technology. They make their money selling products and software, rarely by getting them used at scale. And finally, user adoption programs cost money.

Your true ROI will come from embedding new work practices into the processes, the work flows, and, ultimately, the culture of organizations. Even when the value of adoption is understood, cost containment often takes over. Faced with limited budgets, companies focus on the most tangible part first—deploying the technology. The difficult training and organizational change required for full adoption is left for later, and often, "later" never comes.

This partial implementation drives negativism and can potentially threaten a big part of your digital transformation program. Business users do not see the value and fail to engage in the new digital platforms. The platforms are themselves blamed for the failure. Cynicism sets in. Every additional digital investment is negatively scrutinized, and the whole digital transformation program slows down.

Encouraging employees to adopt digital tools and technologies, and doing so visibly, through role modeling, gamification, rewards, or any other methods, can have a significant impact on behaviors. When adoption programs are well implemented, the benefits become obvious.

Bayer's material science CIO, Kurt De Ruwe, explained how the introduction of a social platform created an irreversible movement: "You can't stop it. Once you make it available to people on the right platform the magic happens . . . Why do I participate? If you don't do it then your internal employees will find a way of leading themselves. Micro-blogging is basically engaging with just anybody in the organization that wants to engage with them. That is totally creating a different culture environment in the organization. Sometimes, if people ask me to quantify in euros or dollars what the platform has delivered to us—I tell them to look at the change of mindset, the open information sharing, and how quickly information passes around Bayer. Things that otherwise may have taken two or three weeks to uncover, now take hours."[11]

But business adoption of digital tools does not happen naturally. It has to be led. So what do you need to do? It often starts with doing fewer things better. You need to plan for adoption from the start—taking into account people, process, and structural changes. Align the investment required to achieve your intended benefits. It will cost money. Aligning rewards and recognition is good practice. And as we've shown earlier, so is leading by example.

Organizations that focus on the business adoption of digital tools get better returns. Your active leadership in adoption will ensure that your digital technology investments benefit the business as intended.

Learn to Fail

With the speed of technology change, your go-to-market and operational processes will often be catapulted into uncharted territory. Not everything you try will succeed. The adage "Fail fast, fail cheap, fail often" is not new, but is very relevant to the business adoption of digital technology. Of course, it's not about encouraging failure. It's about promoting a culture where teams can learn quickly and smartly.

Experimentation can steer you in the right direction. Digital technology enables a multitude of ways to experiment with new business ideas, at relatively low cost. With the right control mechanisms in place, it also provides a continuous stream of data to measure, learn from, and enable adaptation. Time to market becomes more important than perfection. Invariably, despite well-executed experiments, some initiatives will fail to deliver as planned. But this is part of the game.

The important thing is to learn from these failures and, in subsequent attempts, leverage the knowledge gained. Kim Stevenson, CIO of Intel, instituted a simple program to encourage informed risk-taking in her organization. She distributes small cards that read: "I took a risk, it failed, and I learned something and applied it." Each card is a license to experiment and take a risk. When a project fails, team members turn in a card to their manager; managers then decide whether to give the card back.[12] Failure can be a learning opportunity—consider it part of the process.

Institutionalize New Work Practices

Use the power of digital tools to the limit of their capabilities. Encourage new work practices to become the routine way your organization works. Sourcing your internal crowd can both help harness the power of your organization and send a signal that everyone matters, not just the select few on the management committee. Sainsbury, the British-based retailer, runs a panel of more than two thousand employees who give feedback every month about key managerial decisions.[13] Even the process of innovation is being transformed by new digital tools: crowdsourcing, broadcast search, and open innovation. So you need to institute these tools one by one across your organization in search of productivity and efficiency.

But how do you make these changes stick and become routine? You need to adapt your management and people processes to institutionalize the new practices. This should be a key opportunity for your HR or organization development functions to take a leadership role in the transformation. Unfortunately, our research shows that all too often, the employees in these functions don't rise to the task. So challenge them and ask yourself, "Do I have the right support for my ambitions?"

You have signaled the change to your organization, you have engaged communities and champions, and you are actively cultivating new behaviors to move closer to a digital business. Your mobilization task should be well on its way.

So what's new with mobilizing in digital transformation? You can mobilize at scale, whatever the size or complexity of your organization. You can co-design your transformation plans by engaging a wider community. Digital champions who drive the change can be of any age or tenure, not just senior leaders. Even more than in the past, experimentation and tolerance for failure are part of the digital game.

HOW WELL HAS YOUR ORGANIZATION
BEEN MOBILIZED?

Table 11-1 summarizes how you can mobilize your organization in three key steps. Look at the central questions at each step, and give an honest assessment of your company's progress on a scale from 1 to 7 (1 = strongly disagree; 4 = neutral; 7 = strongly agree). For each of the three steps, total your scores across the individual questions.

For each step, we have provided you with a target that places you among the Digital Masters. We've also provided a threshold below which you should start taking action now to improve your situation. If your score is in the Digital Master range, you are ready to move on. If your score is in the middle range, reflect on why. Your team still needs to work out a few things in the mobilizing phase. If your score is below the average of the rest of the sample, it is time for remedial actions. If it is well below, we recommend you design and conduct a full mobilization program with your top team.

TABLE 11.1

How well has your organization been mobilized?

For each of the three questions, rate your company, using a scale from 1 to 7, where 1 = strongly disagree; 4 = neutral; and 7 = strongly agree, and find the recommended action for your score.

Are you marketing your ambitions clearly enough?	Score
Our senior leaders are actively promoting a vision of the future that involves digital technologies.	
Our senior leaders and middle managers share a common vision of digital transformation.	
Our employees understand the benefits of change.	
Total score	

Scoring: **Over 17:** you are doing a good job of marketing your ambitions; **7–17:** isolate which part is not satisfactory, and work with your team to remedy; **less than 7:** consider developing a specific program for signaling the ambition.

Are you building sufficient momentum within the organization?	Score
There are opportunities for everyone in the company to take part in the conversation around digital initiatives	
We have identified the "true believers" who will help mobilize the organization.	
We are building momentum through quick wins.	
Total score	

Scoring: **Over 16 :** you have built sufficient momentum in the organization; **8–16:** you need to look at which component of engagement is below par, and remedy this component; **less than 8:** you need to design and conduct a full engagement program.

Are you actively encouraging a digital culture shift?	Score
Our senior leaders act as role models in the adoption of new behaviors.	
We tolerate and learn from failure in our digital initiatives.	
We are promoting the necessary culture changes for digital transformation.	
Total score	

Scoring: **Over 16:** you have started to shift your organization's behaviors and culture; **7–16:** understand the root causes of your concerns, and work with your team to remedy problems; **less than 7:** you need to start working to create a cultural shift.

CHAPTER 12

SUSTAINING THE DIGITAL TRANSFORMATION

Large transformation programs often fail to reach their goals because they lose their momentum. Digital transformation is no different. It's easy to stay motivated in the early days—T-shirts, baseball caps, regular video communications, visible engagement programs, quick wins, best practices sharing, and new leadership roles. But as time goes by, change fatigue sets in and new ways of working begin to give in to the old way of doing things.

This is the time where skills gaps become obvious; where unaligned metrics and incentives get in the way of doing the right thing; and where leadership teams, busy planning the next strategic move, too often assume that the digital transition is flying on autopilot on its way to completion.

These can be dangerous times. Until new digital practices are rooted into your customer experience, your operations, and your ways of working, there is a real danger that the momentum of your digital transformation will start faltering. Without a concerted effort to sustain the transformation program, your vision and your business objectives may be at risk. Joe Gross of insurer Allianz Group explained: "I think the top challenge for Allianz will be to maintain and accelerate the momentum that we have already generated. It's still an evolving process—we cannot hope to see immediate results. It's also easy for organizations to slip back into old, familiar patterns. The challenge for us is not to go back to our comfort zones and instead always keep looking for new digital opportunities."[1]

What can we learn from Digital Masters about making digital transformations sustainable? Ensuring that you are managing three aspects of your digital transition will help sustain the momentum of your transformation. Ask yourself the following questions:

- *Building foundation capabilities:* Do you have a plan for a ramp-up of digital competence within your organization? Do you have a well-structured digital platform? Do you have strong IT–business relationships?

FIGURE 12.1

The digital transformation compass: sustaining the digital transformation

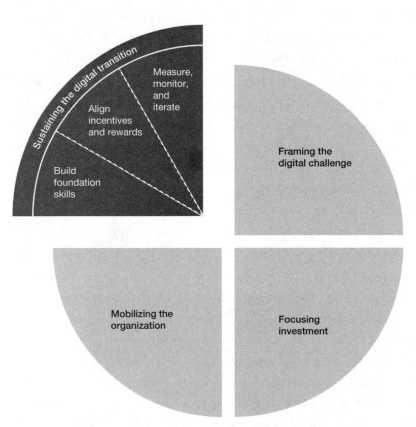

- *Aligning reward structures:* Are your incentives, rewards, and recognitions aligned to your transformation objectives?

- *Measuring, monitoring, and iterating:* Do you have a management process that allows you to measure and monitor the progress of your digital transformation? Do you have enough visibility to adapt your course as needed?

ARE YOU BUILDING FOUNDATIONAL CAPABILITIES?

Technology innovation is outpacing many firms' ability to build organizational capabilities fast enough. In chapter 8 we showed that Digital Masters build three solid foundations to sustain their digital transformation. They build *digital skills*—the experience and knowledge of people. They build a well-structured *digital platform*—the assembly of technology to power their business processes. And they develop strong *IT–business relationships*—trusted, shared, and integrated interactions between technology and businesspeople.

Orchestrate Your Skills Build-Up

Building digital skills is a gradual process. There's no silver bullet, so getting it right won't happen overnight. You need to craft a capability building and organization development plan meshing several complementary approaches—hiring, training, partnering, acquiring, or incubating.

But first, you need to *understand what your skills gap is*. At operational levels, you need to first conduct a proper skill inventory assessment to understand the retooling required in your key functions: what you have today, what your digital transformation requires, and the skill gap that needs to be filled. Ask your HR organization to take a lead on this. And consider all tactics at your disposal.

Hiring

The ability to make good hires is the most obvious tool. External hiring is effective in bringing both digital leadership skills to the senior levels and specific capabilities in the more operational roles.

Start at the top. When you are trying to build up digital skills in your company, bringing in digital awareness and experience at the board level is useful. For example, in 2012, Coca-Cola added Robert Kotick, CEO of game company Activision Blizzard, to its board. Muhtar Kent, chairman and CEO, explained: "Bobby brings an entrepreneurial mindset and a high level of financial literacy and digital knowledge to our company. His global brand expertise and insight will be invaluable as we continue to grow our business and invest in enhancing our digital engagement with consumers and customers around the world."[2] Many organizations also bring in experienced executives to inject digital leadership in their senior executive team. Nestlé, the food giant, brought in Pete Blackshaw as global head of digital and social media in 2011 to harmonize and accelerate the company's digital marketing strategy.[3]

Innovate in your recruitment strategy. Use all of the recruitment channels that digital technologies bring today—social media, online recruitment agencies, and other online communities—as well as more traditional routes. L'Oréal, for instance, developed "Reveal," a recruitment website that takes the form of a business game.[4] Not surprisingly, digital-savvy Generation Y candidates preferred to be engaged through digital means—49 percent of candidates are more likely to consider a job advertised in an innovative way.[5]

Cast your net wide for rare skills. Go and get talents where they are. Look outside your own industry to acquire valuable skills, or partner with academic institutions to get early exposure. This is what Caesars did when it needed to beef up its quantitative skills. The company identified the companies that were, at the time, the most advanced in terms of analytics skills—many were in the financial services sector. Caesars proceeded to attract candidates from these companies to build a solid set of core analytical skills.

Training

Training is essential to grow your capabilities from within. Many of your existing employees will be eager to embark on their personal digital journeys to grow their skills. Training comes in several flavors: digital awareness programs, specific digital skills training and certification, employee exchange programs, reverse mentoring, and even your own internal digital university.

Increase your digital awareness. L'Oréal, for example, wanted to increase digital awareness in several functions, including marketing, research, manufacturing, communication, and sales. The company launched a specific program to train fifteen thousand individuals, including managers, in digital fluency in two years.[6]

Bring employees up to speed in specific digital technologies. Intel started a Digital IQ training program comprising sixty online courses spanning diverse areas, from social media measurement to brand identity. Its success led the company to launch an internal certification called the Digital IQ 500, which licenses employees to practice social media on behalf of the company.[7]

Organize employee exchange programs. Such programs can also be a good way for your company to leverage key partners to improve digital skills. P&G, for example, started an employee exchange program with Google. Employees from both companies participate in each other's training programs and business meetings.[8] This program enabled select P&G employees to gain expertise on digital and search marketing. On the other hand, for Google, which controls about 74 percent of search-term advertising spending, the exchange enables Google employees to gain insight into the working practices and culture of the world's biggest advertiser.[9]

Introduce reverse-mentoring programs. Originally pioneered by GE, reverse mentoring is also a great way to pair your digital-savvy employees with executives in a nonhierarchical way. Krish Shankar, head of HR at Indian telecommunications group Bharti Airtel, explained: "The future of technology will be defined by the youth, and unless we talk to the younger generation and observe them closely, we will not know their demands. A [reverse-mentoring] program like this sends a message that no matter how high up you are, you are never too old to learn."[10]

Consider building your own digital university. Kering, the luxury-brands holding company, set up its own in-house digital academy to increase digital skills globally. The focus is threefold: to develop brand innovation, to build digital awareness among managers, and to create an international community around digital transformation across the group.[11]

Partnering

Partnerships can be very effective when you're *lacking critical skills* that your ecosystem partners already possess. Angela Ahrendts, Burberry's CEO, explained: "We began sharing our vision of our ecosystem with our technology partners. We told them: Burberry is global, dynamic, and has a clear vision. We have an amazing CTO and an IT team that's nimble and fast. So our proposal was: let us be your R&D. Let's experiment together."[12]

Partnerships can also be effective for *accessing specific skills* critical to your product or service innovation. GE, for instance, partnered with Quirky, a social product-development company. The partnership enables the Quirky product-development community to access GE's patents and accelerate advanced innovations in manufacturing. In return, GE encourages product innovation that builds on GE technology without fear of potential infringement.[13] With proper skill-transfer mechanisms, partnering can be very effective.

Acquiring (or "Acqui-Hires")

You can acquire generally small companies purely for their talent. When Walmart Labs wanted to strengthen its offerings across mobile and social media channels, it acquired a range of mobile-related agencies that were focused on product development.[14] When other methods are too slow or when skills are rare, acquisitions can be the answer. But, as with any people-based acquisition, they can be risky to implement.

Incubating

Through incubation, you invest in agile start-ups while providing them access to your company's technical and executive support. By opening up your resources to such start-ups, you can access specialized talent that would otherwise be tough to source. Mondelez, the global snack company, launched its Mobile Futures incubator in 2011 to harness mobile marketing start-up capabilities. The company hopes to launch mobile-focused tech companies out of the process. But more importantly, it wants to garner new capabilities—such as in-store marketing, location-based advertising, and social TV applications to drive innovation.[15] If you want to infuse entrepreneurial spirit and access state-of-the-art digital skills, an incubator model can be very helpful, but it requires strong program management to succeed.

Building strong digital skills is essential to secure the sustainability of your digital transformation program. In some areas, you will need to build capabilities at scale, while in other areas, you may need to target very narrow skills. There is no shortage of methods of how you can get there. What matters is the impact on execution. You need a clear plan, investment, and a concerted implementation with your functions and business units. And don't do it alone. You need your HR and organizational development teams by your side and mandated to implement this complex capability shift.

Build Your Digital Platform

Earlier in the book we described how important it is to have a strong digital platform. Why? Because a well-defined and well-managed platform provides you with the information you need to make decisions and the coordination you need to power your processes as effectively as possible. Great digital platforms are at the same time a bridge to your customers and a gateway to your internal and third-party processes. When it's good, your platform enables you to personalize your customer interactions, perform analytics, optimize your internal processes, manage seamlessly across channels, and have a single view of your customers.

A digital platform is a coherent set of business processes, along with supporting infrastructure, applications, and data, intended to ensure the quality and predictability of core transactions.[16] It should be well defined, well managed, and only as complex as necessary. Great digital platforms make your company's business processes more efficient, less risky, and more agile.[17] Unfortunately, in many large companies, the platform is a mess of spaghetti—overly complex, expensive to run, tough to change, and prone to failure.

If you hope to transform your customer engagements or operations, you'll need to start by transforming your platform. It's what Angela Ahrendts of Burberry did when launching her digital transformation program. It's what Lloyds Banking Group did in setting the stage for new digital banking capabilities. And it's what, in all likelihood, you'll have to do as you get started.

What does it take to build the right digital platform? A useful approach is to think in terms of an enterprise architecture—a roadmap explaining the desired organizing logic of your business processes and underlying technology.[18] Many people find it helpful to think of their enterprise architecture in three different, but coordinated, layers. First, you need a technical architecture comprising existing applications and new ones, as well as the underlying infrastructure for processing, storage, and communication. Some technologies will be managed by you, some by your partners, and some by third-party suppliers—often cloud-based. You also need a business process architecture to understand your desired level of integration and standardization across different parts of the company, and how your business processes make your company work. You should be able to map your current state to your future state with the technical and organizational changes that will be required to get there. Increasingly, companies are building a data architecture. This is an understanding of your content—how information is produced and how it is distributed. Is it structured or unstructured? How will it be used for transactions and for analytics? How will you manage requirements for security, privacy, and data retention? How can you get to a unified view of your customers, processes, and performance?

To move your platform in the right direction, you will need strong digital governance. An effective governance model both rejects requests that will add unnecessary complexity and facilitates initiatives that will improve the platform's capabilities. Governance is essential to build a platform that is standardized enough to provide efficiency and enable changes that affect the whole company, like the platform at pharmacy retailer CVS that we discussed in chapter 8. It should also provide ways that different units can customize parts of the platform or innovate on top of it, as local hotels can do with Caesars Entertainment's corporate web platform.

Building world-class digital platforms is not a job just for your CIO and his or her technical team. They can't do it on their own. It's a job for you and other business executives, working in tandem with your IT leaders. You need the discipline to follow standards and avoid unnecessary exceptions, and the savvy to envision new ways you can work with a great platform and new technologies. Your IT leaders can be valuable partners in helping you build this platform, if you are willing to engage with them.

Develop a Close IT–Business Relationship

In the long-distant past, we were taught that IT was the keeper of technology and that IT leaders were service providers to the rest of the business. Their job was to stay aligned with business strategy, taking orders from the business and delivering new systems. If they kept the systems running and delivered projects on time, then all was good. That time is over, and it has been for many years.

To be effective, digital transformation demands a fusion between IT and business skills. It requires mutual trust and shared understanding. It also requires new methods of working—agile learning-by-doing approaches for fast-moving, customer-facing innovations; more-systematic methods for more-critical and longer-lasting projects, and the wisdom to mix the methods appropriately.

Years of separation can get in the way of building the strong relationships you need. In many organizations, the interaction will not come naturally. But moving from a poor relationship to a state of true partnership between IT and business leaders is possible. We've seen it dozens of times in companies around the world, and there are good guides to help you create that partnership.[19] Unfortunately, achieving the new partnership takes time and effort. Your digital transformation may need to start before you have completely changed the culture of, and the relationship between, IT and business leaders across your organization. We've seen some Digital Masters take different approaches to begin improving the IT–business relationship. Some efforts are top-down, some are project-based, some are governance-based, and some are organizational.

Top-Down

Burberry CEO Angela Ahrendts mandated that the CIO would be part of the senior management team. But just putting him on the team was not enough. She worked closely with him to help him develop into a new role. And she was very clear that the members of her team needed to work on the relationship from their own business-oriented sides.[20] This worked, because the senior-most executive in the company led the IT/business fusion.

Project-Based

Some companies take a Skunk Works approach to digital innovation projects. They extract the resources required from business and IT to deliver a specific initiative for a limited duration. This has the advantage of being easy to set up. But although a project-based approach improves communication, it does not commit the two communities to work together over time.

Governance-Based

Strong governance processes require an integrated IT and business approach to vetting and conducting projects. An integrated approach helps IT and business executives spend time together and to jointly identify how they'll make their initiatives happen. Making business leaders accountable for the financial results of technology projects is one good way to ensure that IT and business are in sync. In a large apparel company, for example, if a unit needs funding for a digital initiative, the president of the business unit makes the pitch directly to an executive steering committee and is required to give a specific, measurable return target. Then, after implementation, the unit president must go in front of his or her colleagues and show whether the return was achieved, as well as why. This kind of accountability drives stronger links between technology and business executives, since the credibility of the business executive depends on working closely with IT to make results happen.

Organizational

Some organizational changes can start to dissolve the distance between IT and business units. For example, TetraPak aligns its IT and business-people around strong business process ownership. The business process owner controls what changes will be made to processes, and coordinates IT and businesspeople to make them happen. Other companies have made technology and operations people report to the same senior executive. Meanwhile, other companies have created specific organizational units to deliver their digital roadmaps. This unit, such as Nike Digital Sport or the one at Lloyds Banking Group, may have its own resources or a combination of owned and shared resources. Or it may be a dual-speed IT arrangement as we discussed in chapter 8.

Whatever the model, getting your IT and business leaders to work more closely together—in an environment of trust, shared understanding, and collaboration—is a prerequisite for sustaining your transformation and gaining the digital advantage of Digital Masters.

ARE YOUR REWARD STRUCTURES ALIGNED
TO YOUR TRANSFORMATION GOALS?

Your company's transformation goals and measures are inextricably linked. Reward structures are the glue that binds them. Many of the challenges labeled as "resistance to change" during a transformation are actually conflicts about measures and rewards. For that reason, two-thirds of Digital Masters in our survey have explicitly tied reward structures to their digital transformation goals.[21] Digital transformation gives business leaders a good opportunity to reassess the combination of financial and nonfinancial incentives that will best serve the company's goals. You need to calibrate your reward structures to overcome conflicts and sustain your digital transformation.

Start at the Top

We've shown in the framing phase the importance of aligning the top team around a vision. We've also discussed the cross-functional nature of digital transformation throughout the book. A collective top team incentive—based on the success or the progress of your digital transformation—is often a good way to facilitate this alignment.

Smooth End-to-End Operations

Operations can constitute a real challenge to aligning digital transformation goals. How can you ensure end-to-end delivery of your core processes or smooth the interface between functions and business units? Some conflicts in your reward structures will be obvious from the early stage, and you will need to fix them. But many won't. They will occur as you get into the depth of your digital conversion. You need to remain alert, as they will act like bottlenecks or excuses for slowing down your transformation efforts. Employee resistance to change was cited as one of the biggest hurdles to implementing digital transformation in our initial phase of interviews.[22]

Consider the retail sector as an illustration. Online channels are fast gaining more traction. One of the biggest challenges facing retailers today is integrating online and offline channels. In 2011, Walmart defined new incentives for its store managers and employees. These people now had to push online sales from their respective territories, just as they did for in-store sales. Following this alignment of rewards, employees started promoting Walmart.com, the new iPad app, and the My Local Walmart Facebook app to the 140 million weekly in-store shoppers.[23]

Similarly, John Lewis, the chain of department stores in the United Kingdom, rolled out a Click and Collect strategy whereby shoppers can collect their online purchases from a brick-and-mortar store. In order to effectively drive offline-online store coordination, the company attributes online sales to the relevant customer's local store. Store managers became accountable not just for in-store sales, but also for overall internet sales in their catchment area. This change motivated managers to influence customers to purchase products from the website. After rolling out its Click and Collect strategy, John Lewis witnessed a significant increase in sales across its online channels. A third of all online orders are now collected in John Lewis or Waitrose (food retail division of John Lewis) stores.[24]

Make Sure the Rewards Are More Than Financial

The reward structures for sustaining digital transformation should not be just financial. Intangible incentives such as status, reputation, recognition, expertise, and privileges are great managerial levers to drive employee motivation, productivity, and ultimately reach your transformation goals.[25] Indeed, research suggests that nonfinancial motivators are sometimes more effective than financial rewards in fostering employee engagement.[26] For example, as we discussed earlier, Chilean mining company Codelco and technology company EMC created internal innovation awards to promote new ideas, encourage workers to innovate, and consequently effect a culture change.

Digital technologies are also enabling new forms of incentives, such as gamification.[27] Intangible rewards, such as recognition and real-time feedback, provided through gamification initiatives, can yield positive results. When a midsized firm installed a new event-logging system for its sales force, the firm found very poor adoption rates from its employees. To rectify this, the company ran a weeklong sales competition where every event logged would receive a point and the employee accruing the highest number of points would receive a $100 gift certificate at a local restaurant. The number of events shot up by 750 percent. Even four weeks into the contest, events logged were six times higher than previous levels.[28]

Extend Reward Structures Beyond Your Corporate Boundary

Part of your digital transformation may require that you extend reward structures beyond your own corporate boundary to suppliers, partners, or even customers. Samsung, the Korean electronics giant, wanted to increase customer advocacy on its Samsung.com portal. The company rolled out a social incentive program, using gamification techniques, to measure, recognize, and reward key customer advocates who could promote Samsung products to their networks. By looking beyond the corporation, Samsung turned passive web visitors into active brand advocates. The site recorded a 500 percent increase in reviews and 200 percent more comments.[29]

Sustaining your digital transformation program will be highly influenced by your ability to align your reward and recognition structures to your goals. It is a complex, multidimensional challenge. Not all the misalignments will be obvious from the start, so you will have to tackle them in stages. But the benefits will outweigh the difficulties. Rewards drive behavior, for better or for worse. And changing people's behavior is what, ultimately, will drive culture change in your organization.

ARE YOU MEASURING AND MONITORING YOUR DIGITAL PROGRESS?

The old management adage "You can't manage what you can't measure" is as true for digital transformation as it is for any other business activity. Digital transformation can't be sustained through just an act of faith from your senior team. Having a proper measurement and monitoring system in place will provide you with confidence that the investments and the business change are bringing real benefits to your organization. In addition, over two-thirds of executives we surveyed think that measurements have a critical effect on changing the culture of an organization.[30] Therefore, metrics should constitute the backbone of your transformation program and the instrument panel with which to guide it

How does measurement work? There are four basic steps to properly measuring and monitoring progress: managing your strategic scorecard, driving an initiative-level business case and KPIs to measure the progress of your digital initiatives, connecting top-down and initiative-level measures, and developing an iterative review process.

Managing Your Strategic Scorecard

Keeping track of your strategic scorecard is the task of senior management. Earlier in the investment-focusing phase, we saw the importance of translating your vision into strategic goals that reflect the final state of what you are trying to achieve. Financial measures will play a big part. But your strategic scorecard should also contain digital goals for customer experience, for operational processes, and for the organizational capabilities that you need to build. The scorecard should provide a basic template for your entire digital transformation effort. You need to manage individual components of your scorecard actively to ensure the balanced progress of your transformation.

A multibrand global company wanted to review the progress of its digital transformation program, so the executive team implemented an executive digital dashboard to ensure proper focus on the right objectives and oversight on the companywide transformation. The company went further by building a virtual digital P&L that included all online activities across the group, independently of the entity that actually generates the revenue or incurs the cost. The executive team also set up a Digital Transformation Index as a compound measure to monitor progress of each business unit. But not everything is top-down.

Drive the Initiative-Level Business Case and Related KPIs

In chapter 10, we also highlighted the need to quantify and monitor the benefits of your digital roadmap—by engaging employees with the right expertise to provide rigor and commitment to the exercise. Clear business cases also act as great motivators for people to transform the business.

Your KPIs will come in different flavors. Some will be high level, and some, very granular. Typically, your process-driven performance measures will be captured by a few key metrics, such as online credit-card application-to-issue time. Others will be more related to experiments and proofs of concept, such as measuring the impact of an online ad campaign on Facebook. The key is to choose the metrics that are critical to attain your long-term transformation objectives.

Connect Top-Down and Initiative-Level Measures

By connecting your top-down and initiative-level measures, you build a coherent business management process. You need to make clear how each of your digital initiatives contributes to your transformation goals and strategic scorecard. You must also understand the cause and effect of each initiative. Establishing such a measurement cascade will ensure that the teams remain focused on delivering the vision and that business leaders have visibility of the business impact.

Develop an Iterative Review Process

An iterative review will allow you to monitor progress and correct your course when necessary. The review needs to be conducted rigorously and frequently, and with the flexibility that digital programs demand. Digital transformation requires constant adaptation as new technology appears and as your teams discover and test new opportunities for improvement. Traditional sectors are learning quickly from born-digital companies. For example, the UK government recently embarked on a Digital by Default program. Mike Bracken, head of the Government Digital Services, explained the government's new iterative approach in the digital space: "Do it quick, fail fast, learn your lessons and continue to change—that's why you need the skills inside the organization."[31]

At the executive level, the iterative review process will help you to choose and prioritize new initiatives—which ones advance your transformation goals, and which are peripheral. It will also help you kill those that do not lead to real benefits. At the operational level, it will ensure that critical digital initiatives are progressing to plan, and raise early warnings when organizational bottlenecks get in the way.

Sustaining the momentum of your digital transformation is critical to long-term success. It requires building new foundation skills that will make the change possible, aligning reward structures to ensure that employees are motivated and organizational bottlenecks are removed, and putting in place an iterative review process to measure progress frequently. When enthusiasm tapers off and you start to encounter more resistance from within your organization, these sustaining interventions will become essential to help you stay the course.

So what's new with sustaining your transformation in a digital world? Even more than in the past, it is essential to truly integrate your technology and business capabilities. Ramping up digital capabilities faster than your competitors is a source of advantage. Building a coherent digital platform will speed up transformation. Digital transformation demands a new fusion of IT and business skills. Aligning online and offline incentives and rewards is more important than ever, and will remove bottlenecks. Digital technology has enabled new forms of incentives, such as gamification. Connecting your top-down and initiative-level digital metrics will make clear how your digital initiatives contribute to your transformation goals.

So, is this end of the journey? Absolutely not. Although you, and your organization, will have applied the approaches that have given Digital Masters the digital advantage, the transformation is never finished. Even if you become a Digital Master, you will need to work to remain one. In the epilogue, we will explain why.

HOW WELL IS YOUR ORGANIZATION SUSTAINING DIGITAL TRANSFORMATION?

Table 12.1 summarizes how you can sustain the digital challenge in three key steps. Look at the central questions at each step, and give an honest assessment of your company's progress on a scale from 1 to 7 (1 = strongly disagree; 4 = neutral; 7 = strongly agree). For each of the three steps, total your scores across the individual questions.

For each step, we have provided you with a target that places you among the Digital Masters. We've also provided a threshold below which you should start taking action now to improve your situation. If your score is in the Digital Master range, you are ready to move on. If your score is in the middle range, reflect on why. Your team still needs to work out a few things in the sustaining phase. If your score is in the lower range, it is time for remedial actions. If it is well below, you run the risk of early burnout. We recommend that you take action on capabilities, rewards, and measurements to make sure your program becomes sustainable.

TABLE 12.1

How well is your organization sustaining digital transformation?

For each of the three questions, rate your company, using a scale from 1 to 7, where 1 = strongly disagree; 4 = neutral; and 7 = strongly agree, and find the recommended action for your score.

Do you have the foundation capabilities you need?	Score
The organization is investing in the necessary skills.	
Where appropriate, we use common digital platforms.	
We have strong IT–business relationships.	
Total score	

Scoring: **Over 16:** you have the foundation capabilities you need for digital transformation; **8–16:** you have started implementing projects aimed at developing capabilities, but more is needed; **less than 8:** you need to consider specific programs for improving foundation capabilities.

Are your reward structures aligned with your transformation goals?	Score
Financial incentives (bonuses, etc.) are aligned with the goals of digital transformation.	
Awards and recognition mechanisms are aligned with the goals of digital transformation.	
Personal rewards (performance reviews, promotions, etc.) are aligned with the goals of digital transformation.	
Total score	

Scoring: **Over 14:** your current reward structures are aligned with your digital objectives; **6–14:** build consensus around a viable reward strategy aligned to digital transformation; **less than 6:** implement specific reward structures that accomplish digital goals.

Are you measuring and monitoring your digital progress?	Score
Digital initiatives are assessed through a common set of key performance indicators (KPIs).	
We have a clear line of sight from project-level KPIs to goals on our strategic scorecard.	
We regularly review with the top team our progress on digital transformation.	
Total score	

Scoring: **Over 15:** you believe you have the necessary KPIs in place; **7–15:** isolate specific measurement parameters, and use them to measure progress; **less than 7:** establish a process to develop KPIs, identify the correct level of measurement, and iteratively track progress.

YOU AIN'T SEEN NOTHIN' YET

In this book, we've presented a case for why your organization should strive to become a Digital Master—an enterprise that's able to use each new wave of technology to radically improve the performance or reach of its business. Our research has shown that Digital Masters enjoy superior performance, which should be reason enough to get leadership teams interested in the concepts presented in this book. But there's also another, even more fundamental, reason: *when it comes to the impact of digital technologies on the business world, we ain't seen nothin' yet.*

TECHNOLOGY: THE ENDLESS AGITATOR OF THE BUSINESS WORLD

The innovations we've discussed in previous chapters, including social networks, mobile devices, analytics, smart sensors, and cloud computing, are certainly powerful and profound. They're reshaping customer experiences, operations, and business models. The pace and impact of these innovations have been nothing short of astonishing, but they're just a prelude for what's to come.

Technology's role as the endless agitator of the business world will not only continue, but will accelerate—exponentially. Moore's Law will continue to be the central drumbeat of the digital future.[1] In five years, technology will be about ten times as powerful as today, for the same price. In ten years, the increase will be a hundredfold. If you find yourself struggling to keep up with waves of change over the past few years, you're in for a rough ride. Keeping up will be even more difficult in the future, unless you develop the skills of the Digital Masters.

The good news is that some of the next transformative techno-logical innovations are already on the horizon. They will continue to reshape customer experiences and operations in fundamental ways. We've seen Digital Masters hard at work figuring those out already.

The most significant innovation is the continuing business impact of data and analytics—the explosive increase in the amount of infor-mation available in digital form, and businesses' ability to use new insights to make smarter decisions. This is a fundamentally important development because data is the lifeblood of science—of improving our understanding of what causes what, and why, and under what cir-cumstances. In the years to come, smart organizations will use big data to become better, smarter, and more rigorous at many key activities: making predictions and forecasts; hiring and promoting people; decid-ing on product attributes; optimizing internal processes; marketing and advertising; and customizing products and services (to name just a few). Companies that use big data to get better at these activities will pull ahead of those that don't, as sure as gamblers who know the odds pull away from those who bet only on gut feel.

Gaining new analytic skills can't happen fast enough, as compa-nies gather richer data on their customers and operations, as unstruc-tured data-analysis techniques open social media to investigation, and as more and more devices report data through the "internet of things." How will your internal processes change when you have detailed infor-mation on the full performance of processes and products in real time? How will your hiring and HR processes change when you have this kind of measurement for employees? How much better will you be able to personalize your services through ever more granular insights into customers' needs and behavior?

Other waves of technology innovation will also be significant. Robotics, additive manufacturing, augmented reality, and wearable technology, among others, will fundamentally change the way businesses operate. They will transform the nature of operations, customer experience, and even business models.

Until recently, industrial robots were expensive, inflexible, and dangerous if people had to work too close to them, but all of that is changing. People work side by side with automatons in many factories now, and human-robot collaborations are only getting closer. Robots are rapidly getting better at seeing, feeling, and otherwise sensing their environments, which enables them to take on more and more work. And they're escaping the factory floor and moving through the economy; driverless cars and other autonomous vehicles are robots, even though they're not anthropomorphic. They'll change the logistics and transportation industries, not just the manufacturing ones. As Watson, the computer that won the TV quiz show *Jeopardy!*, enters law and medicine, what will that mean for the way those fields are managed? How will industrial robots change the shape of your supply chain and logistics management?

Additive manufacturing (also called 3-D printing) will open up further business opportunities. It holds the promise of giving companies the ability to literally print out parts just as easily (if not yet as quickly) as they now print out documents. These parts, which can be made from several materials, including plastic and metal, can have highly complex geometries; additive manufacturing is not constrained in the same ways that traditional fabrication processes are. Already, 3-D printing is being used intensively for prototyping and for small production runs of specialized parts. It will expand much beyond these initial uses. How will your inventory management processes change if you don't have to stock low-volume parts? How would your design and sales activities change if you could print custom parts on demand?

Augmented reality meshes real-world environments with additional data and presents a revised environment with computer-generated sensory forms such as sounds, graphics, and video. This technology will allow consumers to experience what your product or service has to offer like never before. Trying on a new outfit in a virtual changing room, changing its color, adding jewelry to dress it up, or asking your friends on Facebook for comments—all will become the norm. Over time, online shopping may become as immersive as visiting a store.

Augmented reality will also change your internal processes. For instance, your field maintenance engineers could use tablets to visually identify pieces of your infrastructure and automatically overlay all maintenance records and procedures. In one major electronics firm, product designers using 3-D augmented reality discovered that a wire harness would rub repeatedly against another part, causing the harness to break prematurely—a condition they could not see in their 2-D design software. How could you use this technology to increase the prepurchase experience for your customers? Could it help you substantially improve the productivity of your operations?

Wearable technology, as commonly described today, is meshing real-time monitoring and feedback technology with design and mobility. Nike's FuelBand, which we described earlier in this book, is an example. Wearable items will track anything, from your sleep patterns to your heart rhythms. Smart socks will monitor your running technique. You may be able to change the color or thermal properties of your T-shirt at will. Digitized eyewear, such Google Glass, will open up exciting new possibilities. For instance, video images from inside machines can be streamed directly to a technician's eyewear, overlaying machine specification data to sharpen diagnostics, while keeping the worker's hands free to conduct repairs. Could the constant monitoring of how your customers use your products and services uncover new sources of growth? Can you monetize the new data stream that wearable technology brings? Have you considered how much more productive your engineers and technicians could be if they used wearable technology in your core operations?

Fast-moving technologies may also change the way you organize and innovate. The so-called sharing economy is forcing a rethink of large, asset-heavy industries, with important implications for the business models of large firms. Open innovation can build communities of interest, surface new sources of talent, and, for some problems, make progress both more quickly and more cheaply than approaches that rely on internal resources and centralized planning.[2] Social media and the seamless flow of data can bridge organizational boundaries and flatten hierarchies. What is the role of middle management in a digitally transformed enterprise? How might you overcome the nagging limits in your traditional organizational model?

LEADING DIGITAL IS A JOB FOR NOW

Technology is reaching into every corner of the business world—every industry, company, process, decision, and job—bringing deep changes in how companies are structured and led, and how they perform and compete. Over time, it will create a new playing field with new rules— and new winners and losers.

It's not yet clear exactly how any of the innovations we discussed here will progress, or how broad and deep their impacts will be. We think that, individually, each of them is likely to be a big deal indeed in the business world. In combination, their effects will be hugely transformational.

We're also confident that other technologies will be even more transformational; we just don't know what they are. The history of technological progress, and particularly progress with digital technologies, is one of constant surprise. Who knew that, within one generation, the personal computer would become an indispensable tool for virtually every knowledge worker? That a multimedia interface would turn the internet from a geek's network to the world's connective tissue? That phones would become an entirely new category of computing device? That social media, a mere diversion ten years ago, would grow to billions of connected people and become a vibrant organizing force that could topple governments?

This work of innovative astonishment is nowhere near over. The world abounds with ever more potential innovators, entrepreneurs, inventors, tinkerers, and geeks, and they have access to more and more increasingly powerful computing technologies all the time, at lower and lower price points. These tech-savvy people are going to come up with things that change the business world, and hence the world. We're not nearly good enough tech forecasters to predict what all of these advances will be, but we're fully confident that they're coming. We ain't seen nothin' yet.

The best way to get ready for these changes—in fact, probably the *only* way—is to start the work of becoming a Digital Master now. Companies that are indifferent to technology (to say nothing of hostile to it), or that haven't figured out how to make it part of the lifeblood of the enterprise, are going to have an increasingly hard time as the innovations keep mounting and the management breakthroughs keep coming.

We've written this book as a guide to help you in the work of digital mastery. It's not a blueprint—a complete description of everything you need to do to build the technologically adept company—because no such blueprint exists. Every company is different, and so is every company's path to mastery. But the patterns we've seen among those who do it well—the DNA of Digital Masters—can be helpful for any digital transformation.

We hope that the examples, explanations, and frameworks we've shared in *Leading Digital* will be useful to you and will help your organization thrive in a new, digitally transformed, world.

APPENDIX

DIGITAL MASTERY
SELF-ASSESSMENT

To get started in your digital transformation journey, you first need to understand your starting point. Is your company a Digital Master already? Or is somewhere else: Beginner, Fashionista, or Conservative? We've created a simple quiz to help you understand your organization's level of digital mastery.

First, think about how your company uses digital technologies such as social media, mobile, analytics, and embedded devices. Are you building digital capabilities in customer experience or operations? Are you digitally improving your existing business models or launching new ones? Table A.1 can help you assess your digital capabilities.

Next, think about how well your company is leading digital transformation. Do you have a shared transformative vision that is engaging your employees? Are you governing the transformation correctly? Do you have solid technology leadership capabilities in place? Table A.2 can help you assess your leadership capabilities.

Now, use your scores for digital capabilities and leadership capabilities to plot your position in the digital mastery matrix of figure A.1. This will give you a rough idea of where you are starting in your journey.

TABLE A.1

How well is your organization building digital capabilities?

Answer each question, using a scale from 1 to 7, where 1 = strongly disagree; 4 = neutral; and 7 = strongly agree, and then total your digital capability score.	Score
We are using digital technologies (such as analytics, social media, mobile, and embedded devices) to understand our customers better.	
We use digital channels (such as online, social media, and mobile) to market our products and services.	
We sell our products and services through digital channels.	
We use digital channels to provide customer service.	
Technology is allowing us to link customer-facing and operational processes in new ways.	
Our core processes are automated.	
We have an integrated view of key operational and customer information.	
We use analytics to make better operational decisions.	
We use digital technologies to increase the performance or added-value of our existing products and services.	
We have launched new business models based on digital technologies.	
Total score	

Scores for digital capabilities range from 10 to 70. A score from 10 to 41 means you are in the bottom half of the distribution, while a score from 42 to 70 puts you in the top half.

For leadership capabilities, scores range from 10 to 70. A score from 10 to 42 means you are in the left-hand side of the distribution, while a score from 43 to 70 puts you in the right-hand side.

Ask some colleagues to take the same self-assessment, and then compare your answers. Where are you doing best? What areas need work? And where do people in different units, or different levels of the organization, agree and disagree?

Of course, you and your colleagues will soon need to think in much more depth about where you are relative to your competitors. As we discuss in chapter 1, some industries are farther along than others.

TABLE A.2

How well is your organization building leadership capabilities?

Answer each question, using a scale from 1 to 7, where 1 = strongly disagree; 4 = neutral; and 7 = strongly agree, and then total your leadership capability score.	Score
Senior executives have a transformative vision of the digital future of our company.	
Senior executives and middle managers share a common vision of digital transformation.	
There are possibilities for everyone in the company to take part in the conversation around digital transformation.	
The company is promoting the necessary culture changes for digital transformation.	
The company is investing in the necessary digital skills.	
Digital initiatives are coordinated across silos such as functions or regions	
Rules and responsibilities for governing digital initiatives are clearly defined.	
Digital initiatives are assessed through a common set of key performance indicators.	
IT and business leaders work together as partners.	
The IT unit's performance meets the needs of the company.	
Total score	

And, as time goes by, all industries will move ahead. However, this self-assessment can help you think through your strong and weak points.

Now that you know your starting point, you can start charting your course. Do you need to move upward in the matrix? Focus on digital capabilities, which we discuss in part I of the book. Do you need to move rightward in the matrix? Focus on leadership capabilities, which we discuss in part II. Then, once you're ready, you can use the playbook in part III to get started on your journey.

FIGURE A.1

Four levels of digital mastery

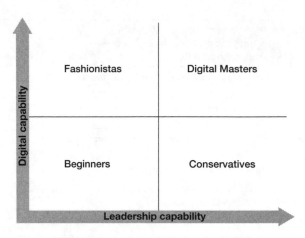

Source: Adapted from George Westerman, Maël Tannou, Didier Bonnet, Patrick Ferraris, and Andrew McAfee, "The Digital Advantage: How Digital Leaders Outperform Their Peers in Every Industry," Capgemini Consulting and MIT Center for Digital Business, November 2012.

NOTES

INTRODUCTION

1. Quentin Hardy, "Just The Facts. Yes, All of Them," *New York Times*, March 24, 2012, www.nytimes.com/2012/03/25/business/factuals-gil-elbaz-wants-to-gather-the -data-universe.html?pagewanted=all&_r=0.

2. Marc Andreessen, "Why Software Is Eating the World," *Wall Street Journal*, August 20, 2011, http://online.wsj.com/news/articles/SB10001424053111903480904576512250915629460.

CHAPTER I

1. "Nike's Just Getting Going: CEO Parker," *Bloomberg*, October 9, 2013, www.bloomberg.com/video/nike-s-just-getting-going-ceo-parker -OdYc8j3aRr2fiNMbiNvpfg.html.

2. Vignette built from public sources and from Maël Tannou and George Westerman, "Nike: From Separate Level Initiatives to Firm Level Transformation," white paper, Capgemini Consulting, 2012, www.capgemini-consulting.com/nike.

3. "Nike's Just Getting Going: CEO Parker."

4. Erica Swallow, "How Nike Outruns the Social Media Competition," Mashable .com, September 22, 2011, http://mashable.com/2011/09/22/nike-social-media/.

5. Asian Paints, "Corporate Information," www.asianpaints.com/company-info /about-us/corporate-information.aspx; currency conversion by oanda.com, accessed May 8, 2014.

6. Capgemini Consulting, "Building a World Leader Through Digital Transformation: An Interview with Manish Choksi," *Digital Transformation Review*, no. 2, January 1, 2012, www.capgemini-consulting.com/digital-transformation-review -ndeg2, 42–47.

7. Ibid.

8. Ibid.; George Westerman et al., "Digital Transformation: A Roadmap for Billion Dollar Organizations," white paper, Capgemini Consulting and MIT Center for Digital Business, November 17, 2011, www.capgemini-consulting.com/digital-transformation -a-road-map-for-billion-dollar-organizations, 14–15.

9. Asian Paints, "About Us," www.asianpaints.com/company-info/about-us /corporate-information.aspx, accessed May 8, 2014.

10. George Westerman et al., "The Digital Advantage: How Digital Leaders Outperform Their Peers in Every Industry," white paper, Capgemini Consulting and MIT Center for Digital Business, November 2012, http://ebooks.capgemini-consulting .com/The-Digital-Advantage/index.html, 9.

11. George Westerman et al., "Digital Transformation," 61.

12. Westerman et al., "The Digital Advantage."

13. Tannou and Westerman, "Nike: From Separate Level Initiatives."

14. Michael Welch and Jerome Buvat, "Starbucks: Taking the 'Starbucks Experience' Digital," Capgemini Consulting, October 4, 2013, www.capgemini.com /resources/starbucks-taking-the-starbucks-experience-digital.

15. Northwestern Mutual case study, interview with author; interviewee has asked to remain anonymous.

16. Interview with author; interviewee has asked to remain anonymous.

17. Westerman et al., "The Digital Advantage," 6.

18. Ibid.

CHAPTER 2

1. George Westerman et al., "Digital Transformation: A Roadmap for Billion Dollar Organizations," white paper, Capgemini Consulting and MIT Center for Digital Business, November 17, 2011, www.capgemini-consulting.com /digital-transformation-a-road-map-for-billion-dollar-organizations.

2. As of spring 2014, Ahrendts is senior vice president for retail and online sales at Apple. Capgemini Consulting, "Burberry's Digital Transformation," *Digital Transformation Review*, no. 2, January 2012, www.capgemini-consulting.com/digital-transformation -review-ndeg2. Austin Carr, "Apple Hires Burberry CEO Angela Ahrendts to Rejuvenate Retail Stores," *Fast Company*, October 15, 2013, www.fastcompany .com/3019981/apple-hires-burberry-ceo-angela-ahrendts-to-rejuvenate-retail-stores.

3. Ibid. Burberry's founder, Thomas Burberry, invented an original design for a coat originally sold to the British Army. The coat was made of a special type of fabric for comfortable, rain-resistant wear.

4. Capgemini Consulting, "Burberry's Digital Transformation."

5. www.burberry.com.

6. http://kisses.burberry.com.

7. Capgemini Consulting, "Burberry's Digital Transformation."

8. Perry Manross, "Three Tenets of a Best Run Business," SAP.info, May 15, 2012, http://en.sap.info/hana-in-memory-sapphirenow-orlando-2012/72972/3.

9. Capgemini Consulting, "Burberry's Digital Transformation."

10. "Burberry Goes Digital," *Economist*, September 22, 2012, www.economist. com/node/21563353; "How Fashion Retailer Burberry Keeps Customers Coming Back For More," *Forbes.com*, October 28, 2013, www.forbes.com/sites/sap/2013 /10/28/how-fashion-retailer-burberry-keeps-customers-coming-back-for-more.

11. Capgemini Consulting, "Burberry's Digital Transformation."

12. For L2 Thinktank ranking, see www.l2thinktank.com/research/fashion -2013. For *Fast Company* ranking, see www.fastcompany.com/most-innovative -companies/2014/industry/retail and www.fastcompany.com/most-innovative -companies/2013/industry/retail. For Interbrand ranking, see www.interbrand.com/en /best-global-brands/2013/Best-Global-Brands-2013.aspx.

13. Michael Welch and George Westerman, "Caesars Entertainment: Digitally Personalizing the Customer Experience," white paper, Capgemini Consulting, April 25, 2013, www.capgemini.com/resources/caesars-entertainment-digitally-personalizing -the-customer-experience.

14. Capgemini Consulting, "Allianz: Creating a Digital DNA," *Digital Transformation Review*, no. 4, May 2013, www.capgemini-consulting.com/digital-transformation -review-4.

15. Michael Fitzgerald, "How Starbucks Has Gone Digital," *MIT Sloan Management Review*, April 4, 2013, http://sloanreview.mit.edu/article /how-starbucks-has-gone-digital/.

16. Martha Heller, "How Vail Resorts Uses IT to Profile Skiers," Cio.com, June 26, 2013, www.cio.com/article/734940/How_Vail_Resorts_Uses_IT_to_Profile_Skiers_.

17. Personae are clusters of users who exhibit similar patterns of behavior in their customer experience. These behavioral patterns are common to a personae type, regardless of age, gender, education, location, or other typical demographic data.

18. Heller, "How Vail Resorts Uses IT to Profile Skiers."

19. Megan Burns, "The State of Customer Experience 2011," Forrester Research, February 17, 2011, 1, 3, www.forrester.com/The+State+Of+Customer +Experience+2011/-/E-RES58635?objectid=RES58635.

20. Fitzgerald, "How Starbucks Has Gone Digital."

21. James Wester, "Starbucks Still Feeling a Buzz from Mobile Payments," Mobilepaymentstoday.com, January 28, 2013, www.mobilepaymentstoday.com /article/207367/Starbucks-still-feeling-a-buzz-from-mobile-payments.

22. Square, Inc., "Starbucks Accelerates Mobile Payments Leadership by Choosing Square for Payments," Square web page, August 8, 2012, https://squareup.com/news /releases/2012/square-starbucks.

23. Starbucks, "Starbucks Coffee 2013 Annual Meeting of Shareholders: Adam Brotman," Starbucks, March 20, 2013, http://media.corporate-ir.net/media_files /IROL/99/99518/asm13/ASM_SHOW_FINAL_AdamBrotman.pdf.

24. Sarah Vizard, "P&G Invests 30% of Media Spend in Digital," *Marketing Week*, January 24, 2014, www.marketingweek.co.uk/sectors/fmcg/pg-invests-30-of-media -spend-in-digital/4009256.article.

25. Gartner, "US Digital Marketing Spending Survey 2013," Gartner, March 6, 2013, www.gartner.com/technology/research/digital-marketing/digital-marketing -spend-report.jsp.

26. "My Starbucks Idea," http://mystarbucksidea.force.com/.

27. Ashton D, "Introducing Starbucks Runner Reward," *My Starbucks Idea* blog, August 27, 2012, http://blogs.starbucks.com/blogs/customer/archive/2012/08/27 /introducing-starbucks-runner-reward.aspx.

28. Starbucks, "Starbucks CEO Hosts 2013 Annual Meeting of Shareholders," transcript, *Yahoo Finance*, March 21, 2013, http://finance.yahoo.com/news/starbucks -ceo-hosts-2013-annual-055406090.html.

29. Andrew McAfee, "Big Data: The Management Revolution," Massachusetts Institute of Technology, Center for Digital Business, Conference, Cambridge, MA, December 12, 2012, https://www.youtube.com/watch?v=T5AkD9gzchs#t=40.

30. Welch and Westerman, "Caesars Entertainment," 3.

31. Liz Benston, "Harrah's Launches iPhone App; Caesars Bypasses Check-In," *Las Vegas Sun*, January 8, 2010, www.lasvegassun.com/news/2010/jan/08 /harrahs-launches-iphone-app-caesars-bypasses-check/.

32. Capital One, "News Release," http://phx.corporate-ir.net/phoenix .zhtml?c=70667&p=irol-newsArticle&ID=1080986&highlight=.

33. Trefis Team, "Capital One Buys Data Analytics Firm to Tap Spending Trends at Local Businesses," *Forbes*, December 6, 2012, www.forbes.com/sites/greatspeculations /2012/12/06/capital-one-buys-data-analytics-firm-to-tap-spending-trends-at-local-businesses/.

34. Julie Shicktanz, "One Year After Its FinovateSpring 2011 Demo, Bankons Inks Deal with Capital One," *Finovate* blog, May 7, 2012, http://finovate.com/2012/05 /one-year-after-its-finovatespring-demo-bankons-is-acquired-by-capital-one.html.

35. John Adams, "Cap One's Jamison Discusses Issuer's New Digital Innovation Lab," PaymentSource.com, November 28, 2011, www.paymentssource.com/news/cap -one-jamison-digital-innovation-lab-3008658-1.html.

36. nGenera, "Business Analytics: Six Questions to Ask About Information and Competition," SAS.com, 2008, www.sas.com/offices/europe/uk/businessanalytics /research-report.pdf.

37. Data from www.google.com/finance; a 2000 net income equaling $467 million and a 2010 net income equaling $2,743 million provide a CAGR of 19.32 percent over ten years.

38. Michael Welch and Jerome Buvat, "Starbucks: Taking the 'Starbucks Experience' Digital," Capgemini Consulting, October 4, 2013, www.capgemini.com /resources/starbucks-taking-the-starbucks-experience-digital.

39. Fred Bernstein, "Technology That Serves to Enhance, Not Distract," *New York Times*, March 20, 2013, www.nytimes.com/2013/03/21/arts/artsspecial/at-cleveland -museum-of-art-the-ipad-enhances.html?pagewanted=all&_r=2&.

40. RightNow/Harris Interactive, Customer Experience Impact Report, RightNow /Harris Interactive, 2011.

41. Forrester, North American Technographics Customer Experience Online Survey, 2010, www.forrester.com/North+American+Technographics+Customer+Exper ience+Online+Survey+Q4+2010+US/-/E-SUS805.

CHAPTER 3

1. Codelco information based on author interviews with CIO Marco Orellana, 2011, and published sources.

2. Marco Orellena, "Digital Codelco," PowerPoint presentation, 2013, http://tinyurl.com/mn8csbq.

3. Christina Torode, "Codelco CIO Transforms Business with Business Process Automation," video interview, SearchCIO, June 15, 2011, http://searchcio.techtarget .com/news/2240036877/Codelco-CIO-transforms-business-with-business-process- automation.

4. Orellena, "Digital Codelco," 30.

5. Torode, "Codelco CIO Transforms Business."

6. Alexei Barrionuevo and Simon Romero, "Trapped 68 Days, First Chilean Miners Taste Freedom," *New York Times*, October 12, 2010, www.nytimes. com/2010/10/13/world/americas/13chile.html?pagewanted=all&_r=0; Faaiza Rashid, Amy Edmondson, and Herman Leonard, "Leadership Lessons from the Chilean Mine Rescue," *Harvard Business Review*, July–August 2013, http://hbr.org/2013/07 /leadership-lessons-from-the-chilean-mine-rescue/ar/1, 113–119.

7. Orellana, "Digital Codelco."

8. Torode, "Codelco CIO Transforms Business."

9. Ibid.

10. James P. Womack, Daniel T. Jones, and Daniel Roos, *The Machine That Changed the World* (New York: Free Press, 2007); Steven Spear and H. Kent Bowen, "Decoding the DNA of the Toyota Production System," *Harvard Business Review*, September 1999, http://hbr.org/1999/09/decoding-the-dna-of-the-toyota-production-system/ar/1.

11. Erik Brynjolfsson and Andrew McAfee, *The Second Machine Age: Work, Progress, and Prosperity in a Time of Brilliant Technologies* (New York: W. W. Norton & Company, 2014).

12. See, for example, Zeynep Ton, *The Good Jobs Strategy: How the Smartest Companies Invest in Employees to Lower Costs and Boost Profits* (Boston: New Harvest, 2014).

13. J. March, "Exploration and Exploitation in Organizational Learning," *Organization Science* 2 (1991): 71–87; M. Benner and M. Tushman, "Exploitation, Exploration, and Process Management: The Productivity Dilemma Revisited," *Academy of Management Review* 28, no. 2 (2003): 238–256.

14. Erik Brynjolfsson and Adam Saunders, *Wired for Innovation: How Information Technology Is Reshaping the Economy* (Cambridge, MA: MIT Press, 2010), chap. 3.

15. Brynjolfsson and McAfee, *The Second Machine Age*, chap. 9. Recent research shows that over the past thirty years, technology has led to a hollowing-out of labor demand, with some routine manual tasks (such as patient care or housecleaning) still performed by people, but middle-skilled routine tasks, such as paper processing or accounting, rapidly being replaced by computers. Nonroutine cognitive tasks such as teaching and financial analysis have traditionally been safe from computerization, but this is changing rapidly.

16. Capgemini Consulting, "UPS: Putting Analytics in the Driver's Seat—Interview with Jack Levis," *Digital Transformation Review*, no. 5, *Gearing Up for Digital Operations*, January 2014, www.capgemini-consulting.com/digital-transformation-review-5.

17. Nadira A. Hira, "The Making of a UPS driver," *CNN Money*, November 7, 2007, http://money.cnn.com/magazines/fortune/fortune archive/2007/11/12/101008310/.

18. Capgemini Consulting, "UPS: Putting Analytics in the Driver's Seat."

19. Ibid.

20. Ibid.

21. Ibid.

22. Interview with author; interviewee has asked to remain anonymous.

23. Asian Paints vignette adapted from George Westerman et al., "Digital Transformation: A Roadmap for Billion Dollar Organizations," white paper, Capgemini Consulting and MIT Center for Digital Business, November 2011, 14–15, and Capgemini Consulting, "Building a World Leader Through Digital Transformation: An Interview with Manish Choksi," *Digital Transformation Review*, no. 2, January 1, 2012, 42–47.

24. Capgemini Consulting, "Building a World Leader Through Digital Transformation."

25. Michael Welch and George Westerman, "Caesars Entertainment: Digitally Personalizing the Customer Experience," white paper, Capgemini Consulting, April 25, 2013, www.capgemini.com/resources/caesars-entertainment-digitally-personalizing -the-customer-experience.

26. Capgemini Consulting, "Building a World Leader Through Digital Transformation," *Digital Transformation Review*, no. 2, July 1, 2011, www.capgemini .com/resources/digital-transformation-review-no-1-july-2011, 42.

27. Ibid.

28. Association of Certified Fraud Examiners, *Report to the Nations on Occupational Fraud and Abuse: 2012 Global Fraud Study* (Austin TX: Association of Certified Fraud Examiners, 2012).

29. G. Collins, "Safeguarding Restaurants from Point-of-Sale Fraud: An Evaluation of a Novel Theft Deterrent Application Using Artificial Intelligence," *Journal of Hotel Business Management* 2 (2013): 105.

30. Lamar Pierce, Daniel Snow, and Andrew McAfee, "Cleaning House: The Impact of Information Technology Monitoring on Employee Theft and Productivity," MIT Sloan Research Paper No. 5029-13, August 24, 2013.

31. Lamar Pierce and Michael Toffel, "The Role of Organizational Scope and Governance in Strengthening Private Monitoring," *Organization Science* 24, no. 5 (October 2013): 1558–1584.

32. Michael Schrage, "Q&A: The Experimenter," *MIT Technology Review*, February 18, 2011, www.technologyreview.com/news/422784/qa-the-experimenter/.

33. K. Nagayama and P. Weill, "7-Eleven Japan, Inc: Reinventing the Retail Business Model," MIT Center for Information Systems, January 2004.

34. Dan Siroker, *A/B Testing: The Most Powerful Way to Turn Clicks into Customers* (New York: Wiley, 2013).

35. James A. Cooke, "Kimberly-Clark Connects Its Supply Chain to the Store Shelf," *Supply Chain Quarterly*, Q1, 2013, www.supplychainquarterly.com/topics /Strategy/20130306-kimberly-clark-connects-its-supply-chain-to-the-store -shelf/?utm_medium=email&utm_campaign=Preview+-+Q1+2013+ -+2013+Mar+15&utm_content=Preview+-+Q1+2013+-+2013+Mar+15+CID_ 3581e3c0e4a6dd35057267737b0b40fc&utm_source=Email%20marketing%20 software&utm_term=Kimberly-Clark%20connects%20its%20supply%20chain%20 to%20the%20store%20shelf.

36. "Zara: A Case of Rapid-Fire Fast Fashion Strategy," IPR Plaza, December 2012. http://ipr-plaza.com/state2/flow14950.

37. Sebastien Veigneau of Air France, interview with authors.

38. Ibid.

CHAPTER 4

1. Mark W. Johnson, *Seizing the White Space: Business Model Innovation for Growth and Renewal* (Boston: Harvard Business Press, 2010).

2. Michael Fitzgerald, Nina Kruschwitz, Didier Bonnet, and Michael Welch, "Embracing Digital Technology: A New Strategic Imperative," *MIT Sloan Management Review*, October 8, 2013.

3. Tom Kaneshige, "Hailo Picks Up Speed as a Digital Disrupter for Taxis," *CIO.com*, March 7, 2013, www.cio.com/article/729877/Hailo_Picks_up_Speed _as_a_Digital_Disrupter_for_Taxis.

4. Capgemini Consulting, "Hailo: Digitally Disrupting a Traditional Market—An Interview with Ron Zeghibe, Co-Founder and Executive Chairman," July 26, 2013, www.capgemini-consulting.com/hailo-digitally-disrupting-a-traditional-market.

5. Ibid.

6. C. Zott, R. Amit, and L. Massa, "The Business Model: Theoretical Roots, Recent Development and Future Research," working paper WP-862, IESE Business School, University of Navarra, Madrid, June 2010.

7. Alexander Osterwalder and Yves Pigneur, *Business Model Generation: A Handbook for Visionaries, Game Changers and Challengers* (New York: John Wiley & Sons, 2010); Mark W. Johnson, *Seizing the White Space: Business Model Innovation for Growth and Renewal* (Boston: Harvard Business Press, 2010); Constantinos C. Markides, *Game-Changing Strategies: How to Create New Market Space in Established Industries by Breaking the Rules* (San Francisco: Jossey-Bass, 2008); Henry W. Chesbrough, *Open Business Models: How to Thrive in the New Information Landscape* (Boston: Harvard Business Press, November 2006).

8. Henning Kagermann, Hubert Osterle, and John Jordan, *IT-Driven Business Models: Global Case Studies in Transformation* (New York: John Wiley & Sons, 2011); James McQuivey and Josh Bernoff, *Digital Disruption: Unleashing the Next Wave of Innovation* (Amazon Publishing, 2013).

9. Thomas Eisenmann, Geoffrey Parker, and Marshall W. Van Alstyne, "Strategies for Two-Sided Markets," *Harvard Business Review*, October 2006, http://hbr

.org/2006/10/strategies-for-two-sided-markets/ar/1. Geoff Parker and Marshall Van Alstyne, our colleagues at the MIT Center for Digital Business, have done pioneering work to understand the theory of two-sided platform strategy. See also Andrei Hagiu and Julian Wright, "Multi-Sided Platforms," working paper 12-024, Harvard Business School, Boston, October 12, 2011; Andrei Hagiu, "Strategic Decisions for Multisided Platforms," *MIT Sloan Management Review*, winter 2014, http://sloanreview.mit.edu/article/strategic-decisions-for-multisided-platforms/.

10. Sangeet Paul Choudary, Geoffrey Parker, and Marshall Van Alstyne, "Outlook 2014: Platforms Are Eating the World," *Wired*, December 26, 2013, www.wired.com/insights/2013/12/outlook-2014-platforms-eating-world/.

11. Tomio Geron, "Airbnb and the Unstoppable Rise of the Share Economy," *Forbes*, January 23, 2013, www.forbes.com/sites/tomiogeron/2013/01/23/airbnb-and-the-unstoppable-rise-of-the-share-economy/.

12. Thomas Friedman, "Welcome to the 'Sharing Economy,'" *New York Times*, July 20, 2013, www.nytimes.com/2013/07/21/opinion/sunday/friedman-welcome-to-the-sharing-economy.html?_r=0.

13. Marriott Hotels, "Welcoming the Collaboration Generation into More Marriott Hotels: Workspace on Demand Expands," press release, *Market Watch*, September 23, 2013, www.marketwatch.com/story/welcoming-the-collaboration-generation-into-more-marriott-hotels-workspace-on-demand-expands-2013-09-23.

14. Zipcar, "Zipcar Reports Fourth Quarter and Full Year 2012 Results," press release, *GlobeNewswire*, February 15, 2013, http://globenewswire.com/news-release/2013/02/15/523986/10021911/en/Zipcar-Reports-Fourth-Quarter-and-Full-Year-2012-Results.html.

15. Beth Gardiner, "Jump In and Drive: Car Hire by the Minute Pulls on to UK Roads," *Guardian*, August 22, 2013, www.theguardian.com/environment/2013/aug/22/on-street-car-hire.

16. Tim Worstall, "Explaining the Avis Takeover of Zipcar," *Forbes*, February 2, 2013, www.forbes.com/sites/timworstall/2013/01/02/explaining-the-avis-takeover-of-zipcar/; Hagiu, "Strategic Decisions for Multisided Platforms."

17. Eisenmann, Parker, and Van Alstyne, "Strategies for Two-Sided Markets"; see also Hagiu and Wright, "Multi-Sided Platforms"; Hagiu, "Strategic Decisions for Multisided Platforms."

18. "The Last Kodak Moment," *Economist*, January 14, 2012, www.economist.com/node/21542796.

19. Australia Post, Annual Report 2012, auspost.com.au, 2012, http://auspost.com.au/media/documents/australia-post-annual-report-2011-12.pdf.

20. Ibid.

21. eBoks, "70-årig er e-Boks-bruger nummer fire million," e-boks.com, November 13, 2013, www.e-boks.com/dk/news.aspx?articleid=337.

22. eBoks, "Save at Least 80% on Postage—and Save Paper," eBoks home page, accessed April 25, 2014, www.e-boks.com/international/default.aspx.

23. Maël Tannou and George Westerman, "Nike: From Separate Level Initiatives to Firm Level Transformation," white paper, Capgemini Consulting, 2012, www.capgemini-consulting.com/nike.

24. Mark McClusky, "The Nike Experiment: How the Shoe Giant Unleashed the Power of Personal Metrics," *Wired*, June 22, 2009, archive.wired.com/medtech/health/magazine/17-07/lbnp_nike?currentPage=all.

25. Austin Carr, "Nike: The No. 1 Most Innovative Company of 2013," *Fast Company*, February 11, 2013, www.fastcompany.com/most-innovative-companies/2013/nike.

26. Trefis Team, "Why Nike Will Outpace the Sports Apparel Market's Growth," Forbes.com, May 3, 2013, www.forbes.com/sites/greatspeculations/2013/05/13/why-nikes-growth-will-outpace-the-sports-apparel-markets/.

27. Maël Tannou and George Westerman, "Volvo Cars Corporation: Shifting from a B2B to a 'B2B+B2C' Business Model," Capgemini Consulting, June 22, 2012, www.capgemini.com/resources/volvo-cars-corporation-shifting-from-a-b2b-to-a-b2bb2c-business-model.

28. Bertrand Dimont, "Mobile Insurance: Are You Well Positioned for This Emerging Channel?" Capgemini Consulting, 2012, http://ebooks.capgemini-consulting.com/Mobile-Insurance/files/assets/basic-html/page5.html.

29. Tokio Marine Holdings, "Evolving to Drive Growth," annual report, Tokio Marine Holdings, 2013, http://ir.tokiomarinehd.com/en/AnnualReport/IRFilingDataDownPar/0/IRFilingDownPar/0/PDFile/AR13_e_All%20pages.pdf.

30. Franklin Rios, "How Analytics Can Transform Business Models," interview by Renee Boucher Ferguson, *MIT Sloan Management Review*, April 16, 2013.

31. Renee Boucher Ferguson, "Luminar Insights: A Strategic Use of Analytics," *MIT Sloan Management Review*, February 2014.

32. Entravision Q4 2013 Analyst Call Transcript from SeekingAlpha, http://seekingalpha.com/article/2057273-entravision-communications-management-discusses-q4-2013-results-earnings-call-transcript.

33. Ibid.

CHAPTER 5

1. Case vignette based on interviews conducted by George Westerman with Jean-Pierre Remy and Nicolas Gauthier in 2011, 2013, and 2014. Information used with permission.

2. Hugh Schofield, "Minitel: The Rise and Fall of the France-Wide Web," *BBC News Paris*, June 27, 2012, www.bbc.co.uk/news/magazine-18610692.

3. Based on author interviews with CEO Jean-Pierre Remy. Used with permission.

4. George Westerman et al., "Digital Transformation: A Roadmap for Billion Dollar Organizations," white paper, Capgemini Consulting and MIT Center for Digital Business, November 17, 2011, www.capgemini-consulting.com/digital-transformation-a-road-map-for-billion-dollar-organizations, 63.

5. Didier Bonnet, George Westerman, and Michael Welch, "The Vision Thing: Developing a Transformative Digital Vision," white paper, Capgemini Consulting and MIT Center for Digital Business, 2013, www.capgemini.com/resources/the-vision-thing-developing-a-transformative-digital-vision.

6. Ibid.

7. Jennifer Van Grove, "How Starbucks Is Turning Itself into a Tech Company," VentureBeat, June 12, 2012, http://venturebeat.com/2012/06/12/starbucks-digital-strategy/.

8. Salesforce, "Burberry's Social Enterprise," video, Salesforce YouTube Channel, uploaded April 7, 2012, www.youtube.com/watch?v=XErGxMYuF2M.

9. Capgemini Consulting, "Beauty and Digital: A Magical Match—An Interview with Marc Menesguen," Capgemini Consulting Digital Leadership Series, 2012, http://ebooks.capgemini-consulting.com/Marc-Menesguen-Interview/index.html.

10. Michael Welch and George Westerman, "Caesars Entertainment: Digitally Personalizing the Customer Experience," Capgemini Consulting, April 25, 2013, www.capgemini.com/resources/caesars-entertainment-digitally-personalizing-the -customer-experience.

11. Commonwealth Bank of Australia, Annual Report, 2012, 5, https://www .commbank.com.au/about-us/shareholders/pdfs/annual-reports/2012_ Commonwealth_Bank_Annual_Report.pdf.

12. Michael Schrage, *Who Do You Want Your Customers to Become?*" (Boston: Harvard Business Review Press, 2012).

13. Novartis, Annual Report, Novartis, 2012, www.novartis.com/investors /financial-results/annual-results-2012.shtml.

14. Proctor & Gamble, Annual Report, 2012, 5, www.pginvestor.com /Cache/1001174630.PDF?Y=&O=PDF&D=&fid=1001174630&T=&iid=4004124.

15. Boeing, "The Boeing Edge," Boeing Company website, accessed April 25, 2014, www.boeing.com/boeing/commercial/aviationservices/integrated-services/digital -airline.page.

16. Ibid.

17. See, for example, Alexander Osterwelder and Yves Pigneur, *Business Model Generation: A Handbook for Visionaries, Game Changers and Challengers* (New York: John Wiley & Sons, 2010); and Mark W. Johnson, *Seizing the White Space: Business Model Innovation for Growth and Renewal* (Boston: Harvard Business Press, 2010).

18. Banco Santander, Annual Report, 2012, www.santanderannualreport. com/2012/en/, 7.

19. General Electric, Annual Report, 2011, 7, https://www.ge.com/sites/default /files/GE_AR11_EntireReport.pdf.

20. Progressive, "Progressive Background," Progressive Company website, accessed April 25, 2014, www.progressive.com/newsroom/press-kit/progressive-background/.

21. Ian Ayres, *Super Crunchers* (New York: Bantam Dell, 2007), 33.

22. Progressive, "Innovative Auto Insurance Discount Program to Be Available to 5,000 Minnesotans," Progressive, August 8, 2004, www.progressive.com/newsroom /article/2004/August/TripSense/.

23. Progressive, "Good Drivers Finally Get the Savings They Deserve as Progressive Unveils Snapshot Discount Countrywide," Progressive Company Website, March 14, 2011, www.progressive.com/newsroom/article/2011/March/snapshot-national-launch/.

24. J. Barney, "Firm Resources and Sustained Competitive Advantage," *Journal of Management* 17, no. 1 (1991): 99–120.

25. Westerman et al., "Digital Transformation"; Didier Bonnet, Andrew McAfee, and George Westerman, "Companies Must Use Digital Technologies to Transform, Not Substitute," *Financial Times*, March 29, 2012, www.ft.com/cms/s/0/4fc3a520-79d4 -11e1-9900-00144feab49a.html.

26. To perform this analysis, two expert coders jointly identified prototypical examples of substitution, extension, and transformation in each of four technologies: social media, mobile, analytics, and embedded devices. Subsequently, they independently coded interviews for each company to identify the most transformative initiative in each company by technology type. Where coding differed for a company, the two coders met to discuss the differences and identify a single answer for each technology for that company.

27. Westerman et al., "Digital Transformation," 63.

28. "Prisa Grasps Liberty Lifeline," Variety.com, November 29, 2010, http://variety .com/2010/biz/news/prisa-grasps-liberty-lifeline-1118028069/.

29. Westerman et al., "Digital Transformation," 56.

30. Capgemini Consulting, "Building a World Leader Through Digital Transformation: An Interview with Manish Choksi," *Digital Transformation Review*, no. 2, January 1, 2012, www.capgemini-consulting.com/digital-transformation-review -ndeg2, 42–47.

31. Ibid.

CHAPTER 6

1. Frederick F. Reichheld and Rob Markey, *Loyalty Rules: How Today's Leaders Build Lasting Relationships* (Boston: Harvard Business School Press, 2001).

2. See, for instance, Michael Beer, *High Commitment, High Performance: How to Build a Resilient Organization for Sustained Advantage* (San Francisco: Jossey-Bass, 2009).

3. Rosabeth M. Kanter et al., *The Challenge of Organizational Change: How Companies Experience It and Leaders Guide It* (New York: Free Press, 1992).

4. For individual and team renewal, see Francis J. Gouillart and James N. Kelly, *Transforming the Organization: Reframing Corporate Direction, Restructuring the Company, Revitalizing the Enterprise, Renewing People* (New York: McGraw Hill, 1995). For psychological alignment, see Beer, *High Commitment, High Performance*.

5. Andrew McAfee, *Enterprise 2.0: New Collaborative Tools for Your Organization's Toughest Challenges* (Boston: Harvard Business Press, 2009).

6. Capgemini Consulting, "Conviviality Goes Digital at Pernod Ricard," unpublished case study, 2014.

7. Ibid.

8. Pernod Ricard, "87% of Pernod Ricard's Employees Recommend Their Company," press release, 2013, http://pernod-ricard.com/8931/press/news-press -releases/headlines/87-of-pernod-ricard-s-employees-recommend-their-company.

9. Capgemini Consulting, "Conviviality Goes Digital at Pernod Ricard."

10. Ibid.

11. Ibid.

12. Ibid.

13. Ibid.

14. Ibid.

15. Ibid.

16. McAfee, *Enterprise 2.0*.

17. Interview with authors, interviewee asked to remain anonymous.

18. Apple, "Serving Up Innovation," 2014, www.apple.com/iphone/business /profiles/kraft-foods/.

19. Mark Fidelman, "The World's Top 20 Social Brands," *Forbes*, November 20, 2012, www.forbes.com/sites/markfidelman/2012/11/20 /the-worlds-top-20-social-brands/.

20. Stuart Elliott, "Coke Revamps Web Site to Tell Its Story," *New York Times*, November 11, 2012, www.nytimes.com/2012/11/12/business/media/coke-revamps -web-site-to-tell-its-story.html?_r=0.

21. David F. Carr, "Coca-Cola on Chatter: Beyond the Secret Formula," *Information Week*, September 20, 2012, www.informationweek.com/social-business/social _networking_private_platforms/coca-cola-on-chatter-beyond-the-secret-f/240007735? pgno=1.

22. Nestlé, "Digital Acceleration Team II," video, uploaded June 13, 2013, www .youtube.com/watch?v=b2KjwoxhvAs.

23. L'Oréal, "Digital for All: Sustainable Development," L'Oréal website, April 17, 2012, www.loreal.com/news/digital-for-all.aspx.

24. Popsi'it, "Management: Innovation Participative: Vos Idées Valent de l'OR," *Popsi'it* blog, February 2014, http://blog.popsiit.com/wp-content/uploads/2014/02/19022014_art__001.pdf, 36–39.

25. George Westerman and Deborah Soule, "Learning to Foster Breakthrough Innovation: The Evolution of EMC's Innovation Conference," MIT Center for Information Systems Research, November 18, 2010.

26. EMC, "EMC Unites Thousands for Fourth Annual Innovation Conference," press release, October 20, 2010, www.emc.com/about/news/press/2010/20101020-01.htm.

27. Westerman and Soule, "Learning to Foster Breakthrough Innovation."

28. See, for instance, Henry William Chesbrough, *Open Innovation: The New Imperative for Creating and Profiting from Technology* (Boston: Harvard Business School Press, 2006).

29. Bruce Brown and Scott Anthony, "How P&G Tripled Its Innovation Success Rate," *Harvard Business Review*, June 2011, http://hbr.org/2011/06/how-pg-tripled-its-innovation-success-rate/ar/1.

30. Procter and Gamble, "What Is Connect and Develop?" Procter and Gamble website, 2014, www.pgconnectdevelop.com/home/pg_open_innovation.html.

31. Brown and Anthony, "How P&G Tripled Its Innovation Success Rate."

32. The remaining quotes in this chapter are from interviewees who asked to remain anonymous.

CHAPTER 7

1. P&G Corporate Video, YouTube, "QA with Bob McDonald—Investing in Digital Technologies at P&G," March 2011, https://www.youtube.com/watch?v=8m5LgZX27c4.

2. Jennifer Reingold, "Brainstorm Tech Video: P&G's Bob McDonald Talks Tech," *Fortune,* July 19, 2011, http://fortune.com/2011/07/19/brainstorm-tech-video-pgs-bob-mcdonald-talks-tech/.

3. Peter Weill and Stephanie L. Woerner, "The Future of the CIO in a Digital Economy," *MIS Quarterly Executive,* June 2013, http://cisr.mit.edu/locker/WeillWoernerMISQE2013FutureofCIO.pdf.

4. I CIO, "Creating the World's 'Most Tech-Enabled Corporation,'" April 2012, www.i-cio.com/big-thinkers/filippo-passerini/item/creating-the-world-s-most-tech-enabled-corporation.

5. Ken McGee, "Interview with Filippo Passerini," Gartner Fellows Interviews, January 2012, https://www.gartner.com/doc/1901015.

6. Heller Search Associates, "The Anticipator CIO: Procter & Gamble's Filippo Passerini," April 2014, http://blog.hellersearch.com/Blog/bid/196094/The-Anticipator-CIO-Procter-Gamble-s-Filippo-Passerini.

7. I CIO, "CEO & CIO United," April 2012, www.i-cio.com/features/april-2012/p-and-g-ceo-bob-mcdonald-and-cio-filippo-passerini.

8. Ibid.

9. "P&G's Global Business Services Organization Earns Praise," P&G Corporate Newsroom, September 21, 2011, http://news.pg.com/blog/innovation/pgs-global-business-services-organization-earns-praise.

10. Filippo Passerini, "Transforming the Way of Doing Business via Digitization," slideshare, November 2, 2011, www.slideshare.net/ericakirichenko/filippo-passerini-goind-digital.

11. TechWeb, "Procter & Gamble CIO Filippo Passerini: 2010 Chief of the Year," December 3, 2010, www.techweb.com/news/228500182/procter-gamble-cio-filippo -passerini-2010-chief-of-the-year.html.

12. Passerini, "Transforming the Way of Doing Business via Digitization."

13. TechWeb, "Procter & Gamble CIO Filippo Passerini."

14. I CIO, "Creating the World's 'Most Tech-Enabled Corporation.'"

15. Ibid.

16. Ibid.

17. *Information Week*, "2010 CIO of the Year," December 2010.

18. McGee, "Interview with Filippo Passerini."

19. *Information Week*, "2010 CIO of the Year."

20. *Wikipedia*, s.v. "governance," last updated March 14, 2014, http://en.wikipedia. org/wiki/Governance.

21. Capgemini Consulting, "Burberry's Digital Transformation," *Digital Transformation Review*, no. 2, January 2012, 10, www.capgemini-consulting.com/ resource-file-access/resource/pdf/Digital_Transformation_Review____Edition_2.pdf.

22. Additional analysis of 2012 global survey data to gain descriptive insights. Difference of 25.9 versus 17.2 on a summed composite of five survey items.

23. Interviewees in our study reported that the pace of business is much faster than five years ago (5.6 on a scale from 1 = much slower to 7 = much faster) and that it continues to accelerate.

24. Maël Tannou and George Westerman, "Volvo Cars Corporation: Shifting from a B2B to a 'B2B+B2C' Business Model," Capgemini Consulting, June 22, 2012, www .capgemini.com/resources/volvo-cars-corporation-shifting-from-a-b2b-to-a-b2bb2c -business-model.

25. Printed with company permission; interviewee asked to remain anonymous.

26. Ibid.

27. Jennifer Van Grove, "How Starbucks Is Turning Itself into a Tech Company," *Venture Beat*, June 12, 2012, http://venturebeat.com/2012/06/12 /starbucks-digital-strategy/.

28. Pete Blackshaw, "How Digital Acceleration Teams Are Influencing Nestlé's 2000 Brands," interview by Michael Fitzgerald, *MIT Sloan Management Review*, September 22, 2013.

29. George Westerman et al., "Digital Transformation: A Roadmap for Billion Dollar Organizations," white paper, Capgemini Consulting and MIT Center for Digital Business, November 17, 2011, www.capgemini-consulting.com /digital-transformation-a-road-map-for-billion-dollar-organizations.

30. Ibid.

CHAPTER 8

1. See, for example, Rosabeth M. Kanter, Barry A. Stein, and Todd D. Jick, *The Challenge of Organizational Change: How Companies Experience It and Leaders Guide It* (New York: Free Press, 1992).

2. Ashley Machin and Zak Mian, Lioyd's vignette written from author interviews. Used with permission.

3. D. Preston and E. Karahanna, "Antecedents of IS Strategic Alignment: A Nomological Network," *Information Systems Research* 20, no. 2 (2009): 159–179.

4. In our analysis: 22.97 versus 17.37 on a summed measure.

5. In our analysis, Digital Masters averaged 5.72, and nonmasters averaged 4.74 on a seven-point scale, in response to the question, "We are in control of our destiny for digital transformation."

6. George Westerman, "IT Is from Venus, Non-IT Is from Mars," *Wall Street Journal*, April 2, 2012, http://tinyurl.com/n6xu7p7.

7. Richard Hunter and George Westerman, *The Real Business of IT: How CIOs Create and Communicate Value* (Boston: Harvard Business Press, 2008), 13.

8. Capgemini Consulting, "Burberry's Digital Transformation," *Digital Transformation Review*, no. 2, January 2012, www.capgemini.com/resources/talking-bout-a-revolution, 12.

9. Westerman, "IT Is from Venus."

10. Hunter and Westerman, *The Real Business of IT.*

11. John Allspaw and Paul Hammond, "10 Deploys Per Day: Dev and Ops Cooperation at Flickr," *Slideshare*, 2009, www.slideshare.net/jallspaw/10-deploys-per-day-dev-and-ops-cooperation-at-flickr

12. Damon Edwards, "What Is DevOps?" Dev2Ops, February 23, 2010, http://dev2ops.org/2010/02/what-is-devops/.

13. Christina Farr, "An Idiot's Guide to DevOps," *Venture Beat*, September 30, 2013, http://venturebeat.com/2013/09/30/an-idiots-guide-to-devops/.

14. Charles Bobcock, "DevOps: A Culture Shift, Not a Technology," *Information Week*, April 14, 2014, www.informationweek.com/software/enterprise-applications/devops-a-culture-shift-not-a-technology/d/d-id/1204425.

15. George Westerman et al., "Digital Transformation: A Roadmap for Billion Dollar Organizations," white paper, Capgemini Consulting and MIT Center for Digital Business, 2011, 39, www.capgemini-consulting.com/digital-transformation-a-road-map-for-billion-dollar-organizations.

16. Average survey responses of Digital Masters and non-masters on a seven-point disagree-agree Likert scale for questions of the form "We have the necessary skills in . . ."

17. Capgemini Consulting, "Burberry's Digital Transformation."

18. Average survey responses of Digital Masters and nonmasters on a seven-point disagree-agree Likert scale for questions of the form "We have the necessary skills in . . ."

19. Capgemini Consulting, "Digital Leadership: An Interview with Markus Nordlin, CIO of Zurich Insurance," 2013, http://ebooks.capgemini-consulting.com/Digital-Leadership-Zurich-Insurance/.

20. Nick Clayton, "E.U. 'Grand Coalition' to Fight IT Skills Shortage," *Wall Street Journal*, March 6, 2013, http://blogs.wsj.com/tech-europe/2013/03/06/e-u-grand-coalition-to-fight-it-skills-shortage/.

21. Gartner, "Gartner Reveals Top Predictions for IT Organizations and Users for 2013 and Beyond," Gartner, October 24, 2012, www.gartner.com/newsroom/id/2211115.

22. Marianne Kolding, Mette Ahorlu, and Curtis Robinson, "Post-Crisis: e-Skills Are Needed to Drive Europe's Innovation Society," *IDC*, November 2009, http://ec.europa.eu/enterprise/sectors/ict/files/idc_wp_november_2009_en.pdf.

23. Gartner, "Key Findings from US Digital Marketing Spending Survey," Gartner, March 6, 2013, www.gartner.com/technology/research/digital-marketing/digital-marketing-spend-report.jsp

24. Barbara Spitzer et al., "The Digital Talent Gap," Capgemini Consulting, 2013, www.capgemini.com/resources/the-digital-talent-gap-developing-skills-for-todays-digital-organizations.

25. Jeanne W. Ross, Peter Weill, and David Robertson, *Enterprise Architecture as Strategy: Creating a Foundation for Business Execution* (Boston: Harvard Business Review Press Books, 2006).

26. Interview with authors; interviewee asked to remain anonymous.

27. Ross et al., *Enterprise Architecture as Strategy;* George Westerman and Richard Hunter, *IT Risk: Turning Business Threats into Competitive Advantage* (Boston: Harvard Business School Press, 2007).

28. Westerman and Hunter, *IT Risk.*

29. Brad Stone, *The Everything Store: Jeff Bezos and the Age of Amazon* (New York: Little, Brown and Company, 2013), 133.

30. Average survey responses of Digital Masters and nonmasters on a seven-point disagree-agree Likert scale for questions of the form "We have an integrated view of . . ."

31. Erik Brynjolfsson and Andrew McAfee, "Investing in the IT That Makes a Competitive Difference," *Harvard Business Review,* July–August 2008, 98–107.

32. Hunter and Westerman, *The Real Business of IT.*

33. P. Weill, C. Soh, and S. Kien, "Governance of Global Shared Solutions at Procter & Gamble," MIT Center for Information Systems Research, Research Briefings vol. VII, no. 3A (December 2007).

34. John Furrier, "Google Engineer Accidentally Shares His Internal Memo about Google+ Platform," *Silicon Angle,* October 12, 2011, http://siliconangle.com /furrier/2011/10/12/google-engineer-accidently-shares-his-internal-memo-about -google-platform/.

35. Hunter and Westerman, *The Real Business of IT.*

36. Capgemini Consulting, "Building a World Leader Through Digital Transformation," *Digital Transformation Review,* no. 2, July 2011, www.capgemini .com/resources/digital-transformation-review-no-1-july-2011, 42.

CHAPTER 9

1. Michael Fitzgerald et al., "Embracing Digital Technology: A New Strategic Imperative," *MIT Sloan Management Review,* 2013, http://sloanreview.mit.edu /projects/embracing-digital-technology/.

2. Ibid.

3. Ibid.

4. Andy Grove, *Only the Paranoid Survive: How to Exploit the Crisis Points That Challenge Every Company* (New York: Crown Business, 1999).

5. Didier Bonnet and Jerome Buvat, "Digital Leadership—Hailo: Digitally Disrupting a Traditional Market," An Interview with Ron Zeghibe, 2013, http://www .capgemini-consulting.com/digital-leadership-hailo-digitally-disrupting -a-traditional-market.

6. Fitzgerald et al., "Embracing Digital Technology."

7. Joe Gross, "Allianz: Creating a Digital DNA," in *Digital Transformation Review,* no. 4, *Accelerating Digital Transformation,* Capgemini Consulting, May 2013, www .capgemini-consulting.com/digital-transformation-review-4.

8. See, for example, Michael D. Michalisin, Robert D. Smith, and Douglas M. Kline, "In Search of Strategic Assets," *International Journal of Organizational Analysis* 5, no. 4 (1997): 360–387.

9. American Bankers Association, "ABA Survey: Popularity of Online Banking Explodes," American Bankers Association, September 2011,

www.ababj.com/197-new-products-a-services/tech-topics-plus5
/3250-aba-survey-popularity-of-online-banking-explodes.

   10. Kevin S. Travis et al., "U.S. Muti-Channel Customer Research 2012: The
Rise of the Virtually Domiciled," Novantas Research, 2012, http://novantas.com
/wp-content/uploads/2014/01/Novantas_US_Multi_Channel_Research_2012.pdf.

   11. Rupert Jones, "Barclays to Sell Customer Data," *Guardian*, June 24, 2013, www
.theguardian.com/business/2013/jun/24/barclays-bank-sell-customer-data.

   12. To analyze your current business model, use the business model canvas concept
in Alexander Osterwelder and Yves Pigneur, *Business Model Generation: A Handbook
for Visionaries, Game Changers and Challengers* (New York: John Wiley & Sons, 2010).
There are also useful approaches to help you structure your business model thinking
in Joseph V. Sinfield et al., "How to Identify New Business Models," *MIT Sloan
Management Review*, winter 2012; Raphael Amit and Christoph Zott, "Creating Value
Through Business Model Innovation," *MIT Sloan Management Review*, spring 2012.
To generate new business model options, see Alexander and Pigneur, "Business Model
Generation"; Mark W. Johnson, *Seizing the White Space: Business Model Innovation
for Growth and Renewal* (Boston: Harvard Business Press, 2010); Constantinos C.
Markides, *Game-Changing Strategies: How to Create New Market Space in Established
Industries by Breaking the Rules* (San Francisco: Jossey-Bass, 2008), 23–54; W. Chan
Kim and Renée Mauborgne, *Blue Ocean Strategy: How to Create Uncontested Market Space
and Make the Competition Irrelevant* (Boston: Harvard Business School Press, 2005);
Clayton M. Christensen, *The Innovator's Dilemma: When New Technologies Cause Great
Firms to Fail* (Boston: Harvard Business Review Press, 1997). To defend and respond to
a new business model, see Markides, *Game-Changing Strategies*, 121–141.

   13. George Westerman et al., "The Vision Thing: Developing a Transformative
Vision," Capgemini Consulting, June 11, 2013, http://www.capgemini-consulting.
com/the-vision-thing-developing-a-transformative-digital-vision; Morten T. Hansen,
Collaboration: How Leaders Avoid the Traps, Build Common Ground, and Reap Big Results
(Boston: Harvard Business Press, 2009), chapter 4.

   14. Michael Fitzgerald, "How Starbucks Has Gone Digital," *MIT Sloan
Management Review*, April 4, 2013, http://sloanreview.mit.edu/article
/how-starbucks-has-gone-digital/.

   15. Fitzgerald et al., "Embracing Digital Technology" (unpublished survey data).

   16. Gross, "Allianz: Creating a Digital DNA."

CHAPTER 10

   1. Michael Fitzgerald et al., "Embracing Digital Technology: A New Strategic
Imperative," *MIT Sloan Management Review*, 2013, http://sloanreview.mit.edu
/projects/embracing-digital-technology/.

   2. Robert S. Kaplan and David P. Norton, *The Balanced Scorecard: Translating
Strategy into Action* (Boston: Harvard Business School Press, 1996).

   3. Tim Kastelle, "Is Your Innovation Problem Really a Strategy Problem?"
Harvard Business Review, February 11, 2014, http://blogs.hbr.org/2014/02
/is-your-innovation-problem-really-a-strategy-problem/.

   4. Jeff Gothelf, "How We Finally Made Agile Development Work," *Harvard
Business Review*, October 11, 2012, http://blogs.hbr.org/2012/10
/how-we-finally-made-agile-development-work/.

5. Michael Fitzgerald, "How Starbucks Has Gone Digital," *MIT Sloan Management Review*, April 4, 2013, http://sloanreview.mit.edu/article /how-starbucks-has-gone-digital/.

6. A control group within an experiment is a group that doesn't receive the treatment being tested. This isolates the treatment's effects on the outcomes and can help rule out alternate explanations of the experimental results. Aim to use a control group wherever possible. If you need to conduct an experiment without a control group, be very careful in using the results. Many other factors besides the treatment you were testing may explain the results. A/B testing (or split-testing) has become a standard real-time testing method for digital experiments. It works by diverting a portion of users to a slightly different version of a given web page or mobile app, for example. The users' behavior is compared with the mass of users on the standard site or app. If the new version shows better results—e.g., more clicks, longer visits, more purchases—it may replace the original; if the new version has inferior results, you can phase out the test, sparing most users from ever seeing it. A/B testing is used in many leading internet firms such as Google and Amazon.com. It allows you to put some data-driven rationale on seemingly subjective questions of design—color, layout, image selection, text, and so forth.

7. Jeanne W. Ross, Peter Weill, and David Robertson, *Enterprise Architecture as Strategy: Creating a Foundation for Business Execution* (Boston: Harvard Business Press, 2006).

8. George Westerman and Richard Hunter, *IT Risk: Turning Business Threats into Competitive Advantage* (Boston: Harvard Business Press, 2007).

9. George Westerman and Michael Welch, "Caesars Entertainment: Digitally Personalizing the Customer Experience," white paper, Capgemini Consulting, April 25, 2013, www.capgemini.com/resources/caesars-entertainment-digitally-personalizing -the-customer-experience.

10. A. G. Lafley and Roger Martin, *Playing to Win: How Strategy Really Works* (Boston: Harvard Business Review Press, 2013).

11. Fitzgerald, "How Starbucks Has Gone Digital."

12. See, for example, Bryan Maizlish and Robert Handler, *IT Portfolio Management Step-by-Step: Unlocking the Business Value of Technology* (New York: John Wiley & Sons, 2005); Robert J. Benson, Tom L. Bugnitz, and William B. Walton, *From Business Strategy to IT in Action* (New York: John Wiley & Sons, 2004); Catherine Benko and F. Warren McFarlan, *Connecting the Dots: Aligning Projects with Objectives in Unpredictable Times* (Boston: Harvard Business Review Press, 2003).

13. See, for example, George Westerman and Garrett Dodge, "Vendor Innovation as a Strategic Option," MIT Sloan School of Management, Research Briefing, March 2008, http://cisr.mit.edu/blog/documents/2008/03/14/2008_03_1c- vendorinnoasstrategicop-westerman.pdf/.

14. CFO Research Services, "Uncrossing the Wires: Starting—and Sustaining—the Conversation on Technology Value," CFO Research Services, March 2012, http:// docs.media.bitpipe.com/io_10x/io_101990/item_457981/Cisco_CFO_SearchCIO_ UncrossingTheWires_031312.pdf.

15. The translation problem for metrics is common in many areas, especially information technology. Doing this correctly can change the nature of the IT–business relationship and improve the value your company gets from IT. For examples and advice on how to do this, see Richard Hunter and George Westerman, *The Real Business of IT: How CIOs Create and Communicate Value* (Boston: Harvard Business Press, 2008).

CHAPTER 11

1. Michael Fitzgerald et al., "Embracing Digital Technology: A New Strategic Imperative," *MIT Sloan Management Review*, 2013, http://sloanreview.mit.edu /projects/embracing-digital-technology/.

2. George Westerman et al., "Digital Transformation: A Roadmap for Billion Dollar Companies," white paper, Capgemini Consulting and MIT Center for Digital Business, November 17, 2011, www.capgemini.com/resources /digital-transformation-a-roadmap-for-billiondollar-organizations.

3. Marc Menesguen, "Beauty and Digital: A Magical Match," *Digital Transformation Review*, no. 1, July 2011, www.capgemini.com/resources /digital-transformation-review-no-1-july-2011.

4. John Young and Kristin Peck, "Pfizer: Think Digital First," *Digital Transformation Review*, no. 3, November 2012, http://ebooks.capgemini-consulting .com/Digital-Transformation-Review-3/index.html#/1/.

5. David F. Carr, "Coca-Cola on Chatter: Beyond the Secret Formula," *Information Week*, September 20, 2012, www.informationweek.com/social-business /social_networking_private_platforms/coca-cola-on-chatter-beyond-the-secret-f /240007735?pgno=1.

6. Ninon Renaud, "La Société Générale phosphore sur la transition numérique," *Les Echos*, July 9, 2013, www.lesechos.fr/09/07/2013/LesEchos/21474-120-ECH_ la-societe-generale-phosphore-sur-la-transition-numerique.htm.

7. Ibid.

8. Alison Boothby, "The End of the Workplace as We Know It?" *Simply-communicate*, January 25, 2013, www.simply-communicate.com/news/event-reviews /engagement/end-workplace-we-know-it.

9. Jorgen Sundberg, "Social Media from the Top: Influential CEO Leadership," Enviableworkplace.com, September 27, 2013, http://enviableworkplace.com /ceos-and-social-media/.

10. Jacob Morgan, "ING Direct CEO Gives Employees 'the Right to Bitch,'" CloudAve, March 19, 2013, www.cloudave.com/27297/ing-direct-ceo-gives -employees-the-right-to-bitch/.

11. Mark Fidelman, "How This CIO Helped Bayer Become Social," *Forbes*, May 28, 2012, www.forbes.com/sites/markfidelman/2012/05/28/how-this-cio-helped-bayer -become-social/.

12. "Video: What Digital Transformation Means for Business," *MIT Sloan Management Review*, August 06, 2013, http://sloanreview.mit.edu/article /video-what-digital-transformation-means-for-business/.

13. Laura Snoad, "The Vital Connection Between Staff and the Bottom Line," *Marketing Week*, November 10, 2011, www.marketingweek.co.uk/analysis/essential -reads/the-vital-connection-between-staff-and-the-bottom-line/3031707.article.

CHAPTER 12

1. Joe Gross, "Allianz: Creating a Digital DNA," *Digital Transformation Review*, no. 4, *Accelerating Digital Transformation*, Capgemini Consulting, May 2013, www .capgemini-consulting.com/digital-transformation-review-4, 13.

2. Coca Cola, "The Board of Directors of the Coca-Cola Company Elects Robert A. Kotick as Director," press release, February 16, 2012, www

.coca-colacompany.com/press-center/press-releases/the-board-of-directors-of-the-coca-cola-company-elects-robert-a-kotick-as-director.

3. Jack Neff, "Nestle Hires Pete Blackshaw as Global Digital Chief," *Ad Age*, February 4, 2011, http://adage.com/article/news/nestle-hires-nielsen-s-blackshaw-global-digital-chief/148679/.

4. L'Oréal, "Reveal," home page, accessed April 25, 2014, www.reveal-thegame.com.

5. Joshua Bjurke, "HR Must Step Up Recruitment/Motivation Game to Keep Employees," Recruiter, June 19, 2013, www.recruiter.com/i/hr-must-step-up-recruitment-motivation-game-to-keep-employees/.

6. Capgemini Consulting, "Beauty and Digital: A Magical Match—An Interview with Marc Menesguen," Capgemini Consulting Digital Leadership Series, 2012, http://ebooks.capgemini-consulting.com/Marc-Menesguen-Interview/index.html.

7. Jeanne C. Meister and Karie Willyerd, "Intel's Social Media Training," *HBR Blog Network*, February 3, 2010, http://blogs.hbr.org/2010/02/intels-social-media-employee-t/.

8. Bryon Ellen, "A New Odd Couple: Google, P&G Swap Workers to Spur Innovation," *Wall Street Journal*, November 19, 2008, http://online.wsj.com/news/articles/SB122705787917439625.

9. Ibid.

10. Warc, "Reverse Mentoring Popular in India," Warc, December 21, 2012, www.warc.com/LatestNews/News/Reverse_mentoring_popular_in_India.news?ID=30801.

11. Kering, "Digital Academy," Kering.com, 2012, www.kering.com/en/talent/digital-academy.

12. Capgemini Consulting, "Burberry's Digital Transformation," *Digital Transformation Review*, no. 2, January 2012, http://www.capgemini-consulting.com/digital-transformation-review-ndeg2.

13. Heather Clancy, "GE, Quirky Collaborate on Sustainable Innovations via M2M," *Business Green*, April 16, 2013, www.greenbiz.com/blog/2013/04/16/ge-quirky-collaborate-sustainable-innovations-m2m.

14. Ryan Kim, "Walmart Labs Buys Mobile Agency Small Society," Gigaom, January 2012, http://gigaom.com/2012/01/04/walmart-labs-buys-mobile-developer-small-society/.

15. Dale Bus, "Mondelez Pairs Brands with 2013 Class of Mobile Futures Startups," January 8, 2013, Brandchannel.com, www.brandchannel.com/home/post/2013/01/08/Mondelez-Mobile-Futures-2013-Class-010813.aspx.

16. Jeanne Ross, Peter Weill, and David Robertson, *Enterprise Architecture as Strategy: Creating a Foundation for Business Execution*, (Boston: Harvard Business Press, 2006).

17. George Westerman and Richard Hunter, *IT Risk: Turning Business Threats into Competitive Advantage* (Boston: Harvard Business Press, 2007).

18. Ross et al., *Enterprise Architecture as Strategy*

19. Richard Hunter and George Westerman, *The Real Business of IT: How CIOs Create and Communicate Value* (Boston: Harvard Business Press, 2008).

20. Capgemini Consulting, "Burberry's Digital Transformation."

21. Michael Fitzgerald et al., "Embracing Digital Technology: A New Strategic Imperative," *MIT Sloan Management Review*, 2013, http://sloanreview.mit.edu/projects/embracing-digital-technology/.

22. George Westerman et al., "Digital Transformation: A Roadmap for Billion Dollar Companies," Capgemini Consulting, November 27, 2011, www.capgemini -consulting.com/digital-transformation-a-road-map-for-billion-dollar-organizations.

23. Jack Neff, "Walmart Brings Bricks and Mortar to Battle with Amazon," *Ad Age Digital*, November 2011, http://adage.com/article/digital /walmart-brings-bricks-mortar-battle-amazon/230986/.

24. Ruddick Graham, "'Success Online? It's All About Shops Actually,'" *Telegraph*, April 20, 2013, www.telegraph.co.uk/finance/newsbysector/retailandconsumer /10007746/Success-online-Its-all-about-shops-actually.html.

25. Andrew McAfee and Michael Welch, "Being Digital: Engaging the Organization to Accelerate Digital Transformation," *Digital Transformation Review*, no. 4, May 2013, www.capgemini-consulting.com/digital-transformation-review-4.

26. John Gibbons, "Employee Engagement: A Review of Current Research and Its Implications," Conference Board, November 2006, www.conferenceboard.ca/e-library /abstract.aspx?did=1831.

27. Gamification helps businesses measure and influence user behavior through the application of game mechanics to reward systems.

28. Mario Herger, "Gamification Facts and Figures," Enterprise Gamification Consultancy, August 23, 2013, http://tinyurl.com/ksnnrsd.

29. McAfee and Welch, "Being Digital: Engaging the Organization to Accelerate Digital Transformation."

30. Fitzgerald et al., "Embracing Digital Technology."

31. Rory Cellan-Jones, "Fail Fast, Move On: Making Government Digital," *BBC News*, July 18, 2013, www.bbc.com/news/technology-23354062.

EPILOGUE

1. Over the years, experts sometimes argue that Moore's Law is coming to an end. However, over the past decades, these predictions have proven to be untrue. See, for example, Rebecca Henderson, "Of Life Cycles Real and Imaginary: The Unexpectedly Long Old Age of Optical Lithography," *Research Policy* 24, no. 4 (July 1995): 631–643. However, even if Moore's Law slows, digital technology's growth trajectory will not screech to an abrupt stop. It will continue to advance powerfully into the future, bringing new business practices, capabilities, and customer demands with it.

2. See, for example, Henry William Chesbrough, *Open Innovation: The New Imperative for Creating and Profiting from Technology* (Boston: Harvard Business School Press, 2006).

INDEX

ACKNOWLEDGMENTS

When the three of us met for the first time in 2010, writing a book was not on our agenda. What happened, however, was a meeting of minds. All three of us had a passionate belief that new forms of digital innovation—mobile devices, analytics, embedded devices, and social media—were going to be a big deal for business and management innovation. We three believed that beyond the companies that do technology for a living, there must be large corporations around the globe doing exciting things with digital technology and getting impressive business benefits from it. But no one was talking about these companies. So we set out to look for them, research them, and engage with their leadership teams. As we shared our findings with senior executives around the world, their enthusiasm and feedback convinced us that we needed to write a book about digital transformation.

A book of this nature is always a collective endeavor. In this particular instance, it became a truly global operation. Acknowledging the many people who contributed to *Leading Digital* is a tall order. We'll never be able to name all the individuals who gave their time and insights to make this book possible. However, you all deserve credit, and we are forever indebted to you all.

Some individuals deserve a special mention. Capgemini CEO Paul Hermelin was a source of constant encouragement and challenge on the impact of technology on business innovation. Claire Calmejane, Maël Tannou, and Mike Welch each spent a year to help with the research that led to this book: Claire with initial interviews and framework development, Maël with survey research and deeper dives on key ideas, Mike with another survey and keeping us on track as we wrote the book's first draft. Nick Carrier managed the process of finalizing the book through revisions, editing, and permissions. Patrick Ferraris, Frank MacCrory, and Jerome Buvat from Capgemini Consulting, and Gregory Gimpel and Deborah Soule from the MIT Center for Digital Business, provided great inputs and contributions throughout.

Xavier Hochet, CEO of Capgemini Consulting, and Pierre-Yves Cros, Group Development Director at Capgemini, not only provided financial support for the research but also gave freely of their time and ideas to make it better. Erik Brynjolfsson, Director of the MIT Center for Digital Business, made this joint research project possible. David Verrill, the center's Executive Director, provided constant encouragement and Zen-like management throughout our efforts.

We owe immense gratitude to all the vice presidents and consultants at Capgemini Consulting who shared their insights and who connected us with their clients to test ideas. Thanks to Marc Burger, Adam Gerstein, Imke Keicher, Stephan Paolini, and Barbara Spitzer for many fruitful conversations about the people side of digital transformation, and to Scott Clarke, Jeff Hunter, and Ravouth Keuky for sharing their expertise on digital strategy and customer experience. Michiel Boreel, Lanny Cohen, Philippe Grangeon, Pierre Hessler, Bob Scott, Olivier Sevilla, Simon Short, Ron Tolido, and Ken Toombs read early drafts of the book and provided valuable suggestions.

We are grateful also to Michael Fitzgerald, David Kiron, and Martha Mangelsdorf of *MIT Sloan Management Review* for partnering in a survey, publishing their own cases and interviews, and volunteering for many conversations about the topic. Thanks also to executives Kamal Bherwani, Katrina Lane, and Jean-Pierre Remy, who made time for frequent exchanges about the digital transformations they were leading.

Our book agent, Carol Franco, helped us translate our original ideas into a clear narrative, connected us with an amazing publisher in Harvard Business Review Press, and offered constant encouragement when the going got tough. Anahid Basmajian and Justin Lockenwitz worked their magic to coordinate the go-to-market plan for the book.

Finally, we would like to acknowledge the great team at the Press. Thanks to Jeff Kehoe, our senior editor, for trusting us in the first place and for being a great partner and mentor throughout. Thanks to four anonymous reviewers who not only encouraged the publication of this book, but also provided helpful feedback to improve the content. We are also indebted to Sally Ashworth, Liz Baldwin, Erin Brown, Julie Devoll, Stephani Finks, Erica Truxler, Sarah Weaver, Tracy Williams, and the many others at the Press who edited, produced, and marketed our work.

Beyond the individual acknowledgements, we owe an immense debt of gratitude to the myriad global business leaders who shared their experiences (good or bad) of conducting digital transformation and who were tolerant of our constant questioning. Some were Digital Masters, and others were just starting their journeys, but all contributed deeply to making this book possible. You are the real heroes of digital transformation. We are grateful to you for showing us the way, and we wish you great success as you navigate your journeys.

ABOUT THE AUTHORS

George Westerman (@gwesterman) is a research scientist with the MIT Initiative on the Digital Economy. His research and teaching focus on digital technology leadership and innovation. George has written numerous contributions for publications ranging from *Sloan Management Review* to *Organization Science* to the *Wall Street Journal*. He is coauthor of two respected books: *The Real Business of IT: How CIOs Create and Communicate Value*, named the Best IT-Business Book of 2009 by *CIO Insight* magazine, and *IT Risk: Turning Business Threats into Competitive Advantage*, named one of the top five books of 2007 by *CIO Insight*. He regularly conducts keynote presentations and senior executive workshops with companies around the world. Prior to earning his doctorate from Harvard Business School, George gained more than thirteen years of experience in product development and technology leadership roles. His blog is georgewesterman.org.

Didier Bonnet (@didiebon) is a senior vice-president at Capgemini Consulting, where he serves as Global Practice Leader and heads Capgemini Consulting's Digital Transformation program. He has more than twenty-five years' experience in strategy development, globalization, internet economics, and business transformation for large global corporations. He has published several articles and book chapters, and is frequently quoted in the press, including the *Wall Street Journal*, *Forbes*, *Financial Times*, and the *Economist*. Prior to Capgemini he was a vice president at Gemini Consulting and a senior associate at economic consulting firm Putnam, Hayes and Bartlett. Bonnet graduated in business economics from a French "Grande Ecole" and earned his doctorate from New College, University of Oxford. His blog is didierbonnet.com.

Andrew McAfee (@amcafee) is a principal research scientist and cofounder of the MIT Initiative on the Digital Economy. He has also held appointments on the faculty of Harvard Business School and as a fellow at Harvard's Berkman Center for Internet and Society. He has written for magazines and journals such as *Harvard Business Review* and *Sloan Management Review*. He is the coauthor, with Erik Brynjolfsson, of *Race Against the Machine* and the *New York Times* bestseller *The Second Machine Age*. He is also the author of *Enterprise 2.0*. McAfee earned his doctorate from Harvard Business School, and completed two Master of Science and two Bachelor of Science degrees at MIT. His blog is andrewmcafee.org.